THE
RECONSTRUCTION
OF SPACE AND TIME

DATE DUE

Demco, Inc. 38-293

THE RECONSTRUCTION OF SPACE AND TIME

MOBILE COMMUNICATION PRACTICES

EDITED BY

RICH LING AND SCOTT W. CAMPBELL

TRANSACTION PUBLISHERS

NEW BRUNSWICK (U.S.A.) AND LONDON (U.K.)

First paperback printing 2010
Copyright © 2009 by Transaction Publishers, New Brunswick, New Jersey.

This book is printed on acid-free paper that meets the American National Standard for Permanence of Paper for Printed Library Materials.

Library of Congress Catalog Number: 2008020073
ISBN: 978-1-4128-0809-5 (cloth); 978-1-4128-1108-8 (paper)
Printed in the United States of America

Library of Congress Cataloging-in-Publication

The reconstruction of space and time : mobile communication practices /
    Rich Ling and Scott W. Campbell, editors.
        p. cm.—(Transaction Books' series on mobile communication)
    Includes bibliographical references.
    ISBN 978-1-4128-0809-5
    1. Mobile communication systems—Social aspects. 2. Interpersonal communication—Technological innovations—Social aspects. 3. Space and time. 4. Spatial behavior. I. Ling, Richard Seyler. II. Campbell, Scott W.

HM1206.R43   2008
304.2'3—dc22   2008020073

Rich Ling:
To my mother, who deserves this recognition.

Scott W. Campbell:
To my new son Fletcher, who reluctantly gave me a chance to finish
this project. And to my wife Faith, who gave me Fletcher.

Contents

Acknowledgments

As with any production, there are a cast of individuals who have worked hard to see it come to fruition. This book is no different. The authors of the papers are perhaps the most worthy of thanks. Their willingness to contribute their work and to go through the process of receiving reviews and then reworking and resubmitting their original contributions puts them into a special class. Each of them is presented in the section describing the contributors. Another group of persons who has contributed is the board of editors for the Mobile Communication Research Series. These are the individuals who have invested their time and energy in the blind reviewing of the papers and they have contributed valuable comments to the aimed at the further development of the work.

These persons are:

Ken Anderson	Intel corporation, US
Naomi Baron	American University, US
Manuel Castells	University of Southern California, US/Spain
Akiba Cohen	Tel Aviv University, Israel
Nicola Döring	Ilmenau University of Technology, Germany
Jonathan Donner	Microsoft Research—Bangalore, India/US
Gerard Goggin	University of Sydney, Australia
Nicola Green	University of Surrey, UK
Leslie Haddon	University of Essex, UK
Keith Hampton	University of Pennsylvania, US
Joachim Höflich	Erfurt University, Germany
Mizuko Ito	University of California, Irvine, US/Japan
Shin Dong Kim	Hallym University, Republic of Korea
Ilpo Koskinen	University of Art and Design, Helsinki, Finland

Patrick Law	The Hong Kong Polytechnic University, Hong Kong
Christian Licoppe	Ecole Nationale Supérieure de Télécommunications, France
Sonia Livingstone	London School of Economics, UK
Steve Love	Brunel University, UK
Kristóf Nyíri	Hungarian Academy of Sciences, Hungary
Leysia Palen	University of Colorado, US
Raul Pertierra	University of the Philippines, Philippines
Madanmohan Rao	Indian Institute of Information Technology, Bangalore, India
Anxo Roibas	University of Brighton, UK/Italy
Harmeet Sawhney	Indiana University, US
Gitte Stald	IT University of Copenhagen, Denmark
Hidenori Tomita	Bukkyo University, Japan
Jane Vincent	University of Surrey, UK
Barry Wellman	University of Toronto, Canada
Peter B. White	La Trobe University, Australia

We wish to thank Mike Traugott and Susan Douglas of the Department of Communication Studies at the University of Michigan, and through them Constance F. and Arnold C. Pohs. Mike and Susan have supported the development of this book in various ways and the Pohs have helped support its development.

We wish to particularly thank James E. Katz of Rutgers University and also the general editor of Transaction Books' series on mobile communication. Jim has been on board with this project from the start and he is a vital member of the mobile communication research community. Without his assistance and insight the study of mobile communication would not be as well developed as it has become. We also want to thank Irving Lewis Horowitz of Transaction Publishers who has shown a great willingness to help us through the publication process.

Finally, and most specially, we want to thank Helen Ho of the University of Michigan. Helen has performed the essential task of editing and formatting the material for this volume. It is no exaggeration to say that without her, this book would not have been published. Thank you Helen.

Introduction

The Reconstruction of Space and Time through Mobile Communication Practices

Rich Ling
Telenor Research/University of Michigan

Scott W. Campbell
University of Michigan

Welcome to the first of what we envision as a series of compendiums examining different dimensions of mobile communication. These volumes are intended to fill a space in mobile communication research that is somewhere between a journal and stand-alone volumes.

In this volume, we examine the theme "The Reconstruction of Space and Time through Mobile Communication Practices." The proliferation of wireless and mobile communication technologies gives rise to important changes in how people experience space and time. These changes may be seen in many realms of social life, such as the transformation of public into private space and vice versa, the blurring of lines demarcating work and personal life, and new patterns of coordination and social networks. Recent scholarship has tried to make sense of these changes in space and time. For example, Manuel Castells (1989) argues that advances in telecommunications have contributed to new spatio-temporal forms, which he describes as "the space of flows" and "timeless time." According to Castells, these new forms mark a shift in the importance of the meaning of a place to the patterns of the de-sequenced, networked interactions that occur in that place. The purpose of this special issue is to continue and deepen the dialogue on how space and time change as a result of the lower threshold for interaction due to mobile communication technologies.

1

We are grateful to the authors who have entrusted us with their articles and we are thankful to the editorial board who has agreed to help with the reviewing of the different articles. We publish material from Denmark, Finland, France, Germany, India, Japan, Norway, the Philippines, Sweden, the UK, and the US. The breadth of methods used by the authors here is quite extraordinary. There is location-based data collection (Diminescu et al.), questionnaires (Julsrud and Bakke; Paragas), classical experimental design (Döring and Pöschl), a five-year panel design (Thulin and Vilhelmson), video/audio data capture (Relieu as well as Arminen, et al.) and of course various forms of interviews, often combined with other forms of data collection (Steenson and Donner; Julsrud and Bakke; Ito, et al.; Light; Thulin and Vilhelmson; Diminescu, et al.). The willingness to use traditional forms of data collection along with the keenness to try new approaches adds both breadth and depth of insight. The authors are to be commended on this.

Coordination and Cohesion across Time and Space

One of the ways that mobile communication influences our understanding of time and space is the way that we coordinate with one another. Mobile communication has meant that we call specific individuals, not general places. Thus, regardless of where we are and where our intended interlocutor is, we are able to make contact. This advancement has changed the way we coordinate interaction. In addition, it has changed our relation to mechanical timekeeping. Instead of agreeing on a particular time to meet, we can iteratively work out the most convenient time and place to meet.

In their chapter "Mobile Phones: Transforming the Everyday Social Communication Practice of Urban Youth," Eva Thulin and Bertil Vilhelmson document how the mobile telephone promoted a different approach to social interaction during the five-year period covered by their study. Their material indicates that the device allowed for more flexible coordination since, for example, the informants did not have to wait at a physical location for a phone call before they could start other activities. The unattached nature of the device seems to both play into and facilitate the mobile lifestyles of these individuals (aged eighteen to twenty-three), who are perhaps in the most nomadic period of their lives. The mobile seemed to result in more intense interaction for many of the individuals. In addition, the device became more integrated into their daily lives, as it became the common way for individuals to coordinate activities, develop plans, and micro-coordinate.

Mobile interaction is not simply instrumental coordination. It also has an expressive dimension, this in spite of the distance between interlocutors. Tom Julsrud and John Willy Bakke examine the use of communication mediation in commercial settings in Chapter 7, entitled "Trust, Friendship, and Expertise: The Use of Email, Mobile Dialogues and SMS to Develop and Sustain Social Relations in a Distributed Work Group." Specifically, they examine how the use of different mediation technologies changes communication patterns and interpersonal dynamics within geographically separated working groups. Their results show that when considering the question of traditional interaction-based social network analysis, the group was rather well integrated in spite of being in two separate locations. There were no persons who were isolated or excluded when using these measures. The email networks were quite dense and there was a high level of reciprocity. Indeed, given the physically distributed nature of the group, email was more inclusive than face-to-face interaction. On the other hand, short message service (SMS) traffic was less dense and was often seen as a more informal channel of communication.

Julsrud and Bakke find that individuals who were seen as experts were not always central in the trust networks. They note that mediated communication mapped well onto the expertise networks within the group. Most interestingly, however, is that trust was more often associated with textual forms of interaction and in particular SMS. This suggests that the transition from email to SMS was also an indication that the relationship between the two individuals had moved from a more formal type of interaction into more of a friendly, informal type of interaction. Indeed, SMS is sent to the individual regardless of where they are, making it slightly more invasive than email. It is also less ephemeral than a mobile phone conversation since it results in a digital artifact. While the expertise interactions were supported by email and telephone dialogues, SMS was the medium of choice for the friendship interactions in this distributed group of workers.

While Julsrud and Bakke focus on interaction in the working world, including the way that trust is developed and managed in mediated settings, Ilkka Arminen examines some of the same issues when considering the situation of friendship groups. He describes how mobile communication increases our potential for autonomous action, but more importantly strengthens social relationships in his chapter "New Reasons for Mobile Communication: Intensification of Time-Space Geography in the Mobile Era" (Chapter 4). Given the ability to connect with peers anywhere at any time, the threshold for interaction is, in effect, lowered. This in turn means that the peer or family group can keep tabs on and remotely integrate themselves with one another. His analysis shows that a large percentage of the calls were related to social coordination. Thus, given the distributed nature of modern society, mobile communication assists us in daily coordination practices. At the same time, when thinking of these coordination activities, mobile communication increases our ability to check on others. It can directly evoke the context of time and space ("Where are you now?" "When are you coming?"). Arminen shows how mobile communication does not free us from the demands of others—as the assertion of individual autonomy might suggest—but rather makes individuals available to peers and family. As such, the interaction within these groups is enriched. It may soften schedules, but at the same time it may enable monitoring and accountability. Arminen posits that the directness of this interaction increases the intensity of the social relationship.

As with the work by Arminen, Fernando Paragas examines how mobile communication has increased the potential for expressive interaction and various forms of coordination and control in his work, Chapter 2 of this book, "Migrant Workers and Mobile Phones: Technological, Temporal, and Spatial Simultaneity." Paragas provides us with personalized insight into the way that mobile communication has changed the situation for overseas Filipino workers (OFWs). Paragas begins by painting a picture of his own experience as a child in a home where his father spent most of the year working in Saudi Arabia. He describes the difficulties of communicating: letters took weeks to deliver and cassette tapes were used to provide vocal contact. Telephone calls were rare since his family did not have a telephone in the home. Phone calls were expensive, costing almost twice the daily wages of a normal worker, and callers had to stand in line for hours in order to use a particular long-distance telephone. Paragas reports that his family bought a mobile phone in the late 1990's—even before his family had a landline phone installed—and that the mobile device changed the nature of interaction with his father. Suddenly, his father was far more accessible since calls could be made quickly, and text messages were relatively inexpensive to send and receive in spite of the distances.

Paragas' experience traces one of the major transitions associated with mobile communication in the developing world. Mobile communication represents one of the easiest ways for families with overseas workers to maintain contact. This is neither a small nor a marginalized portion of the workforce. Paragas notes that 10 percent of the Philippine workforce consists of overseas workers and that they annually remit what amounts to 20 percent of the country's export revenues. Thus, this group represents an important portion of the national economy, and they also represent a significant group interested in adopting mobile communication devices.

In order to extend the analysis beyond his own experience, Paragas interviewed a series of informants and also carried out a survey of 320 persons who were deployed at various overseas posts. Paragas finds that the simultaneity afforded by the mobile phone helps to buffer some of the difficulties of separation, in that the mobile phone serves as a type of umbilical cord to families. In addition to providing a channel through which the families can talk, it can send and receive both text and photos. In countries where computers and the Internet have made only limited progress, the relatively easy to use mobile telephone provides mediated access where none had existed before.

Interestingly, the material gathered by Paragas shows that there are no differences in the use of mobile telephony based on gender or parental status. Thus, men and women, as well as those with and without children, were equally likely to own and use a mobile telephone. This said, there were differences according to the host regions. Those with higher education and those who worked in Europe and the US had access to more advanced mobile technology. Further, younger overseas workers reported having more advanced mobile telephones. In spite of these differences, basic mobile telephony was not as influenced by demographics as other types of technology consumption.

Following the theme of time and space, the ownership and use of mobile communication devices allows overseas workers to maintain a more active profile in the lives of their families. Families now have a more direct line of contact than Paragas experienced as a child. They described how, in addition to expressive communication, the mobile was used for various types of emergency situations and how it facilitated remittances. In some cases, the device was an essential element in various business operations and the overseas workers also used the device to facilitate communication with the expatriate community within the host country. The new simultaneity in the interaction between overseas workers and their families is truly revolutionary in that the distance between a remote posting and the people back home has been dramatically reduced. He discusses how this imagined temporal simultaneity resulted in the absent parent having a more central position in the home, the lives of their children, and decision-making processes. There was an enhanced sense of direct connection in spite of the difficulties imposed by the need to travel to the far corners of the globe in search of economic opportunities.

The material from these authors shows how mobile communication changes our understanding of coordination and control across time and space. It has allowed us to carry out, remotely, both expressive and instrumental interaction. The impact of this can be seen in the spheres of friendship, family, and business.

Managing Mobile Communication and Mobility

Another issue that comes out of the analyses offered in this volume is that individuals use mobile technology for their own purposes. In the previous set of chapters, there was the sense that communication technology was integral to the way that individuals interact with others. We also see that individuals use technology in their daily lives in order to suit their own purposes and their own mobility. In this way, the organization of their lives can take place on the fly; their movement between locations can be made more efficient and their base of operations can be sited in different places as needed.

Chapter 3, by Mizuko Ito, Daisuke Okabe, and Ken Anderson, is entitled "Portable Objects in Three Global Cities: The Personalization of Urban Places," and examines not only the role of mobile communication, but more broadly the role of various personal artifacts in our negotiation of everyday life. They are interested in examining how we use different "informational objects" to colonize personal space, stay in touch, and to mediate our interactions with different institutions. The focus in the chapter is not on the content of interpersonal interaction so much as on the how individuals carry an array of equipment in order to help them through the various exigencies of everyday urban life. This focus on the "stuff" (cards, keys, music players, tickets, mobile phones, receipts, etc.) that people carry about gives a holistic view of not only communicative, but also interpersonal and person-to-institution forms of interaction.

The results show that as individuals move about these urban cityscapes, they selectively draw on various items in their socio-technical kit in order to carry out different tasks. They might use an MP3 player in order to shut out the noise of a tram ride or they might use an access card to get into a training center. Mobile phones and other types of devices are often central objects in these interactions. Based on this analysis Ito, et al. describe three general types of technology use: cocooning, interfacing, and footprinting.

The first of these, *cocooning*, describes how various devices are used to colonize a small portion of an otherwise shared public space. The artifacts used for this can include music players, reading materials, and mobile phones to engage in conversations. The point is often to erect some sort of a shield against the intrusions of other impulses. Another form of cocooning observed—particularly in Los Angeles—included respondents embedding themselves in their automobiles while commuting. In this case, the array of devices included listening to the radio or talking on the mobile phone.

The use of different artifacts for *interfacing* was also a common activity, which includes communicating with others via the mobile phone. Contemporary urban life requires us to authenticate ourselves in different situations as we move from fully public places into those with some form of limited access, such as apartments and workplaces. Thus, keys, key cards, wireless radio frequency identification (RFID) cards—such as the London Underground Oyster card—and membership cards for different organizations become common artifacts for interfacing. Interestingly, some of the functions of these items are being transferred to mobile telephones. The authors also note that various forms of wireless interaction are becoming more common. In addition to mobile telephony, access to WiFi zones via PCs is on the rise. Finally, Ito, et al. observed what they called *footprinting* in that their informants often carried different forms of bonus and loyalty cards for keeping track of their purchases at, for example, coffee shops or other retail outlets.

Ito, Okabe, and Anderson found that the basic kit of mobile phone, wallet, and keys are constant. Through these objects (plus mobile media players), the respondents were able to retreat into a provisional cocoon, interface with their environment to gain access to buildings, services, and other persons, and also to document their interactions with different commercial organizations.

Bringing this into the general stream of this volume, these objects provide us with the ability to be mobile and to alternatively close off or gain access to others as needed. Many of the physical objects described by Ito, et al. are also becoming digital artifacts that in the future may reside on a mobile communication device, which can serve as an access card or means of identification. Thus, it is interesting to speculate how the trinity of keys, wallet, and mobile phone will be folded into a single mobile communications device in the future.

Dana Diminescu, Christian Licoppe, Zbigniew Smoreda, and Cesary Ziemlicki have contributed Chapter 1 of this volume "Tailing Untethered

Mobile Users: Studying Urban Mobilities and Communication Practices."
The chapter uses location-based material along with interview data to
better understand the interaction between location and communication. As with the article by Ito, et al., there is a focus on the way that
individuals rely on technology to facilitate mobility for various persons. Indeed, Diminescu, et al. evoke the work of Ito and Okabe on
tele-cocooning with Licoppe's (2004) "connected presence," as well
as Ling and Yttri's (2002) "micro-coordination" as alternative modes of
interaction. Unlike Ito, et al., however, there is only a focus on the role
of the mobile phone.

Diminescu, et al. draw quite directly on the tradition of "time geography" as outlined by Hägerstrand (1982). They present two cases:
one very routinized person (Patrick) and another who is almost without
routine (Sandrine). In the first case, we observe a man who exclusively
travels between his home in the western suburbs of Paris and his job in
the center of the city. With little variation, his movements were regular,
functional, and periodic. While he had the ambition of moving out of
the city, he had not yet accomplished that. His telephonic interaction
was often associated with coordinating meetings and other instrumental
activities. Few people had his telephone number and he was entrenched
in a lifestyle where there was only marginal use of the possibilities afforded by the mobile telephone.

Patrick is contrasted with Sandrine, who works in the film industry and
often has to find appropriate locations for different film projects. Given
this line of work, there was almost no section of Paris that she had not
visited. As with the individuals interviewed by Ito, et al., Sandrine was
quite active in her use of the possibilities available via mobile communication. She was often in contact with other colleagues, in what Diminescu,
et al. call "ongoing articulation work." Sandrine's workday consisted of
a flow of interactions where locations, props, settings, and the needs of
other persons in the production group were in a constant state of flux.
This meant that mobile communication had a central role in her life.

It is worth noting that the material contributed by Thulin and Vilhelmson also helps us to understand the individuals' increasing dependence
on mobile communication in their negotiation of everyday life. Their
analysis provides insight into how, over the time period of their study,
the mobile telephone had embedded itself into their respondents' lives.
The mobile moved from being an accessory that was "nice to have," to
an essential part of their daily kit. The results from the analysis show
that the intensity of mobile use increased over time: the individuals used

the device more often and used it to develop a more flexible lifestyle. Comparing the adoption of the telephone to the spread of the automobile, the authors argue that the mobile telephone has greatly influenced the organization of daily life.

In a slightly different direction, Chapter 10 by Molly Wright Steenson and Jonathan Donner describes the domestication of the mobile communication technology not only for the individual, but also for those who are able to borrow it. Their chapter, "Beyond the Personal and Private: Modes of Mobile Phone Sharing in Urban India," examines the practice of sharing mobile phones. While there is the general assumption in industrialized countries that there is one phone/subscription per person, this expectation does not hold for users in developing countries such as India.

Steenson and Donner's work helps us to understand that there are various issues associated with the use of mobile telephony, which results in extensive sharing of the technology. The sharing is occasioned not only by economic issues, but also by questions of family mores and literacy. While sharing is rather common, there is also a tension associated with the practice. Not everyone is an equal partner, and the rules determining who is on the inside and who is not are ill defined and often the topic of intense negotiation.

One element in the structure of sharing phones is the economic dimension. Use of mobile telephony in developing countries is quite often associated with economic need. It might be that there is in general little money or that access to economic resources is cyclical. This means that mobile telephony represents a type of resource that needs to be managed. Given this situation, people in developing countries often have two or three different subscriptions that they strategically switch to, given the time of day and the person whom they are trying to reach. Other ways of dealing with the economic issues of mobile telephony include the pooling of minutes and beeping/flashing (Donner, 2005).

Other strategies for extending the reach of mobile communication beyond the intended person-to-person model assumed in many countries is that is the practice of contacting "hub individuals" in the hope that the person they actually would like to speak with is nearby. That is, Steenson and Donner's subjects found specific friends by contacting "someone and not someplace." This practice can be an informal attempt to find a particular person, or it can be more formalized in that one person acts as a message hub for a collection of other persons who do not have mobile phones.

Sharing is not necessarily only based on economic issues, but also questions of family and interpersonal dynamics. The circle of individuals with whom one shares a mobile phone might include parents, children, wives, and business partners or associates. In each case, the sharing of the device makes explicit other, more implicit relationships. The process of sharing and the decisions as to who is a legitimate "sharing partner" also help to make the nature of particular relationships more explicit. Indeed, they draw on the tradition of gifting analysis as developed by Mauss (1990). By examining the economy of sharing, we not only see how sharing mobile phones restructures social space, but are also given insight into individuals' web of interactions.

In this group of chapters, we see that the individuals use mobile communication to facilitate various issues associated with daily life. They might use them to coordinate, protect themselves from the stresses of urban life, or they might use share mobile devices in order to facilitate the resolution of different daily issues.

The Individuals' Relation to Their Co-Present Situation

Another set of chapters focuses on how we as individuals relate to the affordances provided by mobile communication. The making and receiving of mobile telephone calls, by their very nature, mean that the context of the call is ill defined. Using Goffman's phrase, we must somehow "booth" ourselves when making a call (1981, 86): that is, we must negotiate between the physical situation and the concentration required by the communication event. By the same token, the person receiving the call or the text message needs to try and understand not only the content of the communication, but also place it within a broader context where the timing of the communication and the location of the sender/caller might be of relevance.

Chapter 8, "Negotiations in Space: The Impact of Receiving Phone Calls on the Move" by Ann Light, examines our subjective experience of using the mobile phone. The chapter examines how we mentally place ourselves into various thought spaces based on the context of our telephone use. Light was particularity interested in examining how her interviewees discussed their subjective sense of place when using the mobile phone. Using a Heideggerian approach, Light looks at the way in which physical space is juxtaposed with phenomenological space. In order to be considered as "near" in a phenomenological sense, mobile communication must be something that we are dealing with and that requires our attention. Thus, the concern is not based on the objective distance to an object, but rather upon our sense of the object or issue.

The application of this insight is obvious when thinking of mobile communication. Light guides us through a series of interviews where the informants describe their telephonic interaction with persons they know and situations with which they are familiar. Her analysis shows how we, in effect, "live into" the mediated interaction and how the ability to place ourselves into the context of our interlocutor can facilitate the interaction process.

When considering mobile communication, this ability to project ourselves into the context of the interlocutor is no mean trick. Since we call individuals and not places, we are not calling any particularly fixed physical context. This means that perhaps both interlocutors need to be open to their expectations as to what is physically available at the other end of the line. Given the individual nature of the mobile phone, we may come into contact with the person with whom we wish to speak, but do not always know where they are or what they are doing. Thus, both the caller and the receiver need to be open in their assumptions as to the other's situation. Light describes how we "fill in" the image of the location and activities of the person on the other end of the call.

Obviously, in some cases, receiving a mobile phone call can be inappropriate. It is not necessarily possible for the caller to know the situation of the person they call: thus, there is the need to manage the situation with quickly changing contexts, where the recipient of the call must feel a sense of being able to spend the time needed to deal with the situation. Thus, there can be certain vulnerability on the part of the receiver as they try to "stage manage" the call. Goffman (1959) discusses this in terms of front and back stage behavior and the problem of being caught in the wrong context. In other cases, Light's respondents speak of being drawn out of a physical context when they receive a call. She describes respondents who get calls while they are out enjoying a walk and how the call becomes the central focus, pushing the surroundings of their walk into the background. In sum, Light's use of Heidegger's concept of a subjective sense of place shows that it is not only the situation that is important when examining the use of mobile telephony; rather, the ability of the interlocutors to imagine the situation of their counterparts facilitates the interaction.

Arminen's chapter, described above, also resonates with this concept. He examines how mobile communication can affect the intensity of a moment for both those who are co-present and those who are in virtual attendance via a mobile link. The material examined by Arminen shows how interlocutors use the mobile telephone in conjunction with co-present interactions. The mobile communication can augment face-to-face interaction and in turn become a part of the general ballast of the friendship. The connotative meanings become established and help the dyad (or more generally the group) with their organization of further interaction. While the mediated interaction can detract from interactions with co-present others, it can also provide expanded opportunities for contact with those who are not physically present. The increased mediated interaction within the group boosts the web of interaction overall, and in this way increases the cohesion of the group. When seen this way, the mobile phone does not contribute to autonomy, but rather to group integration.

The chapter by Marc Relieu (Chapter 9), entitled "Mobile Phone 'Work': Disengaging and Engaging Mobile Phone Activities with Concurrent Activities," examines some of the same issues as Light's chapter. In both cases, the authors are interested in the question of how the use of mobile communication devices works within individuals' daily lives. However, where Light relies on the use of interview material, Relieu uses a device to directly collect visual material while his subjects used their mobile telephones.

While Light examines how her informants "lived into" their mobile telephone experiences, the work by Relieu documents how his informants went through the process of generating text messages while at the same time maintaining their contact with co-present friends. To do this, Relieu equipped informants with a micro-camera/microphone built into a pair of glasses. The resulting recordings provide very fine-grained examples showing how mobile phone use is interlaced with other social activities, such as chatting with a co-present friend or having a snack in a café.

Relieu notes that when the individual receives a call, he or she is less in control of the situation and must work to place the event into the context of their current surroundings. On the other hand, when an individual creates a call—for example, a text message— they are in control of their situation to a greater degree and are able to weave that activity in with other co-present actions. The composition of a "turn" in an SMS interaction competes with other emergent co-present issues. Since constructing a textual turn does not include the same overhanging demands on focused interaction, the author of the SMS can move attention back and forth between texting and their current physical situation.

Nicola Döring and Sandra Pöschl look beyond the specific content of text messages to examine how people interpret the time and location of the messages they receive in Chapter 5, "Nonverbal Cues in Mobile Phone Text Messages: The Effects of Chronemics and Proxemics." They do this by using an experimental method with which they examine whether or not text messages are interpreted differently, depending on the time at which and the distance from which they are sent. They note, as does Arminen, that providing the context for a mobile phone call is important. It assists in the flow and the interpretation of the interaction. For example, when an interlocutor needs to pause in order to deal with a co-present situation, shared knowledge of their current context means that the other conversation partner has a better sense of what to expect. This common ground is important in facilitating mediated interaction. Playing on Goffman's (1981) idea of signals that are "given" (intentional) and those that are "given off" (unintentional), this meta-information associated with text messages is also available for interpretation.

Döring and Pöschl examine how we give meaning to the timing of text messages. Indeed, we give meaning to the response latency, the synchronicity, the frequency of interaction, and the duration of communication sessions. The "over the top" order from our boss is interpreted differently at 2:00 p.m. than it is if it is sent at 2:00 a.m. The same is true of intimate messages from our significant others. In addition to the importance of how time is interpreted, Döring and Pöschl suggest that the location from which messages are sent is also an issue that is open to interpretation; we might infer different meanings to the same message if it comes from a neighboring room as opposed to coming from a neighboring country.

Their chapter is based on two experiments that asked respondents to give their interpretation of text messages that included a time and a location stamp. In some cases, the text messages were more intimate in nature and in other cases were more authoritative. Their analysis shows that the time stamp influenced the way that the respondents construed the message. Messages sent in the daytime were seen as being more dominant and less intimate while the opposite was true of those with a time stamp from a nighttime hour.

The work of Döring and Pöschl is important since it isolates certain contextual issues associated with the use of mobile communication and examines them using a rigorous experimental approach. Their analysis joins that of Love and Kewley (2005), as well as Cumiskey (2005), in that it applies the insights of psychology to the ownership and use of mobile telephones.

Previous research shows that the anytime, anywhere nature of mobile communication helps bring people together physically and relationally, yet also offers new ways of demarcating and managing boundaries of time and space (see Ling, 2004). The chapters in this volume enrich our understanding of these phenomena by deepening our understanding of how spatio-temporal boundaries are negotiated in a mobile society. In this volume, we gain deeper insights into the ways mobile communication establishes relational rhythms within peer groups, mitigates distance in distributed families, and generates trust among individuals who rarely see each other. At the same time, we also gain deeper insights into the ways that spatio-temporal boundaries are erected through mobile technology to maintain social separation. This can be seen through practices such as "cocooning" and routinizing communication patterns.

Beyond providing a more nuanced understanding of existing concepts, the contributions to this volume also highlight more novel areas of change in how space and time are (re)constructed through mobile communication. For example, we see how the sharing of mobile devices can restructure social space in developing countries. Another relatively novel area of scholarship is the inter-subjectivity involved in imagining an interlocutor's spatial context while a caller is situated in his or her own physical environment. Collectively, the contributions to this volume make an important step forward for the burgeoning new field of mobile communication studies. As such, we would again like to express gratitude to the authors for sharing their cutting-edge work in this venue. We are also grateful to the reviewers and the editorial board members whose help made this project possible. Finally, we hope that you, the reader, get as much out of consuming this volume as we have in putting it together.

Bibliography

Castells, Manuel. *The Informational City: Information Technology, Economic Restructuring and the Urban-Regional Process.* Oxford, UK: Blackwell Publishers, 1989.

Cumiskey, Kathleen M. "'Can You Hear Me Now?' Paradoxes of Techno-Intimacy Resulting from the Use of Mobile Communication Technology in Public." In *A Sense of Place: The Global and the Local in Mobile Communication,* edited by Kristóf Nyíri, 91-98. Vienna, Austria: Passagen Verlag, 2005.

Donner, Jonathan. "The Rules of Beeping: Exchanging Messages Using Missed Calls on Mobile Phones in Sub-Saharan Africa." Paper delivered at the 55th Annual Conference of the International Communication Association. 27 May 2005, New York, NY.

Goffman, Erving. *The Presentation of Self in Everyday Life*. New York, NY: Anchor, 1959.

Goffman, Erving. *Forms of Talk*. Philadelphia, PA: University of Pennsylvania Press, 1981.

Hägerstrand, Torsten. "The Impact of Social Organization and Environment upon the Time-use of Individuals and Households." In *Internal Structure of the City: Readings from Urban Form, Growth and Policy*, edited by Larry S. Bourne, 118-123. Oxford, UK: Oxford University Press.

Licoppe, Christian. "'Connected' Presence: The Emergence of a New Repertoire for Managing Social Relationships in a Changing Communication Technoscape." *Environment and Planning D: Society and Space*, 22.1 (2004): 135–156

Ling, R. 2004. *The mobile connection: The cell phone's impact on society*. San Francisco, CA: Morgan Kaufman.

Ling, Richard S. and Birgitte Yttri. "Hyper-Coordination via Mobile Phones in Norway." In *Perpetual Contact: Mobile Communication, Private Talk, Public Performance*, edited by James E. Katz and Mark Aakhus, 139-169. Cambridge, UK: Cambridge University Press, 2002.

Love, Steve and Joanne Kewley. "Does Personality Affect Peoples' Attitude Towards Mobile Phone Use in Public Places?" In *Front Stage - Back stage: Mobile Communication and the Renegotiation of the Social Sphere*, edited by Rich Ling and Per Pedersen, 139-169. Grimstad, Norway: Springer, 2005.

Mauss, Marcel. *The Gift: The Form and Reason for Exchange in Archaic Societies*. London, UK: Routledge, 1990.

1

Tailing Untethered Mobile Users: Studying Urban Mobilities and Communication Practices

Dana Diminescu
Ecole Nationale Supérieure des Télécommunications

Christian Licoppe
Ecole Nationale Supérieure des Télécommunications

Zbigniew Smoreda
France Telecom R&D

Cezary Ziemlicki
France Telecom R&D

In the past few years the question of mobilities has become inseparable from reflection on territories and their development (Rallet, 2004; Veltz, 2004). In the Urban Studies tradition, Doreen Massey (1993) notes that it is impossible to think of an ordinary shopping street in London without mobilizing half the globe and the history of the British Empire. Urban dynamics are accelerated by new techniques for storing goods and information, and for transporting them and human beings. With humans, in particular, these changes raise the question of the forms of mobility and encounter that are made relevant by the ways territories are equipped for different types of flow.

Regarding mobilities, the work initiated by John Urry and his colleagues suggests a transition between a displacement paradigm, in which mobility is simply a means to other ends (moving from A to B to do something and trying to minimize the costs of that displacement) and a mobility paradigm, in which mobility becomes a creative experience and an end in itself, blurring the boundaries between places, activities, and people (Sheller and Urry, 2006; Urry, 2004). In the latter case, individuals must be viewed as equipped with a set of artifacts which facilitate mobility and allow for access to spatially distributed resources. They compose a mobile habitat that is also a habitat for mobility (Boullier, 1999). Cities and public spaces are increasingly pervaded by fields of signs, which rely on the cognitive capacities of their inhabitants (Amar, 2004; Ascher, 2004)—provided that the profusion of signs does not dull their senses and induce indifference (Simmel, 1989). They are simultaneously "augmented" in a pragmatic sense, with diverse services accessible via the growing number of artifacts that mobile city dwellers carry on themselves.

Regarding encounters and communication, the distinction is rather between an older model of the city as a mosaic of smaller village-like communities and cities as a whole as the source of opportunities for the constant mingling of hordes of strangers (Lofland, 1973, 1998) who politely ignore one another (Goffman, 1963). One trend of urban development has been to design public places so that they afford more opportunities for encounters between people who know one another or for strangers to become acquainted in a polite fashion. This resonates with one of the spontaneous uses of Information and Communication Technologies (ICTs) between family and friends, which relies on the ubiquity of communicational resources so that mobile and connected users can maintain a "tele-cocoon" of favorite contacts with whom they constantly stay in touch (Ito and Okabe, 2005), solving micro-coordination problems on the move (Ling and Yttri, 2002). With "connected presence" (Licoppe, 2004; Licoppe and Smoreda, 2005), a sense of intimacy with distant others pervades all the places we come across.

These two lines of questioning have inspired a new thrust of technological development, urban computing, characterized by devices that exploit mobile networks and terminals and thus allow for new forms of encounter and socialization "on the move." One form of mobile technology, for instance, aims to equip users with "digital auras": the mobile terminal projects the user's profile in his or her immediate proximal environment (e.g., via Bluetooth local connectivity technology) thus enabling him or her to be matched up with others when they are similarly equipped and their profiles correspond (e.g., by SMS) when they happen to be co-located (that is, close enough). This is the idea behind services such as Lovegety[1] (Iwatani, 1998) and Jabberwocky[2] (Paulos and Goodman, 2004) and practices such as "toothing"[3] both of which aim to afford new opportunities for strangers to meet in public spaces for mediated encounters.

Another line of technological development exploits the possibilities of location awareness to enable mobile users to detect one another's presence at a distance, and to read and write localized e-graffitis, as in the ActiveCampus experiment (Griswold, et al., 2003). The geo-location of mobile terminals also makes it possible to determine users' positions on a continuous basis, for institutional purposes. Emergency services such as 911 may be enhanced, for example, so that the caller is automatically located at the time of the call (E-911). Other configurations of geo-located services are designed to produce emergent communities, where the users of such services may constantly monitor their positions. This enables them to develop highly original forms of mobility, encounters, and association, as in geo-located multiplayer mobile games (Licoppe and Inada, 2006).

Theoretical concerns and technological developments share a growing focus on questions of territories and mobilities, coordination, and communication. The aim of this chapter is to show how it is possible to systematically analyze mobilities and communication practices on the basis of location-specific data. We have developed an original protocol in which we combined the systematic collection of data on location and on communication acts performed on mobile terminals by a given user with the qualitative descriptions and interpretations elaborated by the same user during in-depth interviews. Our approach relates to two other research trends. The first is time geography, which endeavors to reconstruct 4-D patterns of practices by asking individuals to fill in log books in which they describe certain practices and index the places and times of their occurrence, and by analyzing the corresponding corpus (Hägerstrand, 1970; Janelle, et al., 1998; Kwan, 1998). The second is the analysis of social networks that has made it possible to explore the relations between the structure of networks and mediated communication practices (Chabrol and Périn, 1997; Claisse and Rowe, 1993; Rivière, 2000). However, most of these different types of research rely on self-report diaries, which generally limit the temporal range of studies to one or two weeks. One step forward has been to study the electronic traces left by calls in itemized billing databases (Smoreda and Licoppe, 2000; Licoppe and Smoreda, 2005).

The purpose of our research was to take this idea further by simultaneously drawing on a collection of location data and details of communication acts, and thus to propose what, to our knowledge, is the first systematic and combined study of communication practices and mobility ranging over a period of several months. This chapter explains the methodology and the various questions and perspectives that it opens, and describes the initial results of the research that has been undertaken thus far.

Approach to the Study

The methodology on which the experimental protocol is based consists of three parts: (1) an empirical apparatus for collecting and aggregating data concerning the locations of users and their communication practices; (2) two series of interviews over ten days, in which they were shown these objective data and questioned about their interpretation; and (3) use of the previous interviews to qualify the data gathered over six months.

Apparatus for Collecting Data on Communication and Mobile Practices

The data collection device relies on a probe or a software application functioning on terminals running the Symbian operating system. Users simply have to download the probe via one of the interfaces (GPRS, Bluetooth, infrared) managed by the terminal. They can deactivate it at any time if they wish to be "invisible," and then reactivate it again. This software can be modulated and extended to various modes of use of the terminals. At this stage we have focused on the software functionalities that enabled us to trace and collect the cells of the network visited (location data) and the details of the interpersonal communication acts performed (voice calls or SMS, incoming or outgoing, time, correspondent's number, etc.).

The collection of location data is based on the properties of a mobile network such as GSM.[4] The antennae of this network delimit "cells" by triangulation. Each of these cells has a unique identity number. The network automatically locates terminals that are within the perimeter of the cells. In urban environments, the range of these cells is between 100 and 300 meters, depending on the density of the radio network. Presence in a particular cell may be associated with the user's location in the urban zone, with an accuracy of within 100 to 200 hundred meters. When the user leaves the zone of coverage of one antenna and enters the zone of the neighboring antennae, the terminal detects this event. The probe stores each of these "mobility events" and records them in the form of a list of all the identities of the cells passed through with the time of the event. The same is done for each communication act. Whether they concern a voice call, an SMS, or an MMS, incoming or outgoing, these data will be recorded and enhanced by the identity of the cell(s) where the communication act was performed.

These data are sent to a centralized database.[5] The next step consists of decoding the data for analysis. The location data and the identities of the cells recorded by the probe are combined with a reference map that specifies the geographic position of each identity. Thus, movements can be mapped and the places visited most often can be visualized. By linking tables showing mobility data with those showing communication data, mixed indicators can be constructed and certain places identified, for instance those in which the most calls, or the most SMS, etc., are made or received. The aim is to construct a typology that combines mobilities and communication practices on the mobile terminal, on the basis of several months of observation.[6] This is where the main advantage in this method lies. When compared to traditional self-report diaries, there is generally only the ability to collect observations for shorter periods, commonly only up to two weeks. This is because of the very heavy constraint of the respondent having to continually fill them in.

The geo-located observation platform allowed us to build an external diary of several months of observation of users' movements and communication practices. This served as a basis for the processing of statistics. In-depth qualitative work was nevertheless necessary, for at this stage users' geographic positions were represented only by the antennae postal address,[7] that is, "physico-geometric" data of very limited significance from users' perspectives. It was therefore necessary to ask users to describe these quasi abstract positions in terms of the places they used to visit and the activities they conducted there. However, this was only a part of the qualitative survey apparatus that we implemented.

Socio-Graphic Approach and Qualification of Practices Recorded in the Logbooks

The data collection described above was carried out between two sets of interviews with the individuals studied. The first set had two objectives: to collect general descriptions of mobility and communication practices and to situate these with respect to current biographies. In this way, personal histories of mobility, both long- and short-term, private and professional, recurrent and occasional, could be constructed. These were completed by specific work on the personal artifacts supporting "on the move" mobility. This part of the interviews focused on the collection and ranking, by order of importance, of the objects that the person carried on him or herself and that afforded access to various places, services, and people.

The second set of interviews was very different. Before the visit, we used the data collected automatically to produce a logbook of the locations of the cells visited and the communication acts performed by the person with the corresponding times. This automatically generated diary covered ten consecutive days in the preceding two weeks, so that the relevant information was still fairly fresh in the user's mind. The survey data was turned into a time ordered printing that could be read as a personal diary (see Figure 1.1). The respondent was asked to describe and qualify, in his or her own words, the type of place and activity corresponding to the cells visited, moment by moment, and to categorize the people contacted as well as his or her relationship with them.

Figure 1.1

Note: Extract of a logbook concerning places and telephone practices (top) and for interactions and consultation of SMS (bottom). Both were presented separately and successively, for reasons of legibility. This short sequence of calls and consultations in a very short space of time (between 14:12 and 14:16) corresponds to a "coordination knot," or a rapid sequence of calls.

We soon noticed that these interviews provided much richer information than the frame of data qualification we had set. In the situation that we had constructed, we actually showed our respondents an objectified representation (the "-etic" type) of their practices. This prompted them to take up these data—that were external but closely concerned their personal "information preserve" (Goffman, 1971)—by producing their own account (the "-emic" type) of the events represented,[8] thus reassuming some form of epistemic priority through their own reactive assessment (Heritage and Raymond, 2005). This way of responding to their public confrontation with the technological traces left by their own practices was highly sensitive to the interviewees' perception of any kind of incoherence between the data and their own memory of what they had done. Every time such a discrepancy was revealed, the subjects worked very hard to make sense by themselves by using the data presented to them. They turned themselves into investigators of their own deeds, commenting aloud—for their own benefit and that of the observer—on their navigation between the clues provided by the data and their own memories. This went on until they were able to produce a satisfactory account for all practical purposes.

This particular research situation revealed some unexpected objects, such as "coordination knots," to use a concept from activity theory.[9] These are very rapid sequences of calls going both ways, lasting only a few minutes, and using varied numbers and media (e.g., fixed professional and mobile phones, voice and SMS, etc.) between two or three participants, generally to ensure some form of coordination within the larger frame of a joint action. The respondents never stopped at simply qualifying their correspondents; they always tried to give coherent meaning to such sequence, that is, to the coordination knot. They described their actions as a sort of emergent process in which, rather than having defined an action plan for once and for all, they used the multiple technological resources enabling them to reach one another, to co-elaborate and co-produce by trial and error the subsequent action that would be relevant in relation to the general orientation of the activity under way. Coordination knots seem to constitute a fairly common mode of coordination in highly connected worlds where the other person's reachability can be anticipated via one of several possible mediations. Their function is not only instrumental; participants were thus also re-experiencing their mutual reachability and re-activating the strength of their bonds.

The second set of interviews was therefore an opportunity for the qualification of the places visited, the correspondents, and the intentions behind mobile communication practices. The particular situation that stemmed from it—a subject's examination of an objectified list of his or her practices—was at the origin of the production of accounts that enabled the subject to reclaim primary rights to his or her own experience by assessing the data we had provided him or her. Our protocol therefore allowed for the production of both objective and interpretive rich data on mobile communication practices. To implement it, we chose to work on a limited but structured sample.

Composition of the Sample

The configuration of the sample used in our survey was limited by the hybrid aspect of our methodology (qualitative but also quantitative and automated) and especially by the need to be able to compare the different subjects while ensuring that there was a significant contrast in their various mobility and communication practices. The sample was first limited to twenty-four representative individuals, all of whom lived in the same city (Paris); this was important since mobile practices are highly sensitive to the type of environment in which people move. They were chosen from the same age group (thirty to forty-five) and all had children (all except one had children and none had more than two), since the coordination constraints weighing on people and their mobility varies widely, depending on age group and family structure.

We chose to differentiate participants along two axes: type of job and previous experience in mobility. With respect to jobs, we chose individuals employed in different kind of jobs requiring disparate forms of mobility: occupations with more or less routine commuting, stable work that required some form of mobility on a regular basis, flexible employment that prompted a sequence of temporary labor contracts with changing mobility constraints, and precariousness where the jobs were not only temporary but also bordered on illegality. Our hypothesis is that these diverse employment configurations are articulated differently to the opportunities and constraints of mobility and communication. In regards to the residential biographies, we chose subjects from within three categories: those who had not changed their address in the past ten years, those who had moved at least once (but still within France) in the past ten years, and those who had moved in the past ten years and had lived abroad at some point during that time. The underlying hypothesis is that any prior experience of residential mobility can influence the user's forms of daily mobility and uses of communication devices. On this basis we recruited twenty-four individuals to whom we gave mobile phones equipped with probes and all agreed to comply with our research protocol.

We introduced a secondary element of differentiation into the sample by recruiting some non-French subjects who were migrants (in the sense of being people who in their history of mobility had at least one event of international migration). We relied on a hypothesis that runs counter to a traditional sociology of migrations that distinguishes between migrants and sedentary people, migratory trajectories and urban ones, and transnational displacements and domestic ones. In this work, research issues are centered on problems of territory, cultural identity, and social or institutional integration. The definition of migrants usually focuses on a series of fateful oppositions, which are constantly highlighted as the organizing principle of theoretical reflection on shifting populations: mobile/immobile, neither there/nor here, absent/present, in the centre/on the margin, etc. It seems necessary to turn from such distinctions and start instead with the idea that "what defines the contemporary world is flows, more than structures and stable organizations" (Urry, 2000: 5). In this way, displacements and mobilities are placed at the heart of the human sciences, as Urry proposed for sociology or Clifford (1997) for anthropology. Many people today are able to take for granted the fact that they or their children will probably end up living and working in a place other than their hometown. Forms of mobility are multiplying and merging: migrants who trade under cover of a tourist visa; tourists who travel and end up staying in the country in which they spent their holidays; immigrants who, once they have obtained access to a new nationality, carry on moving; young highly qualified executives; confirmed travelers, and the like. All juggle with different mobilities in search of a form of stability. We posit that the generic rift between migrant, immigrant, nomadic, and even sedentary is tending to fade completely or at least beginning to take on more subtle forms. Our objective is to identify these forms in the entanglement of practices involving mobility and uses of remote communication devices.

Finally, we chose a relatively long period (six months) of collection and aggregation of data. This enabled us to capture a fairly wide spectrum of each individual's more occasional mobilities, such as journeys and long visits (more than a few days) to other towns or abroad. We thus observed changes in the picture (apart from two people who "disappeared" from our observations). Consequent to biographic events, the social status of certain individuals changed during the survey. Some who were flexibly employed obtained permanent jobs, two had one more child, one divorced, and two separated from their partners.

"Paradigm of Displacements" and "Paradigm of Mobilities": Two Extreme Cases

To illustrate the interest of our approach and the type of results that it allows us to obtain, we have chosen here to arrange the discussion around two cases that display diametrically opposed experiences of mobility and communication.

An "Immutable Mobility"[10]

At the time of our survey, thirty-two-year-old Patrick had recently married and had no children. He was a computer technician in a public institution. The first interview enabled us to reconstruct a "biographical mobility" that was relatively average compared to recent trends in personal histories of mobility (what certain authors have called "mobility transition").[11] Patrick was born in the suburbs of Paris where he lived in his parents' home from 1973 to 1982. The family moved successively to Cherbourg, where they lived from 1982 to 1984, and then back to the Paris area, where they lived from 1984 to 2001. Patrick started his first job in Caen in 2001 and arrived at Mantes-la-Jolie (near Paris) in 2002 to be closer to his parents who had moved in the meantime. He said he lived in two places: his own flat in Mantes-la-Jolie and that of his wife in Cherbourg, where she worked. He considered himself to be constantly between these two places. During the week he was in the Paris area, commuting daily between Mantes-la-Jolie and Paris, where he worked, while most weekends were spent in Cherbourg with his wife.

This particular form of mobility constructed around a stable job and two different homes was prominently displayed in the artifacts composing his mobile habitat: he constantly carried with him several heavy sets of keys (a set to his home, a set to his wife's, and a set to his parents' home). It was also characterized by extensive use of both local and national public transportation networks, combined with movement on foot and by car (when he was in Cherbourg).

The second interview and comparison with the logbooks enabled us to characterize the places visited and to show highly regular mobile behavior over almost two weeks. This was further confirmed when these data were used to examine Patrick's movements over a six-month period. Qualifying the places visited over ten days was enough to identify 96 percent of the locations (in terms of cells) visited in six months! This individual's mobility can be summed up as consisting essentially of short movements (including intra-cell, on the scale of two hundred meters that our apparatus cannot distinguish) around his places of work and residence, and of his daily or weekly journeys between these places (see Figure 1.2).

Figure 1.2a

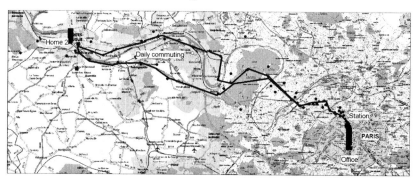

Figure 1.2b

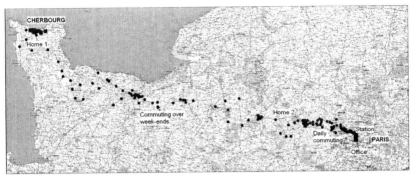

Note: Map of Patrick's displacements over six months. 1.2a shows his daily repetition of the same journey between his home in the suburbs and his job in the Paris area, and 1,2b, at national scale, shows his commuting path over weekends, with the Paris-Cherbourg train journey standing out prominently.

As far as his communication practices were concerned, Patrick identified his main correspondents when he confronted the logbook. It showed that communication with his wife accounted for over 90 percent of his mobile calls during the whole observation period. Moreover, he had given his mobile number to very few people (his wife, his parents, a few friends, and two close colleagues in his computing team). Most interactions took place in the evening after work or over the weekend at his wife's home in Cherbourg, even though his mobile phone was left on all the time. He used it while traveling only when he had forgotten something or was late at the station; these were about 5 percent of his calls, almost all of which were with his wife (see Figure 1.3).

In regards to mobility, Patrick's movements were regular, periodic, and functional. They were the means to an end: going to work, going home, going to see his wife on the weekend. In fact, they were experienced as a constraint that he tried to minimize, even if it meant making big changes. Patrick's plan for the future was to "find a job in Cherbourg," so that he could live and work in the same town. He did not perceive his movements and places of transit during his mobility (railway stations, trains, etc.) as opportunities to do something else. This was particularly true with social networking. He very seldom used his journeys and the time they afforded him to use his mobile phone for the purpose of maintaining personal relationships or managing professional ones (very few people had his mobile number). Mobility was therefore both a constraint and a means to other ends; an experience that Patrick went through while remaining true to himself, in a sense. It was not seen as an opportunity

Figure 1.3

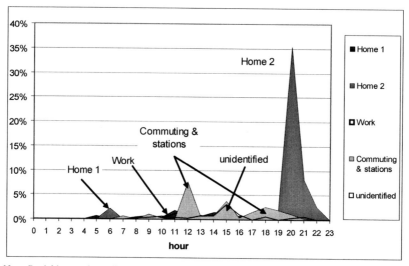

Note: Patrick's outgoing calls. Most of his calls were with family and were made or received at home in the evening or over the weekend. A few calls were made while waiting in the station during his trips to Cherbourg and were mostly related to journey-relevant arrangements.

to use his mobile phone creatively, to weave together the places he had gone through, the modes of transport and the communicational resources used, into an original experience. Patrick is an almost perfect example of the "displacement paradigm" (Sheller and Urry, 2006).

The Opportunistic Exploitation of Communication and Mobility Resources: Constrained Autonomy

At the time of our survey, thirty-six-year-old Sandrine was living with a partner and expecting a child, due near the end of the observation period. She had never left Paris but had moved more than fifteen times after leaving her parents' home at the age of eighteen. She was a filmmaker by profession and had a part-time job as a production assistant for television. This job entailed a great deal of traveling, either for location scouting or for shooting films. She also taught filmmaking in a non-profit association and produced her own films. Examination of the logbook data of the two weeks preceding the interview showed numerous daily movements and a high level of overlap of all her activities everywhere.

Sandrine moved about between several stable places: her home, her office in a production company north of Paris, and the association where she taught. The intensity of her movements was amplified during periods of shooting films, as in the week preceding the interview. On a Friday afternoon she spent several hours in the east of Paris in search of a suitable location. With a vague idea of what she wanted, she drove around in her car until, by chance, she came across the ideal cul-de-sac, the "perfect décor" for her film. She carried on researching on the following Monday afternoon and then spent the entire day on Tuesday at the location. Many of Sandrine's urban movements were turned into opportunistic and creative experiences, oriented by her search for locations. More generally, as she drives around in her daily life she constantly keeps an eye open for suitable spots that might one day come in useful professionally. Far from being journeys that she tries to minimize, she engages in urban mobility in an exploratory mode, characterized by a particular openness and vigilance. Within a fairly flexible schedule she combines varied forms of regular mobility related to her multiple but recurrent personal and professional commitments, with a multitude of occasional movements. This clearly shows up when her mobility data in the Paris area over a period of several months is aggregated (see Figure 1.4). The places identified from the logbook kept for ten days account for only half of the places visited in six months (whereas with Patrick, two weeks gave an almost complete idea of his movements over six months) and compose a mosaic

Figure 1.4

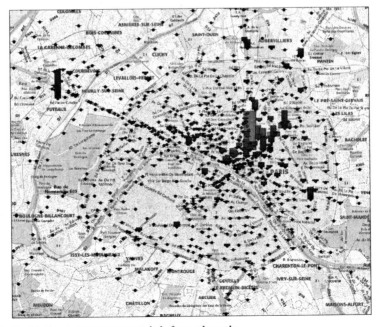

Note: Sandrine's movements over a period of several months.

of points sprinkled across the city. These points are scattered so widely and at the same time are so dense that they almost create a pointillist picture.

The places in which Patrick spent most of his time were clearly characterized by a type of activity: place of work, family space, or leisure. Overlaps were rare and limited, and almost exclusively concerned calls from his wife at work. In Sandrine's case, it is far more difficult to characterize each place since she moved about so much. When she spent an afternoon at home during the week it was to "do paperwork," for either personal reasons (health insurance related to her pregnancy) or professional reasons (applying to the unemployment fund which may have entitled her to benefits due to her borderline status), or to prepare her lessons and work on her films a little. This was equally true of her office and the association from which she sent personal faxes and made phone calls whenever convenient. This entanglement was temporally oriented, insofar as Sandrine was constantly busy preparing what she was going to do next, wherever she was. Each place visited, whether repeatedly or occasionally, was both a place in which she carried out specific activities associated with it, and an almost constant "articulation work"[12] oriented toward the remote organization and preparation of future mobilities and tasks. As she put it, she had to "adapt quickly" and organize things as she went along. In this sense she was both present and on the move.

Sandrine's communication practices reflected this approach to mobility. She exploited all available technological artifacts opportunistically: telephones, fax, computers, or photocopy machines, depending on the place. Her mobile phone played a key part, due to the specific characteristics of her job that had a "strong relational dimension." As she put it, one constantly has to "call and call back" and "keep contact." A dull, constant pressure weighed on her availability: "I've been doing this for 15 years; I had a mobile very early on, because you've got to be reachable immediately otherwise everyone knows, they'll call the next person."[13]

One of the clearest signs of this constant concern to remain available was the frequency with which she consulted her messages. The voice-mail number accounted for over 30 percent of all the calls she made. Each move, each place, and each stop was potentially an opportunity to call or call back, and thus to pursue ongoing "articulation work." This was evident in the complex shape of the diagrams representing her localized uses of the telephone and her voicemail over a six-month

Figure 1.5a

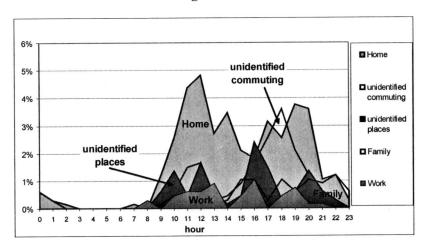

Figure 1.5b

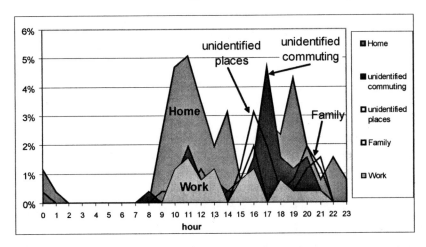

Note: Figure 1.5a shows the daily distribution of calls for different categories of places, relative to Sandrine's mobility, and Figure 1.5b shows similar data for her use of her mobile voicemail. Compared to Patrick's case, one could say she calls and checks her voice message quite often and in every kind of place she stays in. The similitude between both figures is a sign of the entanglement of phone calls and message checks that is characteristic of highly mobile and connected patterns.

period: she telephoned and consulted her messages almost everywhere and anywhere, in a relatively distributed way, depending on the type of place (see Figure 1.5).

Unlike Patrick, Sandrine embodies the "mobility paradigm." Sheller and Urry (2006) define an emergent experience of mobility, in which places and people are mutually constituted through the activities accomplished. Mobilities produce situations filled with opportunities for action, which are grasped by subjects oriented towards a creative exploitation of their stays in different places, relative to the multiple activities in which they are engaged: "The place is not set as much as it is involved in complex networks through which the hosts, guests, buildings, objects, and machines are gathered together contingently to produce certain performances in certain places and at certain time" (208). Sandrine's case enables us to add nuances to this picture by incorporating the dimension of constraint. Her opportunistic exploitation of mobility is partly imposed, due to flexible professional engagements that are always likely to be revised by the organizations to which she contributes. Moreover, unlike Patrick, Sandrine's long-term project is not to minimize her displacements but to stabilize and institutionalize more soundly her professional engagements so that she can manage them better. She would like to stop being "borderline-because-temporary," in short, to acquire more autonomy without giving up her form of mobility and multi-activity.

The constant exploitation of communication resources in situations of mobility is closely coupled with fragmentation, the proliferation of tasks, and the uncertainty surrounding their accomplishment. Sandrine attests to an adaptation to this form of mobility, tightly linked to the use of remote communication resources. She highlights the way in which the triangulation of different forms of competence—opportunistic and creative mobility, management of relational networks, and use of diverse resources for contact and communication—enables her to ensure a form of continuity in an uncertain multi-activity, to manage dispersion in a particular way. These challenges grow (as does the constraint) with the increasing fragility of professional engagements. In the case of another subject in this study who lived on short three-month contracts with architects, she constantly had to call on all her contacts in firms of architects (while she was working) to secure and prepare the next job, and to minimize her unemployment periods in between. Having found a stable, long-term job during the survey, she described how suddenly the pressure lifted with her immediate freedom from this articulation work. For those with less luck or no interest in such stability, it is the skills associated with a fluid and orderly management of mobilities and with the exploitation of the relational and communicational opportunities of the different places visited that allow the specter of precariousness to be kept at bay. The person can thus remain within the professional world by continuously converting places and solidarities into productive and economically effective relations.

The Inter-Relations between Mobility and Communication Practices

We have shown how it is possible to combine mobile phone-based communication data with geo-location data (i.e., the location of the successive cells of the mobile network in which an individual has used his or her phone). The precision of these data is more limited than that of global positioning service (GPS) systems (typically, user locations are known only within a 100-meter radius in town) so that very small-scale mobility cannot be analyzed in this way. However, with the combination of such location and communication data, individuals' medium-scale and large-scale movements, as well as the spatiotemporal distribution of their communication practices, can be mapped over extensive periods of time, a few months or more (several times more than the scale allowed for by methodologies based on logbooks kept by users).

Irrespective of the strength of methods based on the gathering and analysis of traces left by uses of information and communication technologies, they cannot be deployed fully without a qualification of the data. To be interpreted, location data require the individuals' relations between geographic locations and the places in which they carry out their activities to be specified in the users' own terms. This type of research has the capacity to make empirically visible new objects, such as coordination knots, where individuals' spatial coordination (and their experience of the place they occupy or inhabit at a point in time) become emergent features of their communication practices. Rather than operating with a predefined sense of shared purpose, individuals let their joint action emerge from a trial-and-error-based exploration that relies on their quasi-constant mutual accessibility. Instead of one-time coordination within a single mediated encounter, they multiply communication acts through different channels, so that something can be jointly achieved as on ongoing process.

This is also one of the only possible ways of showing the empirical relevance of theoretical distinctions proposed to account for contemporary transformations of mobility, such as the contrast between the "displacement paradigm" (movement as a means to an end) and the "mobility paradigm" (mobility as an end in itself, weaving together the spatial displacements and the social and artifactual resources available in the places people go through). By way of two ideal-type case studies, we have shown how the combined analysis of movements and communication practices enable us to account for the relevance of this analytical frame with respect to people's actual practices. The preliminary analyses of our corpus of mobility and communication patterns suggest that the rest of the sample can probably be located along a continuum between these two configurations. A given person may also switch from one form of mobility to another, according to his or her biographical trajectory (this happened, for instance, to one subject who lost her job during the study). Finally, although it does not seem that households' cultural competence with respect to mobility (as seen in their history of moving in and moving out) plays a significant role, this is not the case with forms of professional engagement. Flexible and temporary forms of work are a powerful lever for developing the mobility paradigm, especially due to the importance of "the job of preparing the next job."

Conclusion

We have simply caught a glimpse of the full potential of the methodology developed here. From a quantitative point of view, it should allow for the creation of indicators which are radically new in the way in which they combine mobility and communication—for instance the propensity to telephone from a type of place at a particular time. From a qualitative point of view, the analysis can be pursued in other directions, such as the link between "mobility capital" (that is, the skills and resources that are involved in the achievement of varied forms of mobility) and the way in which it may support social bonding and integration. Note, finally, that the current development of mobile context-sensitive services based on geo-location is oriented towards the challenge of revealing forms of proximity (between people, and between people and places) and giving them an economic and social content, for example, by facilitating different forms of encounter and transaction. The importance of inter-relations between mobility and communication practices will necessarily grow in coming years.

Notes

1.   The idea is to predetermine preferred activities, such as communicating or playing, and to put neighboring users into contact when they have a common interest.
2.   The service signals the other users to its own user, especially when they have frequently been near to one another.

3. In toothing, a Bluetooth device is used to "discover" other enabled devices then send the expression "Toothing?" as an initial greeting. The greeting seems to be used to generate encounters (often on a sexual basis) in some public settings and is an example of localized social networking.

4. See also: Faessler, 2006.

5. The telephone was synchronized automatically each night via GPRS connection with a distant server (sending data and synchronising the internal device clock).

6. Our survey consisted of six months of observation for each subject.

7. We have systematically transformed the X-Y coordinates into a classical address format, street and street number of the antenna location, in order to facilitate the place recognition by the subject.

8. Certain artists, like Sophie Calle in *Filatures* (1981), worked on the effects of meaning that emerge from the juxtaposition of a personal diary written in the first person singular (here, by the artist) and a diary of her activities kept by an outside observer (a private detective whom she herself had paid, unknown to him, to watch her and draw up a report).

9. Yrjö Engeström refers to "knotworking" to describe the way in which the course of activity can be concentrated in a very short period, extremely densely packed, with actions that jointly steer the activity toward its object (Engeström, et al., 1999).

10. We paraphrase the concept introduced by Latour (1987) to take into account distant action in socio-technical networks.

11. The mobility transition concept was formulated in the early seventies by Zelinsky (1971) with the intention of conceptualizing population movements in the period between the end of traditional society and the development of modern society. We have followed the approach of Knafou (2000) who uses the concept of mobility transition "as a dynamic analysis tool for verifying the existence of the shift in our society from a dominantly sedentary situation to dominant hypermobility."

12. We have borrowed this concept from Strauss (1988) who describes, in the context of activities structured into a complex project, the constant process of participants' interactional alignment and coordination of modules and sub-tasks, so that the project as a whole can take place fluidly, without too many hiccups or disruptions.

13. This is evident in the particular distribution of outgoing calls. While calls to her husband account for 20 percent of all Sandrine's calls, the rest of her calls are spread across 150 different correspondents, of whom the most frequently called number accounts for no more than 2 percent of all calls made.

Bibliography

Amar, Georges. "Notes sur la Mobilité à l'âge du Signe." In *Mobilités.net: Villes, Transports et Technologies Face aux Nouvelles Mobilités*, edited by Daniel Kaplan and Hubert Lafont. Paris, France: FING, 2004.

Ascher, François. "Les Sens du Mouvement: Modernités et Mobilités." In *Les Sens du Movement*, edited by Sylvain Allemand, François Ascher, and Jacques Lévy, 21-34. Paris, France: Belin, 2004.

Boullier, Dominique. *L'urbanité Numérique: Essai sur la Troisième Ville en 2100*. Paris, France: L'Harmattan, 1999.

Calle, Sophie. *Filatures Parisiennes (1978/1979)*. Exhibition. Paris, France: Centre Pompidou, 1981.

Chabrol, Jean-Louis and Pascal Périn. "Les Usages du Téléphone en France et aux Etats-Unis au Début des Années 90." *Réseaux*, 82-83 (1997): 255-267.

Claisse, Gerard and Franz Rowe. "Téléphone, Communications et Sociabilités: Des Pratiques Résidentielles Différenciées." *Sociétés Contemporaines*, 14/15 (1993): 165-189.

Clifford, James. *Routes: Travel and Translation in the late Twentieth Century*. Cambridge, MA: Harvard University Press, 1997.

Engeström, Yrjö, Ritva Engeström, and Tarja Vähäaho. "When the Center Does Not Hold: The Importance of Knotworking." In *Activity Theory and Social Practice: Cultural-Historical Approaches*, edited by Seth Chaiklin, Mariane Hedegaard, and Uffe J. Jensen. Aarhus, Denmark: Aarhus University Press, 1999.

Faessler, Jean-Daniel. "La Géolocalisation." 2006. http://www.ib-com.ch/pages/archives/05.06/ 05_06_com_techno_geolocalisation.htm (accessed January 8, 2007).

Goffman, Erving. *Behavior in Public Places: Notes on the Social Organization of Gatherings*. New York, NY: Free Press, 1963.

Goffman, Erving. *Relations in Public*. New York, NY: Harper, 1971.

Griswold, William G., Patricia Shanahan, Steven W. Brown, Robert Boyer, Matt Ratto, R. Benjamin Shapiro, and Tan Minh Truong. "ActiveCampus: Experiments in Community-Oriented Ubiquitous Computing." *Computer*, 37 (10, 2004): 73-81.

Hägerstrand, Torsten. "What about People in Regional Science?" *Papers in Regional Science*, 24 (December 1970): 6-21.

Heritage, John and Geoffrey Raymond. "The Terms of Agreement: Indexing Epistemic Authority and Subordination in Talk-in-Interaction." *Social Psychology Quarterly*, 68 (March 2005): 15-38.

Ito, Mizuko and Daisuke Okabe. "Intimate Connections: Contextualizing Japanese Youths and Mobile Messaging." In *The Inside Text: Social, Cultural and Design Perspectives on SMS*, edited by Richard Harper, Leysia Palen, and Alex Taylor, 127-146. Berlin, Germany: Springer, 2005.

Iwatani, Yukari. "Love: Japanese style." *Wired News*. June 1999. http://www.wired.com/culture/lifestyle/news/1998/06/12899.

Janelle, Donald G., Michael F. Goodchild, and Brian Klinkenberg. "The Temporal Ordering of Urban Space and Daily Activity Patterns for Population Role Groups." *Geographical Systems*, 5.1-2 (1998): 117-138.

Knafou, Rémy. "Les Mobilités Touristiques et de Loisir et le Système Global des Mobilités." In *Les Territoires de la Mobilité*, edited by Michel Bonnet and Dominique Desjeux, 193-204. Paris, France: PUF, 2000.

Kwan, Mei-Po. "Space-time and Integral Measures of Individual Accessibility: A Comparative Analysis Using a Point-based Framework." *Geographical Analysis*, 30 (July 1998): 191-216.

Latour, Bruno. *Science in Action*. Cambridge, MA: Harvard University Press, 1987.

Licoppe, Christian. "'Connected' Presence: The Emergence of a New Repertoire for Managing Social Relationships in a Changing Communication Technoscape." *Environment and Planning D: Society and Space*, 22.1 (2004): 135-156.

Licoppe, Christian and Yoriko Inada. "Emergent Uses of a Multiplayer Location-aware Mobile Game: The Interactional Consequences of Mediated Encounters." *Mobilities*, 1 (2006): 39-61.

Licoppe, Christian and Zbigniew Smoreda. "Are Social Networks Technologically Embedded? How Networks are Changing Today with Changes in Communication Technology." *Social Networks*, 27 (October 2005): 317-335.

Ling, Richard S. and Birgitte Yttri. "Hyper-Coordination via Mobile Phones in Norway." In *Perpetual Contact: Mobile Communication, Private Talk, Public Performance*, edited by James E. Katz and Mark Aakhus, 139-169. Cambridge, UK: Cambridge University Press, 2002.

Lofland, Lyn H. *A World of Strangers: Order and Action in Urban Public Space.* Prospect Heights, IL: Waveland Press, 1973.

Lofland, Lyn H. *The Public Realm: Exploring the City's Quintessential Social Territory.* Hawthorne, NY: Walter de Gruyter, Inc., 1998.

Massey, Doreen. "Power-geometry and a Progressive Sense of Place." In *Mapping the Futures: Local Cultures, Global Change*, edited by Jon Bird, Barry Curtis, Tim Putnam, George Robertson, and Lisa Tickner, 59-69. London, UK: Routledge, 1993.

Paulos, Eric and Elizabeth Goodman. "The Familiar Stranger: Anxiety, Comfort, and Play in Public Places." Paper delivered at the annual conference on Human Factors in Computing Systems, 29 April 2004. Vienna, Austria.

Rallet, Alain. "Les Mobilités Urbaines à L'heure du Commerce Electronique." In *Les Sens du Movement*, edited by Sylvain Allemand, François Ascher, and Jacques Lévy, 190-197. Paris, France: Belin, 2004.

Rivière, Carole. "Les Réseaux de Sociabilité Téléphonique." *Revue Française de Sociologie*, 41 (2000): 685-717.

Sheller, Mimi and John Urry. "The New Mobilities Paradigm." *Environment and Planning A*, 38.2 (2006): 207-226.

Simmel, Georg. *Philosophie de la modernité*. Paris, France: Payot, 1989.

Smoreda, Zbigniew and Christian Licoppe. "Gender-Specific Use of the Domestic Telephone." *Social Psychology Quarterly*, 63 (September 2000): 238-252.

Urry, John. *Sociology Beyond Societies: Mobilities for the Twenty-first Century*. London, UK: Routledge, 2000.

Urry John. "Connections." *Environment and Planning D: Society and Space*, 22 (January 2004): 27-38.

Veltz, Pierre. "L'économie de Toutes les Mobilités." In *Les Sens du Movement*, edited by Sylvain Allemand, François Ascher, and Jacques Lévy, 49-59. Paris, France: Belin, 2004.

Zelinsky, Wilbur. "The Hypothesis of the Mobility Transition." *Geographical Review*, 61 (February 1971): 219-249.

2

Migrant Workers and Mobile Phones: Technological, Temporal, and Spatial Simultaneity

Fernando Paragas
University of the Philippines

Simultaneity, or living lives that incorporate daily activities, routines, and institutions located both in a destination country and transnationally, is a possibility that needs to be theorized and explored. Migrant incorporation into a new land and transnational connections to a homeland or to dispersed networks of family, compatriots, or persons who share a religious or ethnic identity can occur at the same time and reinforce one another. (Levitt and Schiller, 2004: 1003)

When my father started working in Saudi Arabia in 1983, nine years after the Philippine government first sponsored the export of Filipino workers, he became part of what would become the diasporic community of overseas Filipino workers (OFWs). For more than ten years, he worked under a contract that entitled him to an annual month-long vacation in the Philippines. Thus, during the eleven months he was away, we were in contact primarily through letters, pictures, and cassette tapes that could be sent only through the inefficient postal system or through his friends who returned home. It would take, at best, a full month before he would get our reply to any of his questions. Simultaneity was, to us, an alien concept because of the asynchronous nature of our correspondence given the media at our disposal. We were not part of what Castells (2001) would later call the space of flows, a space that "links up distant locales around shared functions and meanings on the basis of electronic circuits and fast transportation corridors, while isolating and subduing the logic of experience embodied in the space of places" (155-178).

Back then, telephone calls were rare. In the late 1980s, the Philippine Long Distance Telephone Company (PLDT) opened phone booths in their offices for long-distance calls. However, international calls were expensive. Using the 1989 exchange rate, each three-minute call cost US$13.40, which was much more than the Philippine daily income of US$8.25. Beyond the cost, calling my father meant having to queue during office hours. Because of the time difference, it meant we had only a two-hour timeframe to talk to him. We wanted a phone line of our own, but so did one million other households not served by PLDT. It took eight years, as many years since the government began deregulating the telecommunications industry, before we got a landline phone in 1997. In fact, we had gotten a mobile phone a year earlier to communicate with my father just before he returned home for good. With the mobile phone, contact with my father suddenly became fast and affordable—which meant he could monitor us more closely. Suddenly, there was potential for simultaneity for our transnational family, but my father ended his tenure abroad before we could truly realize it.

The deregulation of the telecommunications industry both in the Philippines and abroad helped lower the price of a mobile phone call from the Philippines to anywhere in the world to US$0.50, or 5 percent of the daily income in 1996.[1] My father thus worked abroad as our telecommunications industry went through major changes (Paragas, 2003) that have since resulted in the perpetual contact that today's transnational migrants, or "transmigrants," (see Schiller, 1999) theoretically have with their family members, friends, and organizations (Katz and Aakhus, 2002).

The diversification of communication technologies through which OFWs exchange information with their communication partners comes at a time when the deployment of OFWs itself is increasing and changing. There are estimated to be four million OFWs, with annual deployment nearing one million. Representing over 10 percent of the Philippine workforce, OFWs annually remit a total of US$8.5 billion to the Philippines, an amount equal to 9 percent of the Gross National Income or nearly 20 percent of the country's export revenues. The face of the OFW community itself is changing. More women and more professionals who work in the same capacity (rather than being underemployed) abroad are entering the migrant workforce, showing a shift from the predominantly male blue-collar OFW labor pool that worked in the Middle East in the mid-70s (Hochschild, 2003; Tyner, 1996; Tyner, 2004; Huang, et al, 2004). Spread across nearly all states and territories around the world, OFWs constantly communicate with the people in the Philippines as they negotiate their different cross-territorial and cross-cultural circumstances.

In this chapter, I locate the mobile phone in the midst of the changing arena of transnational communications and explore how it contributes to the simultaneous sharing of experiences among OFWs and their communication partners who otherwise live in different places and spaces. I attempt to answer three questions:

1.   How have changes in communication media helped facilitate transnational simultaneity among OFWs?
2.   How do access and ownership of mobile phones differ (a) from those of other communication media, (b) across respondent groupings, and (c) within and beyond the host country?
3.   How are mobile phones being used to protect and promote the welfare of OFWs?

In so doing, I argue that the ubiquity and multi-stranded utility of mobile phones in the local, transnational, and global communications of OFWs make them a pivotal medium to explicate the concept of technological, temporal, and spatial simultaneity among migrants.

The data I used in this article came from interviews with 16 organizational informants and from a random survey of 320 respondents deployed in the top 16 destinations for OFWs (15 countries and off-shore/sea-based operations). Survey data were gathered in mid-2005 at the Manila head office of the Philippine Overseas Employment Administration, which most OFWs visited to renew their work papers. I decided to use gender (male and female), age (younger and older than thirty-four years old), parental status (with or without children), host regions (East Asia, West Asia, North America/Europe, Sea-based), work (professionals/associate professionals or services/trades workers), and income (monthly salary below or above one thousand dollars) as comparison variables. These variables represented the changing dynamics of migrant employment: the increasing number of female, young, professional, and higher-income workers who were deployed in an expanding base of destinations. Informants, meanwhile, represented governmental, profit, and non-profit private organizations that provided products and services for OFWs.

Research Findings

Changing Media and Transnational Simultaneity

Changing communication technologies have increased the potential for simultaneity among OFWs and their organizations in the host country and their family, friends, and institutions in the Philippines. Until the arrival of mobile phones, OFWs depended upon very asynchronous modes of communication such as letters, cassette tapes, and pictures sent through the postal system.

Sampson (2003) noted seafaring OFWs valued letters even if these contained old news because these provided a tangible link with the Philippines. The letters, she said, represented "the packaging and sending of love and affection" (268). This sentiment of OFWs about letters was earlier articulated by a labor migrant who responded to a study by the Catholic Institute for International Relations (1987: 8):

> My homesickness somehow disappears whenever I receive letters from you. . . . It really feels good to at least have something to read upon returning to our barracks. Please write a longer letter next time. . . . Send pictures of the kids and, most especially, of yourself. Homesickness really strikes strong out here!

Recent studies, however, revealed the shift from letters, photographs, and taped messages sent by post (Catholic Institute for International Relations, 1987) to phone calls as the primary means of contact between OFWs and the Philippines (Parreñas, 2002; Alegado, 2003). Caregivers in the US, for example, would often call their families in the Philippines since flying home was expensive, while seafarers would call the Philippines twice a month even while out at sea (Sampson, 2003).

It was through the phone that OFWs who had children exercised their parenting duties—at a monthly bill that ranged between US$150 and US$400. The large bill, which respondents felt was a necessary expense, was due to their conversations with other relatives to verify the stories of their children (Tung, 2000). Parreñas (2001a) found a particular sense of transnational mothering among the female OFWs she interviewed in Rome and Los Angeles, noting how "the pain of family separation creates various feelings, including helplessness, regret, and guilt for mothers and loneliness, vulnerability, and insecurity for children" (361). However, in her subsequent study, Parreñas (2002) found that children who realized the sacrifices of their mothers were "less likely to feel abandoned and more likely to accept their mother's efforts to sustain close relations from a distance." Asis (2004) said children from two-parent families were able to cope with migration better than the children of single mothers who went abroad to work. She qualified that while her survey depicted a generally positive image of migrant work's impact on children, the focus groups she conducted revealed some emotional difficulty among adolescent participants. The debate on whether children could be considered as abused by transnational parenting was thus recurrent among migrant workers, as Parreñas (2001c) inferred from her analysis of the articles in *Tinig Filipino* [Voice Filipino]—a newsletter of, by, and for OFWs.

The fact that mobile phones enabled parents and children to talk simultaneously about their experiences helped them to discuss the difficulties of separation. The constant sharing of daily lives revealed the nuances and travails of migrant employment to such detail that was not afforded by asynchronous communications through letters, tapes, and pictures. Indeed, in a study I completed in 1999, just a couple of years after the introduction of the mobile phone, I already met a mother working in Hong Kong who stopped writing letters altogether as she could simply and constantly contact her children via the mobile phone (Paragas, 2005b). As she discussed how she would micro-coordinate her family's affairs even from abroad, she represented the dramatic expansion of the array of media that OFWs could use to communicate (Ling and Haddon, 2001).

Victor Fernandez, a former OFW who is now president of the Philippine Association of Service Exporters, Inc. (PASEI—a large labor recruitment agency), told how the industry has been changed by the emergence of newer media in the last two decades. He said:

> When I started the business in 1980, what we were using was telex. . . . [It was] very expensive but it was amazing because you type a letter here, [and] the guy on the other end could also respond. . . . I worked as an OCW [Overseas Contract Worker] before I put up my own business, and because of the telex, I did not get homesick. I could communicate with my office three, four times a day. My wife was the one operating my office. I could get in touch with them. "How are you? How are the kids?" . . . So it was just like I was attending a meeting in the next few days. I did not get homesick. I stayed there as a contract worker—say, working for one year; sometimes it was even longer—but I did not get homesick because of the telex.
>
> You know, the telephone came before the telex, but it was very expensive. The cost was very prohibitive. The telephone was there but hardly any contract worker was using the telephone. Even I who owned my business did not call my office. I cheated in trying to be able to use the telephone. . . . If I went to clients, and the clients told me to recruit someone, I would say that if they wanted fast service, they should let me call my wife. [So I would use my clients' phone to talk to my wife about business, but], then the clients would say, "Why don't you say hello to your wife." That way I would be able to talk to my wife, and also do business. Afterwards my wife would say to keep in touch through the telex.
>
> Then came mobile phones, around the same time as computers and the Internet. But there were different mobile phone networks, and it was only recently that they are becoming universally accessible. Now even our domestic helpers and other workers around the world have mobile phones, which actually help reduce homesickness.
>
> These technologies benefit OFWs, and help reduce the incidence of repatriation. (Personal communication, July 28, 2005)

The Universality of Mobile Phones

My own story with my father, as well as Fernandez's, showed the importance of exploring how their tenure abroad had impelled OFWs to avail themselves of the increasingly varied ways to communicate across borders. These stories underscore the importance of mobile phones to two individuals, but they raise questions as to whether they hold true for the mass of OFWs. Thus, this section locates mobile phones with respect to other media, across respondent groupings, and across territories.

Mobile Telephony and Other Media

The dominance of mobile phones as the medium of choice among OFWs reflected trends within the Philippines itself. In the Philippines, more respondents had a mobile phone than a landline phone. Indeed, 83 percent of the respondents had a mobile phone that was subscribed to a network in their country, while 78 percent had a mobile phone that was subscribed to a network in the Philippines (Table 2.1). That 70 percent of the respondents maintained two phones abroad validates the findings of my earlier exploratory qualitative research on OFWs (Paragas, 2005). While either mobile phone could technically be used across state borders through global roaming capabilities, the informants said they liked the idea that their family could immediately contact them through the Philippine-connected mobile phone. Cost was a consideration, though it was not a major factor since the informants primarily used the Philippine mobile phone for text messaging. The Philippine mobile phone, in the imagination of the respondents, thus served as an umbilical cord to their loved ones back home.

Compared to the nearly universal ownership of mobile phones, only 24 percent of respondents had their own landline phone, in addition to 54 percent who had access to one.[2] Over half (52 percent) of the respondents who owned a mobile phone said their unit had a camera, while another 46 percent said they owned a digital video camera. Five percent and 10 percent had access to a mobile phone camera or a video camera respectively. This meant a majority of the respondents were able to digitally take pictures and, with Internet or mobile phone connection, to send these electronically. Thus, mediated communication facilitated the exchange of both sound and images instantaneously.

Ownership of and access to TV (96 percent), radio (93 percent), DVD/VCD players (91 percent), and cable TV (82 percent) complemented the ownership of mobile telephony abroad. The OFWs thus lived in an

Table 2.1
Media ownership and access while abroad (In percentages, N=320)

Medium	Ownership	Access	Neither
Mobile phone with host country SIM	82.5	04.4	13.1
Mobile phone with Philippine SIM	76.3	03.8	20.0
Radio	72.2	20.6	07.2
TV	63.8	32.5	03.8
VCD/DVD player	59.1	31.9	09.1
Mobile phone with camera	51.6	05.0	43.4
Cable TV	42.2	39.7	18.1
Landline	24.4	53.8	21.9
Computer	16.9	52.8	30.3
Web camera	15.9	32.5	51.6
Internet	13.8	51.6	34.7

environment that enabled downstream and upstream flows of information. National and global events gleaned from traditional media were discussed at the personal level through mobile communications. Conversely, personal stories exchanged over the phone are contextualized in public events. Across all media, it was the Internet that had the least number of subscribers. Only 14 percent of all respondents subscribed to it, while another 52 percent had access to it. Two reasons could be given for these relatively low statistics. On the one hand, many OFWs engaged in service (i.e., domestic and care giving work) and trade (i.e., construction work) activities did not have the skills and equipment needed to surf the Internet. On the other hand, there was low Internet penetration and subscription rates in the rural areas in the Philippines because of logistical (unstable electricity, unfriendly Internet café staffers, difficulty in understanding English) and social (discrimination based on gender, religion, and levels of education) concerns (Umali and Paragas, 2006: 256).

Mobile Telephony across Respondent Groupings

The heterogeneous profile of the OFW community necessitated closer inspection of interpersonal media (landline phones, mobile phones, and the Internet) ownership and access across respondent groupings according to sex, age, parental status, host regions, work, and income (Table 2.2).

Gender and parental status did not have an impact upon interpersonal media ownership, contradicting two general perceptions: First, men were not more connected to the mobile network than women, showing that mobile telephony was not gendered. Mobile phone use was thus differentiated from other media that were known to be biased towards men. Second, parent respondents were no less accessible than those without children. It would have been logical to argue that parents would have greater ownership of and access to mobile phones because of their desire to exercise their parental duties across distances (Parreñas, 2001a; 2002). Instead, practical concerns among parent respondents, such as smaller disposable incomes compared to respondents without children, precluded greater mobile phone ownership and access, as well as other interpersonal media.

Though gender and parental status did not have an impact upon interpersonal media ownership, age did. A larger share of younger respondents (62 percent) than older (42 percent) respondents owned a mobile phone with a camera, indicating greater interest, and ability to purchase, phone units with more complex features.

Similarly, host regions and work significantly differentiated respondents from each other. Respondents who worked in a professional capacity, and those in North America and Europe, were distinguished by significantly higher ownership of all interpersonal media. This reflected the dominant flows of specific occupations to particular destinations (i.e., nurses to the UK and domestic workers to Hong Kong) which had since resulted into skewed economic OFW profiles across host regions.

However, unlike the access to landline phone and Internet services, mobile phone ownership and access did not significantly differ across income groups. This means two things. First, mobile telephony is not influenced by work-related characteristics that give some OFWs a comparative advantage over others. Second, respondents purchased and maintained a basic mobile phone regardless of their capacity to pay the bills.

Thus, across media, it was basic mobile telephony that was nearly universal among respondents. However, more advanced features (such as cameras) and uses (e.g., of multiple units) could still characterize OFWs

Table 2.2

Interpersonal media access and ownership across respondent groupings (In percentages, N=320)

Item	Gender		Age		Parental Status		Regions				Work		Income[a]	
	Male (n=142)	Female (n=178)	21 to 34 years old (n=161)	35 to 57 years old (n=159)	No children (n=145)	With children (n=175)	West Asia (n=100)	East Asia (n=120)	North Am & Europe (n=80)	Sea-based (n=20)	Prof'l & Assoc. (n=113)	Service & Trade (n=207)	Lower (n=196)	Higher (n=122)
Landline														
Ownership	20.4	27.5	21.7	27.0	20.7	27.4	24.0	21.7	35.0		37.2	17.4	17.9	34.4
Access	53.5	53.9	57.8	49.7	60.7	48.0	50.0	55.0	46.3	95.0	46.9	57.5	59.7	45.1
Neither	26.1	18.5	20.5	23.3	18.6	24.6	26.0	23.3	18.8	5.0	15.9	25.1	22.4	20.5
Chi-square	$\chi^2 (2, N = 320) =$ 3.68, $p = .16$		$\chi^2 (2, N = 320) = 2.18$, $p = .34$		$\chi^2 (2, N = 320) = 5.14$, $p = .07$		$\chi^2 (6, N = 320) = 20.27, p < .01$				$\chi^2 (2, N = 320) =$ 16.08, $p < .01$		$\chi^2 (2, N = 320) =$ 11.63, $p < .01$	
Mobile phone with host country SIM														
Ownership	80.3	84.3	85.1	79.9	79.3	85.1	85.0	80.8	87.5	60.0	91.2	77.8	81.1	85.2
Access	4.9	3.9	3.7	5.0	6.9	2.3	2.0	4.2	2.5	25.0	0.9	6.3	5.6	2.5
Neither	14.8	11.8	11.2	15.1	13.8	12.6	13.0	15.0	10.0	15.0	8.0	15.9	13.3	12.3
Chi-square	$\chi^2 (2, N = 320) =$ 0.87, $p = .65$		$\chi^2 (2, N = 320) = 1.51$, $p = .47$		$\chi^2 (2, N = 320) = 4.27$, $p = .12$		4 cells (33.3%) have n < 5.				$\chi^2 (2, N = 320) =$ 9.99, $p < .01$		$\chi^2 (2, N = 320) = 1.91$, $p = .38$	

Table 2.2 (cont.)

Mobile phone with Philippine SIM														
Ownership	81.0	72.5	77.0	75.5	73.8	78.3	82.0	70.8	78.8	70.0	86.7	70.5	71.9	82.8
Access	3.5	3.9	2.5	5.0	4.8	2.9	5.0	2.5	1.3	15.0	2.7	4.3	4.6	2.5
Neither	15.5	23.6	20.5	19.5	21.4	18.9	13.0	26.7	20.0	15.0	10.6	25.1	23.5	14.8
Chi-square	$\chi^2(2, N=320)=3.38, p=.18$		$\chi^2(2, N=320)=1.45, p=.48$		$\chi^2(2, N=320)=1.28, p=.53$		$\chi^2(2, N=320)=15.43, p=.02$				$\chi^2(2, N=320)=10.76, p<.01$		$\chi^2(2, N=320)=4.91, p=.09$	
Mobile phone with camera														
Ownership	54.2	49.4	61.5	41.5	55.2	48.6	42.0	52.5	63.8	45.0	70.8	41.1	41.8	66.4
Access	5.6	4.5	5.0	5.0	4.8	5.1	5.0	0.8	5.0	30.0	2.7	6.3	5.6	4.1
Neither	40.1	46.1	33.5	53.5	40.0	46.3	53.0	46.7	31.3	25.0	26.5	52.7	52.6	29.5
Chi-square	$\chi^2(2, N=320)=1.19, p=.55$		$\chi^2(2, N=320)=13.50, p<.01$		$\chi^2(2, N=320)=1.41, p=.49$		$\chi^2(2, N=320)=40.13, p<.01$				$\chi^2(2, N=320)=25.92, p<.01$		$\chi^2(2, N=320)=18.32, p<.01$	
Internet														
Ownership	12.0	15.2	13.7	13.8	14.5	13.1	8.0	13.3	25.0	0.0	26.5	6.8	6.1	26.2
Access	55.6	48.3	57.1	45.9	55.9	48.0	51.0	55.8	43.8	60.0	60.2	46.9	52.6	50.0
Neither	32.4	36.5	29.2	40.3	29.7	38.9	41.0	30.8	31.3	40.0	13.3	46.4	41.3	23.8
Chi-square	$\chi^2(2, N=320)=1.79, p=.41$		$\chi^2(2, N=320)=4.78, p=.09$		$\chi^2(2, N=320)=2.99, p=.224$		$\chi^2(6, N=320)=16.28, p=.01$				$\chi^2(2, N=320)=46.42, p<.01$		$\chi^2(2, N=320)=28.77, p<.01$	

*Two respondents did not answer.

with more resources. While most OFWs could reduce the impact of time and distance through their mobile phones, those with more resources have a stronger possibility to do so with greater nuance through images, networks, and options. Comparatively, access to basic landline phone and Internet services is already skewed towards higher income professionals, preventing them from being universal.

Mobile Telephony across Territories

The multi-territoriality of the lives of OFWs—living in the host country but virtually connected to the Philippines—differentiates their daily activities from most people. Their everyday communications straddle state boundaries and cultural borders.

Mobile phones were rated most highly as the media of choice in making phone calls both within ($M = 4.0$, $SD = 1.6$) and outside ($M = 4.1$, $SD = 1.5$) the host country. Text messaging was rated second ($M_{Host} = 3.6$, $SD = 1.8$; $M_{Outside} = 3.6$, $SD = 1.8$). Traditional letters, long the staple of OFW transnational communication (Paragas, 1996 and 1999; Catholic Institute for International Relations, 1987) were rated the lowest among the choices. Communication by landline, meanwhile, still rated higher than online chats or e-mails. There was generally no difference between the use of media in and across states, except for traditional letters for cross-border communication and landline phones for intra-country calls (Table 2.3).

The use of mobile phones, texting, and landline phones as the primary media for communication within and to outside the country was generally the same across respondent groupings. However, as with ownership and access, age, host region, work, and income were significant comparison variables. In particular, age was the only variable that limited the universality of mobile phones as a mode of communication for OFWs across different demographic attributes within and beyond the host country. Younger respondents, more often than older ones, gave significantly higher ratings in their use of mobile phones and text messaging, as well as e-mail and online chat both within and outside the host country (tables 2.4 and 2.5).

Still, mobile phone use within and across territories was less likely to be influenced by demographics, unlike other media. For instance, ratings for the intra-country use of e-mail, online chat, and landline phone were significantly different across host regions, work, and income groupings (Table 2.4). North America/Europe, professional/associate, and higher income respondents consistently gave significantly higher ratings for their

Table 2.3

Frequency of use of interpersonal media to communicate with conversation partners within and outside the host country (Means and standard deviations, N=320)

Medium	Across territories	In the host country	To outside the country	Paired samples test (two-tailed) for in and to outside the host country		
				T-test	df	Sig ≤
Mobile phone	4.1 (1.4)	4.0 (1.6)	4.1 (1.5)	-1.5	319	0.10
Texting	3.6 (1.6)	3.6 (1.8)	3.6 (1.8)	0.1	319	0.90
Landline phone	2.8 (2.0)	2.8 (2.0)	2.6 (2.0)	2.1	319	0.01
E-mail	1.9 (1.8)	2.0 (2.0)	1.9 (1.9)	0.8	319	0.40
Internet chat	1.5 (1.7)	1.6 (1.9)	1.5 (1.8)	0.5	319	0.60
Traditional letters	0.8 (0.9)	0.6 (1.0)	1.0 (1.4)	-5.1	319	0.01

Note: Based on a scale of 0 (never) to 5 (very frequent).

Table 2.4

Frequency of use of interpersonal media to communicate with conversation partners within the host country[1] (N=320)

	Gender		Age		Parental Status		Regions				Work		Income[2]	
	Male (n=142)	Female (n=178)	21 to 34 years old (n=161)	35 to 57 years old (n=159)	No children (n=145)	With children (n=175)	West Asia (n=100)	East Asia (n=120)	North Am & Europe (n=80)	Sea-based (n=20)	Prof'l & Associate (n=113)	Service & Trade (n=207)	Lower (n=196)	Higher (n=122)
Mobile phone														
Mean (SD)	4.1 (1.5)	3.9 (1.7)	4.3 (1.4)	3.8 (1.8)	4.1 (1.6)	3.9 (1.7)	4.0 (1.7)	4.1 (1.7)	4.2 (1.4)	3.4 (1.8)	4.5 (1.2)	3.8 (1.8)	3.9 (1.7)	4.2 (1.5)
Significance test[3]	$t(318) = .92, p = .36$		$t(300) = 2.63, p < .01$		$t(318) = 1.26, p = .21$		$F(3,316) = 1.44, p = .23$				$t(305) = 4.01, p < .01$		$t(280) = -1.57, p = .12$	
Texting														
Mean (SD)	3.6 (1.5)	3.6 (1.7)	4.0 (1.6)	3.3 (1.9)	3.7 (1.8)	3.5 (1.8)	3.5 (1.9)	3.7 (1.8)	3.6 (1.7)	3.5 (1.9)	3.9 (1.6)	3.5 (1.9)	3.6 (1.8)	3.6 (1.8)
Significance test[3]	$t(318) = -.38, p = .70$		$t(303) = 3.62, p < .01$		$t(318) = 1.07, p = .29$		$F(3,316) = 1.65, p = .18$				$t(264) = 2.16, p = .03$		$t(316) = -0.08, p = .94$	
Landline phone														
Mean (SD)	2.7 (1.9)	2.9 (2.0)	2.7 (1.9)	3.0 (2.0)	2.8 (2.0)	2.9 (2.0)	2.7 (2.1)	2.8 (2.0)	3.3 (1.7)	2.1 (1.9)	3.1 (1.9)	2.7 (2.0)	2.6 (2.0)	3.2 (1.9)
Significance test[3]	$t(318) = -.88, p = .38$		$t(318) = -1.44, p = .15$		$t(318) = -0.11, p = .91$		$F(3,316) = 2.92, p = .04$				$t(246) = 1.94, p = .05$		$t(316) = -2.84, p < .01$	
E-mail														
Mean (SD)	2.0 (2.0)	1.9 (2.0)	2.3 (2.0)	1.6 (1.9)	2.3 (2.1)	1.6 (1.9)	1.7 (1.9)	2.1 (2.0)	2.3 (2.0)	0.9 (1.4)	3.1 (1.9)	1.4 (1.7)	1.5 (1.8)	2.7 (2.0)
Significance test[3]	$t(318) = .24, p = .81$		$t(318) = 3.28, p < .01$		$t(294) = 3.23, p < .01$		$F(3,316) = 3.91, p < .01$				$t(210) = 7.80, p < .01$		$t(234) = -5.33, p < .01$	

Table 2.4 (cont.)

Internet chat											
Mean (SD)	1.6 (1.9)	1.5 (1.9)	1.8 (1.9)	1.3 (1.7)	2.0 (2.0)	1.2 (1.7)	1.3 (1.7)	1.8 (1.9)	1.8 (1.9)	0.7 (1.3)	2.2 (1.9) 1.2 (1.7) · 1.3 (1.8) 2.0 (1.9)
Significance test [3]	$t(318 = .33, p = .74)$		$t(315 = 2.87, p < .01)$		$t(280 = 3.82, p < .01)$		$F(3,316 = 3.16, p = .02)$				$t(208 = 4.63, p < .01)$ · $t(243 = -3.45, p < .01)$
Traditional letters											
Mean (SD)	0.6 (0.9)	0.6 (1.0)	0.6 (1.0)	0.6 (1.0)	0.5 (0.9)	0.7 (1.0)	0.6 (1.0)	0.5 (0.8)	0.7 (1.1)	0.9 (0.9)	0.6 (0.9) 0.6 (1.0) · 0.6 (0.9) 0.6 (1.0)
Significance test [3]	$t(318 = -.26, p = .79)$		$t(318 = -.19, p = .85)$		$t(318 = -1.78, p = .08)$		$F(3,316 = 1.20, p = .31)$				$t(318 = -0.47, p = .64)$ · $t(316 = -0.67, p = .50)$

[1] Based on a scale of 0 to 5, where 0 is never, 1 is very infrequent, 2 is infrequent, 3 is neither infrequent nor frequent, 4, is frequent, and 5 is very frequent.

[2] Two respondents did not answer.

[3] T-test (two-tailed) for gender, age, parental status, work, and income; ANOVA for regions.

use of e-mail, chat, and landline phones. Sea-based workers, meanwhile, posted low ratings for e-mail and online chat.

Similarly, the use of landline phones, e-mail, and online chat for cross-border correspondence was significantly higher among professionals and higher income respondents, most of whom work in North America/Europe (Table 2.5). These findings indicated an Internet-based digital divide among the respondents, a divide that is not as widely observed in mobile telephony.

Ellene Sana, Executive Director of the Philippine-based non-government organization (NGO) Center for Migrant Advocacy, explained the importance of the divide in considering the use of newer technologies such as Voice Over Internet Protocol (VOIP):

> Of course this is already a given—not only on who [among OFWs] has access, but also on who is literate in it. Just because there is ICT [Information and communication technology] doesn't mean domestic workers will be OK with accessing it. The point is, we should look at opportunities to improve our cause. (Personal communication, July 29, 2005)

Indeed, while a majority (54 percent) of the respondents used the Internet, this statistic is skewed towards younger, childless, professional, and higher-income respondents who used the Internet more than their counterparts. Interestingly, the Internet was used less as a mass medium than as a personal medium for correspondence (92 percent) and chatting (76 percent).[3] Surfing the World Wide Web for leisure (73 percent) and work (34 percent) were the other main activities online. Florence May Cortina of the Kanlungan [Refuge] Center Foundation, an NGO for OFWs, had an explanation for both the popularity of mobile phones and the niche audience of online correspondence. She said:

> Those who chat are those who have access to computers. For example, they would set an appointment for chatting. But, our tradition is more oral in nature. That is why chatting is not really a match for us. Usually, intellectuals and professionals are [the ones who are] able to write a lot. (Personal communication, July 20, 2005)

However, she did note that this is changing after some probing about the written nature of chatting. Cortina said that earlier generations were much more oral in their communications, compared to the generation today that liked to chat online.

The departure from orality was also observed by Father Fabio Baggio of the Scalabrini Migration Center, a non-profit research and extension organization on migration. The organization's research revealed that parents and children were enjoying better transnational communication,

Table 2.5

Frequency of use of interpersonal media to communicate with conversation partners beyond the host country[1] (N=320)

	Gender		Age		Parental Status		Regions				Work		Income[2]	
	Male (n=142)	Female (n=178)	21 to 34 years old (n=161)	35 to 57 years old (n=159)	No children (n=145)	With children (n=175)	West Asia (n=100)	East Asia (n=120)	North Am & Europe (n=80)	Sea-based (n=20)	Prof'l & Associate (n=113)	Service & Trade (n=207)	Lower (n=196)	Higher (n=122)
Mobile phone														
Mean (SD)	4.3 (1.4)	4.0 (1.7)	4.4 (1.2)	3.8 (1.8)	4.2 (1.6)	4.1 (1.5)	4.3 (1.4)	4.3 (1.5)	3.8 (1.8)	4.3 (1.4)	4.3 (1.4)	4.1 (1.6)	4.2 (1.5)	4.0 (1.6)
Significance test[3]	$t(318) = 1.46, p = .15$		$t(279) = 3.44, p < .01$		$t(318) = 0.22, p = .82$		$F(3,316) = 1.84, p = .14$				$t(259) = 0.98, p = .33$		$t(316) = 1.13, p = .26$	
Texting														
Mean (SD)	3.7 (1.8)	3.6 (1.9)	3.9 (1.7)	3.3 (2.0)	3.6 (1.9)	3.6 (1.8)	3.4 (1.9)	3.8 (1.8)	3.4 (1.9)	4.2 (1.5)	3.7 (1.8)	3.6 (1.9)	3.7 (1.8)	3.5 (1.9)
Significance test[3]	$t(318) = .44, p = .66$		$t(308) = 2.70, p < .01$		$t(318) = -0.09, p = .92$		$F(3,316) = 1.44, p = .23$				$t(318) = 0.42, p = .68$		$t(316) = 1.05, p = .29$	
Landline phone														
Mean (SD)	2.5 (2.0)	2.7 (2.0)	2.6 (2.0)	2.7 (2.0)	2.8 (2.0)	2.5 (2.0)	2.2 (2.0)	2.7 (2.0)	3.2 (1.8)	2.2 (2.2)	2.7 (1.9)	2.6 (2.0)	2.3 (2.0)	3.0 (1.9)
Significance test[3]	$T(318) = -.93, p = .35$		$t(318) = -.40, p = .69$		$t(318) = 1.11, p = .27$		$F(3,316) = 4.80, p < .01$				$t(342) = 0.86, p = .39$		$t(316) = -3.04, p < .01$	

Table 2.5 (cont.)

E-mail												
Mean (SD)	2.1 (2.0)	1.8 (1.9)	2.2 (1.9)	1.6 (1.9)	1.8 (1.9)	2.0 (1.9)	2.1 (2.0)	1.2 (1.9)	3.0 (1.8)	1.3 (1.8)	1.5 (1.8)	2.6 (2.0)
Significance test[3]	$t(318=1.29, p=.20)$		$t(318=2.45, p<.01)$		$F(3,316=1.44, p=.23)$				$t(318=7.85, p<.01)$		$t(241=-5.22, p<.01)$	
Internet chat												
Mean (SD)	1.6 (1.8)	1.5 (1.8)	1.7 (1.8)	1.3 (1.8)	1.3 (1.7)	1.7 (1.9)	1.7 (1.9)	0.9 (1.6)	2.1 (1.9)	1.2 (1.7)	1.2 (1.7)	2.0 (1.9)
Significance test[3]	$t(318=.33, p=.74)$		$t(318=2.02, p=.04)$		$F(3,316=1.91, p=.13)$				$t(206=4.54, p<.01)$		$t(239=-3.83, p<.01)$	
Traditional letters												
Mean (SD)	0.9 (1.3)	1.1 (1.4)	1.1 (1.4)	0.9 (1.3)	0.9 (1.3)	1.0 (1.3)	0.9 (1.3)	1.6 (1.9)	0.9 (1.2)	1.0 (1.4)	1.0 (1.4)	0.9 (1.2)
Significance test[3]	$t(318=1.10, p=.23)$		$t(318=.91, p=.36)$		$F(3,316=1.65, p=.18)$				$t(318=-1.12, p=.26)$		$t(316=0.47, p=.64)$	

[1] Based on a scale of 0 to 5, where 0 is never, 1 is very infrequent, 2 is infrequent, 3 is neither infrequent nor frequent, 4, is frequent, and 5 is very frequent.

[2] Two respondents did not answer.

[3] T-test (two-tailed) for gender, age, parental status, work, and income; ANOVA for regions.

especially through text messages. The low subscription fees charged by Philippine mobile phone service providers, he said, had given families the opportunity to keep in touch everyday. Victor Fernandez of PASEI, meanwhile, said:

> Even domestic helpers, once they go abroad, know how to manipulate their mobile phone, even if they don't know how to use a computer. And this phone, we have noticed, has been able to help reduce homesickness. It helps them discuss their home-sickness with their family. This helps the industry in a way because we have fewer complaints about people coming home unless they are already maltreated. (Personal communication, July 28, 2005)

Mobile phone companies are aware of the increasing importance of their services among OFWs. Globe Telecommunications, one of the two biggest mobile phone service providers in the Philippines, launched *Globe Kababayan* [Globe Compatriot] to target the niche audience of OFWs. The program enables *Globe* subscribers to share the pre-paid credit on the mobile phone transnationally. It also allows them to automatically add to that pre-paid credit even when they are out of the country as well as to remit money by text messaging (see Pickens and Richardson, 2007). Globe Kababayan also has regular promotions that range from special rates for international long distance calls between the Philippines and specific countries to raffle contests where vehicles could be won. The latter program, in particular, was conducted in tandem with government agencies for migrant workers. However, *Globe Kababayan* still had a poor participation rate among OFWs as it earned a mean rating of 0.81 on a scale of 0 (never used) to 5 (frequently used).

Mobile Phones and Organizational Linkages

Access to a phone, especially a mobile phone, is important not only for communicating with the family. They can also serve as a lifeline for distressed workers. Ellene Sana said the Center for Migrant Advocacy was developing a database of OFW mobile phone numbers that could be used as a reference for some surveys on OFWs. Moreover, mobile phones could serve as an SOS hotline when migrants required assistance with their problems. She explained:

> Mobile phones are accessible worldwide and text messages can be forwarded. Thus, we can receive an SOS request, which we can forward immediately to the Department of Foreign Affairs. We can also monitor the progress of assistance through the phone. (Personal communication, July 29, 2005)

However, while such assistance can indeed be facilitated faster over the phone, Florence May Cortina said it was not foolproof:

> [A] family here receives a request for assistance from their relative in Saudi Arabia through the mobile phone. The OFW can describe over the phone what is happening to him/her, but he/she has to do it surreptitiously because the employer may get the unit. (Personal communication, July 20, 2005)

Indeed, employers have become very aware of the mobile phone's ability to connect distressed OFWs to support individuals and agencies. Thus, they either confiscate the phone or curtail the length of time that these OFWs can use it, as explained by domestic workers who served as panelists in the Philippine TV show "Moms," in its August 21, 2006 episode.

Cognizant of the importance of communication in the lives of OFWs, the Overseas Workers' Welfare Administration (OWWA), the government agency primarily tasked with improving the plight of OFWs, had worked with Scalabrini Migration Center to investigate the exchange of messages between parent-OFWs and their children. OWWA Director Rustico De la Fuente said their research showed how the use of media technologies has "mitigated the social cost of migration." He explained,

> We could see now that migrants can chat the whole hour without worrying about the expenses. And you know the net effect is that the migrants out there have regained their lost role as decision makers. They are now part of the decision making of the family on a daily or hourly basis. . . . Of course, others are kidding [with it]. . . . even the migrants themselves out there in the Middle East, could see the pictures of a prospective boyfriend or girlfriend. They communicate, if not with the computer, then through text messages. (Personal communication, July 19, 2005)

Beyond family matters, interpersonal media were also used for transnational businesses. Sari Cañete of Unlad Kabayan (Progress Nation), an NGO that focused on promoting entrepreneurship among OFWs, explained they would use SMS to coordinate the transfer of loans and investments. She said, "For example, our clients would text us, `Have you transferred our money to this particular enterprise?' Then we would text back." However, Cañete did note differences in interpersonal media use within East Asia. Their Hong Kong clients usually coordinated with them by text, while those in Taiwan did so by e-mail because the latter would first meet as a group and write their correspondence. She added that texting was more feasible in Hong Kong because of their more intimate relations with the workers there. She said, "Perhaps because we have been in Hong Kong for a long time we have established a lot of personal relations already" (personal communication, July 26, 2005).

The interplay between interpersonal media such as the mobile phone and actual interpersonal relations was also important in promoting simultaneity within and across borders. Ellene Sana, for instance, described how access to interpersonal media can be extended to other OFWs through their face-to-face relations:

> For example, in Saudi Arabia, there are a couple of Filipinos in the telephone company who are active in coordinating with us. One of them is in charge of troubleshooting equipment, so if everything is working well, then he has a lot of free time to correspond with us. (Personal communication, July 29, 2005)

The same relay system worked in shipping vessels, too. Carolina de Leon of the POEA Sea-based Center said a ship usually had a communication group that included a radio operator and telecommunications and internet managers. These people usually relayed job openings to their friends for direct hiring by the vessel itself.

Summary

The asynchronous nature of traditional letters, cassette tapes, and pictures sent through the postal office marked the early communications of OFWs with their family and friends in the Philippines. Since it would take at least a month for OFWs to receive a message and reply to it, the sharing of personal experiences with their transnational communication partners was anything but temporally and spatially simultaneous. OFWs, for instance, had to send birthday greetings to the Philippines two weeks in advance, and pictures of the celebration of that particular birthday would reach the OFWs a fortnight later. In order to negotiate the spatial distance between them, OFWs and their correspondents in the Philippines thus had to tweak the temporality with which they transnationally observed events and addressed concerns. In the absence of simultaneity, OFWs and their conversation partners were not part of a space of flows as conceptualized by Castells (2001).

Among the many media that were available to them, it was mobile phones that the most number of OFWs had used to connect themselves to their own spaces of flows because mobile phones entail relatively less hardware, skills, and costs to purchase, use and maintain. Also, the mobile phone, as a deeply personal medium, imbued OFWs with an intimate sense of connection to their otherwise geographically distant relations. This rise of mobile phones as the most universally accessible communication medium for OFWs across demographic characteristics has since resulted in technological, temporal, and spatial simultaneity among them and their conversation partners.

Technological Simultaneity

Simultaneity would have been possible all along for migrant workers and their partners in the Philippines since state-sponsored migrant employment began only thirty-two years ago, when analog landline telephone technology was already well developed. However, the poor landline telecommunications infrastructure in the Philippines prevented access to telephones for many Filipinos, and expensive international call tariffs made it prohibitive for those who had telephones to use their units regularly.

The deregulation of the Philippines telecommunications industry began in 1989, with the revised National Telecommunications Development Plan. The plan opened the industry to multiple companies, among them the mobile phone service providers that would establish the country's cellular network and slash international long distance call rates from the Philippines, as has been explained earlier.

With the extensive cellular network and cheaper call rates, the potential for simultaneity between OFWs and their family and friends in the Philippines had increased because of mobile phones. Indeed, OFWs had significantly taken to mobile phones as their medium of choice to communicate synchronically across borders.

Their use of mobile phones to call and text during their tenure as migrant workers had grown more radically compared to their use of landline phones and other traditional media such as television and radio. The OFWs' use of landline phones in the host country had not risen because access to the units was often shared with other people, precluding their viability for personal conversations.

Newer media, such as the Internet, could also realize simultaneity for OFWs and their partners through e-mails and online chats. However, access to the Internet—through cybercafés, workplaces, or personally owned computers—was significantly skewed towards professionals and higher-income OFWs, especially those in North America and Europe since Internet use entailed relatively advanced computer skills. There was no need to train OFWs in the use of mobile phones for transnational communications, just as the Philippine government and a private software company had been doing in an educational program to promote computer and Internet literacy for migrant workers and their families. Thus, while there were other ways to achieve simultaneity, mobile phones made it easiest.

Spatial Simultaneity

The simultaneity that mobile phones promoted among OFWs also related to issues about migrant employment that were more complex than simply the choice of media for transnational conversations.

For many underemployed OFWs, working abroad entailed what Parreñas (2001b) calls "contradictory class mobility." As they moved across state boundaries for better economic rewards, they were socially demoted. For instance, schoolteachers in the Philippines who became domestic helpers in Hong Kong enjoyed higher incomes in exchange for a lower social status. Thus, OFWs who were otherwise in lower-end service occupations abroad represented a sizeable portion of the middle-class in the Philippines. Since they acted according to what they perceived was their occupational identity while in the host country by not telling their superiors that they had their own property and household help in the Philippines (Lan, 2003; Constable, 2003), the mobile phone then became the arena for them to exercise their persona as household heads and breadwinners. Thus, as the mobile phone connected OFWs to their family it also enabled them to articulate their position as the dominant figure in their Philippine household. Spatial simultaneity in this regard was not simply about the synchronous communications across territorial borders, but also the confluence of one's multi-stranded standing in transnational social spaces.

The increasing deployment of non-underemployed professionals abroad mitigated the impact of "contradictory class mobility" since these usually high-salaried OFWs generally maintained their social status across borders. These OFWs now comprise their own segment of migrant workers that rarely socializes with other OFWs in the lower-end occupations. Indeed, while basic mobile phone ownership was almost universal among OFWs, those who had higher incomes had more advanced phone units that enabled them to practice simultaneity with the greater nuance of still and moving images.

With these professional OFWs, two OFW communities have emerged abroad, differentiated by the social circumstances founded upon occupation and income. OFWs of lesser means now have to negotiate at least two types of social spaces: their ironic social standing because of their simultaneous economic promotion and social demotion across borders, and their disconnected social space with other OFWs who otherwise share their connection to the Philippines and their experiences as migrant workers.

These dichotomous networks of OFWs are being bridged by NGOs. Through mobile phone calls and text messages, these organizations connected professional OFWs who had greater resources to mobilize communication technologies to less-endowed OFWs who were more prone to problems and abuses owing to their "3D" (dirty, demeaning, and dangerous) jobs abroad (Lan, 2003). Even from the Philippines, NGOs were able to use mobile phones to coordinate the rescue of distressed OFWs with the help of government agencies and other, more privileged OFWs. In this case, mobile phones facilitated the simultaneity of OFW spaces. That mobile phones were also the dominant medium for communication for OFWs within the host country made them readily useful for connecting the eccentric networks of OFWs abroad.

Temporal Simultaneity

The synchronicity and constancy of mobile phone calls immediately attest to how mobile phones enable OFWs and their conversation partners to simultaneously share experiences across borders. With the mobile phone as a personal unit, OFWs can call their family and friends in the Philippines and elsewhere anytime, sometimes irrespective of time differences. They no longer need to wait for after-work hours to use their shared landline units and for weekends to use public payphones, both of which automatically would limit the simultaneity of their transnational lives.

However, mobile phones, beyond enabling calling and texting, also facilitate an imagined temporal simultaneity. Many OFWs had a mobile phone unit, or at least a Subscriber Identity Module (SIM) card, and subscribed directly to a Philippine service provider for a sense of direct connection, regardless of time zones, with their family and friends back home. While a mobile phone that was connected to a service provider in the host country could technically be used to call the Philippines, OFWs maintained their "Philippine" mobile phone. It imbued them with a feeling of security and stability. They could immediately contact or be contacted by people in the Philippines.

The recent export of Filipino media products and services through cable networks such as *The Filipino Channel* and *GMAPinoyTV* and online media such as *Inq7.net* and *Philstar.com* means OFWs can easily access information about news and events in the Philippines as well as update themselves with the latest in the national popular culture. Mediated political, economic, and cultural discourses are thus received by OFWs in generally the same format and packaging as those received by people back home. This rich array of transnational information about the motherland thus becomes contextualized personal discourses over the mobile phone. The temporal urgency with which the media report news events and portray popular trends is translated into mobile phone conversations as instantaneous calls to check on mutual safety and welfare as well as to get "insider"—that is, from inside the motherland—information about the mediated material. The insider information then becomes cultural capital for OFWs to share with their colleagues. Thus, even across distances, OFWs share the latest tidbits from the mainstream media with the addition of local flavor as gleaned from a mobile phone conversation.

Given the breadth of the deployment of OFWs, international events are automatically framed as OFW concerns. The Iraq War became the story of a kidnapped OFW driver, while the Israel-Lebanon War became the tale of OFWs in exodus. The personal discourses of OFWs are thus elevated to the national stage, with the mobile phone as an uncanny medium for temporal simultaneity. Government agencies, NGOs, media organizations, and OFWs coordinated, using mobile phones, to rescue OFWs out of the war zone—a massive version of what NGOs had already been doing to salvage distressed individuals through the help of other OFWs and their partner organizations abroad. The different stakeholders of the migrant employment industry became simultaneously aligned through the mobile phone in these moments of distress.

Conclusion

I often wonder, in retrospect, how differently my family would have been if our transnational experience had taken place now, with the many avenues for simultaneity, especially as afforded by the mobile phone. The first Gulf War transpired during my father's stint abroad, and we were on tenterhooks as he traveled across Saudi Arabia to escape the fighting taking place near the eastern border. We only received intermittent landline calls from him, via our neighbors who were fortunate to have their own telephone installed. Juxtapose this against those who had gone through their own Mid-East war armed with a mobile phone with which they could call and be called by their families and support organizations.

Asis (2003) explained how new media helped mitigate the social costs of migrant employment. While parent OFWs were no more connected by mobile phones or other media than OFWs without children, mobile phones still enabled them to exercise their parental duties with greater influence today than ever before. It would take a month for my father's admonition for a misdeed or congratulations for an award to reach me or my sister while he was abroad. Now, both scolding and felicitations can be simultaneous. If there would be one misgiving about the instantaneity of mobile phone conversations, it is that its speed has parlayed the packaging of information as gift to OFWs (Catholic Institute for International Relations, 1987). Friends and family members no longer have to sit down together before a cassette recorder to reflect on news and to express affection to their OFW. Instead, they now give and get personalized sound bytes—quick and constant updates about the here and now.

Simultaneity among families rendered transnational by migrant employment is thus realized through the mobile phone. True, this simultaneity remains highly nuanced, with some groups still more technologically privileged by their resources. However, just as advanced mobile phones differentiate OFW communities in this regard, mobile telephony itself potentially connects them. Through the mobile phone, they can reach out to each other despite their different social circumstances, as organizations have been trying to facilitate.

Thus, mobile telephony promotes temporal and spatial simultaneity not only because it connects people across territorial boundaries and time zones using transnationally available technologies. It helps OFWs realize simultaneity because it bridges social spaces among OFWs themselves as well as contradictions in OFWs' social standing because of our dualistic world economy. Finally, it helps OFWs negotiate personal, national, and international concerns and discourses by temporally aligning them through a mobile phone conversation. OFWs, through the mobile phone, create their own space of flows (Castells, 2001).

Acknowledgment

The writing of this paper was supported by the PhD Incentive Grant Program of the Office of the Vice Chancellor for Research and Development of the University of the Philippines Diliman.

Notes

1. In 1996, GNI PC PPP was US$3,905, which meant daily income was US$10.70 (World Bank, 2007). In December 1995, the exchange rate was PhP26.21 = US$1 (Wong, 2000).
2. By ownership, I mean the respondents owned and used the unit exclusively or paid for its subscription on their own. By access, I meant the respondents either had shared use and/or subscription, usually paid for by the employer.
3. One of the findings from a study on Internet use in the rural Philippines was that Internet cafés had families of migrant workers as their primary clientele (Umali and Paragas, 2004). An hour's rental of an online computer at such a café usually cost US$0.50, which equals one minute of an international long distance call.

Unlimited monthly Internet subscriptions range from US$10.00 for dial-up to US$40.00 for broadband connections.

Bibliography

Alegado, Dean. "International Labor Migration, Diaspora and the Emergence of Transnational Filipino Communities." In *Filipino Diaspora: Demography, Social Networks, Empowerment and Culture,* edited by Tsuda Mamory, 1-22. Quezon City, Philippines: Philippine Migration Network and Philippine Social Science Council, 2003.

Asis, Marjua M.B. "The Social Costs (and Benefits) of Migration: What Happens to Left-behind Children and Families?" In *Proceedings of the World Conference of OFWs: Shaping the Future of Filipino Labor Migration,* 63-74. Quezon City, Philippines: Philippine Migrants Rights Watch, 2004.

Castells, Manuel. "Internationalism and the Network Society." In *The Hacker Ethic and the Spirit of the Information Age,* edited by Pekka Himanen, 155-178. New York, NY: Random House, 2001.

Catholic Institute for International Relations. *The Labour Trade: Filipino Migrant Workers Around the World.* Nottingham, UK: Russell Press Ltd, 1987.

Schiller, Nina Glick. "Transmigrants and Nation-States: Something Old and Something New in the U.S. Immigrant Experience." In *The handbook of international migration: The American experience,* edited by Charles Hirschman, Philip Kasinitz, and Joshua DeWind, 94-119. New York, NY: Russell Sage Foundation, 1999.

Hochschild, Arlie R. "Love and Gold." In *Global woman: Nannies, Maids, and Sex Workers in the New Economy,* edited by Barbara Ehrenreich and Arlie R. Hochschild, 15-30. New York, NY: Metropolitan Books, 2003.

Huang, Shirlena, Brenda S.A. Yeoh, and Richard T. Jackson. "Domestic Workers and Transnational Migration: Perspectives from the Philippines and Singapore." In *Labour in Southeast Asia: Local processes in a Globalized World,* edited by Rebecca Elmhirst and Ratna Saptari, 329-357. London: Routledge Curzon, 2004.

Katz, James E. and Mark Aakhus, Eds. *Perpetual Contact: Mobile Communication, Private Talk, Public Performance.* Cambridge, UK: Cambridge University Press, 2002.

Ling, Rich S. and Leslie Haddon. "Mobile Telephony, Mobility and the Coordination of Everyday Life." In *Machines That Become Us: The Social Context of Personal Communication Technology,* edited by James Katz, 245-266. New Brunswick, NJ: Transaction Publishers, 2001.

Paragas, Fernando. "Dramatextism: Mobile Telephony and People Power in the Philippines." In *Mobile Democracy: Essays on Society, Self and Politics,* edited by Kristóf Nyíri, 258-284. Vienna, Austria: Passagen Verlag, 2003

Paragas, Fernando. "A Case Study on the Continuum of Landline and Mobile Phone Services in the Philippines." In *When Mobile Came: The Cultural and Social Impact of Mobile Communication,* edited by Sin Dong Kim, 178-197. Seoul, Korea: Communication Books, 2005.

Paragas, Fernando. "Migrant Mobiles: Cellular Telephony, Transnational spaces, and the Filipino Diaspora." In *A Sense of Place: The Global and the Local in Mobile Communication*, edited by Kristóf Nyíri, 241-250. Vienna, Austria: Passagen Verlag, 2005.

Paragas, Fernando. "Distant Voices, Proximate Purses." Paper presented at the Advertising Asia Congress of the Asian Federation of Advertising Associations. Pattaya, Thailand, November, 1999.

Paragas, Fernando. "Distant Voices." Undergraduate thesis, University of the Philippines, 1996.

Parreñas, Rhacel. "Human Sacrifices: What Happens When Women Migrate and Leave Families Behind? The Case of the Philippines Raises some Troubling Questions." *Women's Review of Books*, 19 (February, 2002): 16.

Parreñas, Rhacel. "Mothering From a Distance: Emotions, Gender, & Inter-Generational Relations in Filipino Transnational Families." *Feminist Studies*, 27 (Summer 2001): 361-390.

Parreñas, Rhacel. *Servants of Globalization: Women, Migration and Domestic Work*. Stanford, CA: Stanford University Press.

Parreñas, Rhacel. "Transgressing the Nation-State: The Partial Citizenship and 'Imagined (Global) Community' of Migrant Filipina Domestic Workers." *Signs*, 26 (Summer 2001): 1129-1154.

Pickens, Mark and Brian Richardson. "Mobile Wallets and Virtual Currencies." 2007. *ICT Update 36.* http://ictupdate.cta.int/index.php/en/feature_articles/ mobile_wallets_and_virtual_currencies (11 July, 2007).

Sampson, Helen. "Transnational Drifters or Hyperspace Dwellers: An Exploration of the Lives of Filipino Seafarers Abroad and Ashore." *Ethnic & Racial Studies*, 26 (2, 2003): 253-277.

Tung, Charlene. "The Cost of Caring: The Social Reproductive Labor of Filipina Live-in Home Health Caregivers." *Frontiers*, 21(1/2, 2000): 61-82.

Tyner, James. "The Gendering of Philippine International Labor Migration." *Professional Geographer*, 48 (November, 1996): 405-416.

Umali, Violela and Fernando Paragas. "The Philippines." In *Cyber Communities in Rural Asia: A Study of Seven Asian Countries,* edited by Kavita Karan, 236-272. Singapore: Times Academic Press, 2006.

Wong, Ka Fu. "Historical Exchange Rate Regime of Asian countries." 2000. *International Economics.* http://intl.econ.cuhk.edu.hk/exchange_rate_regime/ (10 July, 2007).

World Bank. World Development Indicators, 2007.

3

Portable Objects in Three Global Cities:
The Personalization of Urban Places

Mizuko Ito
Keio University

Daisuke Okabe
Keio University

Ken Anderson
Intel Research

Much of the public discourse and research on mobile media has focused on how they transcend the constraints of time and space, in the process often disrupting the integrity of face-to-face encounters and locations such as restaurants, movies, and public transportation. In addressing these issues, research has tended to focus on a specific device, the mobile phone, and on interpersonal communication as the primary mode of usage. While private communication on the mobile phone continues to be an important social and research site, we shift our focus towards mobile media that involve interfacing with particular locations and infrastructures. We examine not just the mobile phone, but also the whole range of portable objects that people use to inhabit, navigate through, and interface with urban environments. This includes objects like media players, books, keys, credit and transit cards, as well as identity and member cards that comprise the information-based "mobile kits" of contemporary urbanites. By expanding the object of mobile media studies to include this more diverse ensemble of portable informational objects, we seek to understand the diverse ways in which information and communication technologies (ICTs) shape our experience or urban space and time. The expanded focus also enables us to consider the convergence between objects like transactional cards, media players, and keys with the mobile phone or personal data assistant (PDA).

This chapter reports on a study conducted in three global cities—Tokyo, London, and Los Angeles—where we tracked young professionals' use of portable objects. By examining the ensemble of objects in a mobile kit, this study seeks to understand how portable devices construct and support an individual's identity and activities, mediating relationships with people, places, and institutions. By examining the use of portable objects for navigating, interfacing, and transacting with urban locations and services, we shift our focus away from private, interpersonal communication towards more public, impersonal, and instrumental kinds of social exchanges. What kinds of social and informational activities does an individual engage in when moving about different urban environments and between home and work? How do portable ICTs change how we occupy urban space and time? After first introducing our study and research approach, we discuss three ways of being present in urban space that involve the combination of portable media devices, people, infrastructures, and locations: cocooning, camping, and footprinting.

Research Framework

The study reported here was conducted as a collaborative effort between the Docomo House research lab at Keio University and the People and Practices group at Intel Research. Our goal was to document what people carried around with them in locations outside of the home and office, how these objects were used for transactions and communication, and how they differ between different cities around the world. We were also interested exploring new methods for documenting practices that are very low-key, ongoing, and difficult to observe. All of these research objectives were extensions of our existing research in mobile communications where we seek to understand how information and communication technologies are being integrated into ongoing, pervasive, everyday social interactions and transforming them in subtle ways.

The study centers on a diary-based methodology, adapted from the "communication diary" studies we have used to study mobile communication and camphone use (Grinter and Eldridge, 2001; Ito and Okabe, 2005; Okabe, 2004). We adapted these methods to include a larger set of portable objects and to take into account the specificities of different urban contexts. For example, the record keeping via mobile text input which works well in the pedestrian context of Tokyo was not appropriate for the car-centered infrastructures of Los Angeles. Study participation took place in four stages:

1. An initial interview, including a survey of everything participants were carrying in their car, pockets, bags, wallets, etc.
2. One or two days of diary keeping, where participants documented every time they used something out of their mobile kit. The actual method of self-reporting this data varied by site: paper diaries (London), voice recorders (LA), and moblogs (Tokyo). The media for recording were meant to cause the least amount of intrusion in the particular city's infrastructural context.
3. A "shadowing" session in which a researcher accompanied a participant on a normal or routine activity such as shopping, commuting, or other trip through the city.
4. A final interview, including a review of their diary and a photo-elicitation exercise. The interviews relied on the diary records as the primary basis for discussion, and these are the source of all the quotes reported on in the body of this chapter.

In all three cities, we recruited young professionals, aged twenty-two to thirty-two, aiming for an even split between genders. The participants were recruited through local academic and professional contacts. As is common in ethnographic work, the sample was selected for theoretical interest and trust relationships with the researchers rather than for statistical representation. Our research seeks to understand current patterns among specific populations, as well as considering the ways in which technology uses are likely to evolve in the future. Thus, we sought young professionals who were likely to be leading-edge users of new mobile technologies and spend time in a diverse range of urban spaces. Teens have been the early adopters of many mobile technologies centered on social uses. For this study, however, we were interested not only in social communication but also in issues such as financial transactions and work related uses among a population that has the resources and freedom to make full use of urban space. For these reasons, many participants were in the area of new media, including design and media industries, and we recruited a substantial proportion of freelancers who were engaged in work outside of the home or office. We focused on individuals transitioning into the workforce from study at elite universities, as they could be expected to be both technologically savvy and confronted with novel challenges, and thus potential early adopters and influencers. A total of twenty-six individuals participated, with twelve in London, eight in Los

Angeles, and six in Tokyo. These sites were selected as major world cities with differing cultural, physical, and technological infrastructures. The differences in number of participants in each city was due to practical issues in recruiting and the time that researchers had at each location to conduct the fieldwork.

Conceptual Framework

Research on mobile phone use has thus far focused on interpersonal communication rather than impersonal or transactional social exchanges. One of the most significant technosocial changes heralded by the mobile phone was the shift in the locus of remote communication away from location-based networking to person-based networking. Reflecting this, study of mobile communications has tended to focus on a specific device (the mobile phone) and a specific set of activities (personal communication). What are the implications for interpersonal relationships and interactions when communication is channeled through a personal communications device? Research in a variety of locations around the world has documented the implications of this shift for interpersonal communication, examining the rise of "virtual walled communities" (Ling, 2004), "telecocoons"(Habuchi, 2005), "networked individualism" (Wellman, 1999), or "full-time intimate communities" (Yoshii, et al., 2002). Given this focus on personal communications and personal addressing, research on place and time in relation to mobile communication has centered on the disruptive effects of private communication in public space (Ling, 2002; Murtagh, 2002; Okabe and Ito, 2005; Plant 2002; Weilenmann, 2003). Private communications via the mobile phone were seen as transcending the constraints of local place and time, often disrupting the social logic of public places.

Our work thus far has also focused on personal communication, but we are beginning to turn our attention to a more diverse set of social interactions and transactions being mediated by portable ICTs. Although mobile phones are multi-function devices that can include games, calculators, planners, and information access capabilities, very little social research has examined these types of features. With the expansion in function of the mobile phone to include photos, videos, music players, digital cash, more sophisticated games, and web applications, we are beginning to see more research on uses of the mobile phone that are not exclusively about interpersonal communication. For example, research on camera phones has opened up a dialogue about photography and visual archiving in relation to mobile media and communications (Kindberg, et al., 2004; Rivière 2005; Van House, et al., 2004; Koskinen, 2005; Ling and Julsrud, 2005; Van House, et al., 2005; Okabe and Ito, 2006). Other emerging research on mobile media includes work on electronic wallets (Cooper, et al., 1999; Mainwaring, et al., 2005), mobile gaming (Licoppe and Inada, 2006; McGonigal, 2006), and much research in the area of ubiquitous and pervasive computing. As we have shifted our focus towards practices such as media capture, consumption, and economic transactions, our analytic focus has also shifted to include a different set of social negotiations—including different ways of understanding the relationship between mobile media, place, and time. In this chapter, we are specifically interested in the question of how portable ICTs change our relationships to urban space and services.

In a location-centered analysis, the issue of private communication in public places is just one of many forms of social frames that people nego-tiate with their mobile communications technologies. As people navigate the urban environment, they selectively display aspects of their public identities to interface with local social and infrastructural resources: swiping a transit card at a ticket wicket or displaying a membership card to get into the gym. They appropriate public and semi-public spaces by pulling out a laptop in a café, or donning headphones in a crowded train to create a private cocoon. Our focus in this chapter is on these ways of interfacing with an urban place and social transactions with anonymous others, media, infrastructure, and services. Here we deal with private communication only to the extent that it represents a posture within public space, such or as when somebody will become absorbed with their mobile phone in a bar or train to avoid contact with others in the shared physical space. In other words, we are not analyzing the content of private communications and relations, but rather the ways in which communication and identity play out in public and semi-public places and infrastructures.

The study of interfacing with infrastructures and urban locations has unique methodological problems that differ from the challenges we have faced in the study of private communication. Unlike interpersonal relations where most people have a great deal of personal and emotional investment, relations with urban infrastructures and locations often barely rise to the level of consciousness for most people. As Susan Leigh Star (1999) has suggested, ethnography of infrastructure is the "study of boring things" (377). Star also argues, however, that it is crucial that infrastructure be examined from a social and cultural perspective, and that these embedded and often unnoticed structures represent some of the most pervasive and foundational scaffolds of everyday social life. Building on Star's framework, Paul Dourish and Genevieve Bell (2007) have suggested that the study of technology and place, and ubiquitous computing in particular, needs to be informed by looking at "infrastructures as fundamental elements of the ways in which we encounter spaces—infrastructures of naming, infrastructures of mobility, infrastructures of separation, infrastructures of interaction, and so on." Their project is to examine "how the infrastructures of space and pervasive computing are mutually, reciprocally coupled to social and cultural practices." As new kinds of instrumental, transactional, and media related functions are being implemented for mobile phones, it becomes even more crucial that mobile communications research look at these more infrastructural and impersonal forms of social and cultural practice. Infrastructure represents social negotiations embedded in taken-for-granted technical forms. Steven Jackson, Paul Edwards, Geoffrey Bowker, and Cory Knobel, in their report "Understanding Infrastructure" (2007) note:

> infrastructure is a deeply distributed phenomenon, involving actors of many types and levels. The variety of positions vis-à-vis infrastructure can lead to widely variant experiences and responses to infrastructure—many or all of which will need to be taken into account if the process of infrastructural development is to move forward effectively. (27)

This chapter is an effort to understand the experience of people on the "end-user" side of the infrastructure equation—people who are not part of the high stakes political and economic negotiations around infrastructure development, but who are nonetheless vital participants in the process.

Dourish's (2001) phenomenological approach to pervasive computing, which he describes in greater detail in his book on embodied interaction, provides a conceptual bridge between infrastructure studies and our prior frameworks for studying private communication in public spaces (Ito, et al., 2005; Okabe and Ito, 2005). In our past work, we have relied on an adaptation of Goffman's (1963) approach to how people behave in public space to examine new hybrid "technosocial" settings for behavior that hybridize public and private frames (Ito and Okabe, 2005). With this chapter, we adapt this framework to consider how people display identity and mobilize communications technology not only for other people, but also in order to interface with locations, services, and infrastructures. Dourish (2001) describes how computers have "moved off the desktop" and "designers of interactive systems have increasingly come to understand that interaction is intimately connected with settings in which it occurs" (19). By examining how portable technologies are part of our embodied presence in specific locations of interaction, we can begin to understand new technosocial configurations that couple devices, locations, infrastructures, and behavior into recognizable genres of social practice. Just as how, in prior work, we have identified new "technosocial situations" for behavior structured by text messaging, in this chapter we suggest certain behavioral frames, or "genres of presence," in public space that involve people's use of portable information technologies to inhabit locations and interface with infrastructures.

Managing Presence in Urban Space and Time

In our analysis of our participants' mobile kits, we identified a wide range of different types of objects, including the mobile phone, snacks, toiletries, record-keeping devices (such as planners or receipts), and access mechanisms (such as ID cards, member cards, and keys). In this chapter, we focus only on those objects and activities that center on managing presence in urban space. Our three genres of presence (which can also be considered a form of place making) are cocoons, encampments, and footprints. These are technosocial modes of engaging with urban spaces that rely on a stabilization of technology, social practice, and infrastructural standards. These are also genres of presence that we saw occurring in all three of the cities we studied, despite substantial differences in urban contexts. Clearly some of the specificities of the technology and practice varied depending on factors such as the prevalence of digital cash systems or the centrality of public transportation. We discuss the variability of practices across locations in the course of the following description. Although we cannot verify this through this study, given its limited scope, our sense is that factors such as generational identity, class identity, and profession may be factors that are as important as national context in determining variability in how people mobilize different genres of presence in urban space. And, clearly, the difference between the dense urban contexts we have examined here and suburban and rural contexts will even more decisively inflect different genres of presence. Comparisons of this kind, however, are beyond the scope of this current analysis.

We describe our material in terms of there genres of presence in urban space: cocooning, camping, and footprinting.

Cocooning

One of the primary functions of mobile media that is carried in public and semi-private places is to provide a personalized media environment that is attached to the person and not the physical place. Almost all of our research participants carried around devices and media that were meant to create a cocoon that sheltered them from engagement with the physical location and co-present others—a private territory within the confines of urban space. Mobile phones can function as a cocooning technology, such as when people text message or browse the web when they are alone in places like trains and cafés. Portable media devices of various kinds, however, are more emblematic of this kind of social function in that they are explicitly carried to provide a focus of attention that shelters an individual from local social and spatial interactions. These include music players, as well as books, newspapers, and magazines. Cocoons are micro-places built through private, individually controlled infrastructures, temporarily appropriating public space for personal use. They involve a complex set of negotiations that take into account the presence of others in the vicinity, while also working to shut them out. These cocoons also have specific temporal features, functioning as mechanisms for "filling" or "killing" in-between time when people are inhabiting or moving through places within where they are not interested in fully engaging. We see cocoons operating most commonly when people are in transit or when they are killing time while waiting in a location that doesn't otherwise contain much of personal interest. In other words, cocoons transform "dead time" in incidental locations into time that is personally productive or enriching.

The most common type of cocoon we documented was the use of different media devices in public transportation. In London and Tokyo, where all of our participants relied on public transportation, some kind of cocooning media in addition to the mobile phone was always present in the mobile kit. Without exception, all participants in London and Tokyo regularly carried reading material with them. With the exception of two participants in London and two in Tokyo, all of the participants from these two locations also carried a music player as a standard part of their mobile kit. Cocooning technologies are considered crucial for people who have commutes of any length. Music players are particularly valuable in environments that are very crowded. As one subject in Tokyo notes, "without my MP3 player, crowded trains would be unbearable." A woman in London says that she uses her iPod on the tube "to avoid unwanted conversations." She finds that there are men "who take the tube as an opportunity to try to pick up women . . . there aren't many of them but it happens to me at least a few times a week but never when I have my iPod on."

The combination of a music player, headphones, and reading material creates an ideal, compact cocoon that enables effective escape from involvement in the physical setting in a way respectful to others in the vicinity. For example, in London, "Peter" takes a *National Geographic* with him on all commutes. He connects his iPod, then opens up the *National Geographic* and reads all the way home. He has the *National Geographic* timed to take just about two weeks of commutes. He then switches over to a business magazine. The *National Geographic,* however, is "his time"—a time of "retreat" from daily life and to "refresh." When he is done, he leaves the magazine on the tube as a present for other travelers to enjoy—a chance for them to go "on holiday on the way home."

In Los Angeles, with its more sprawling urban environment and car-centered transport system, the dynamics of cocooning differ substantially from Tokyo and London. The car functions as a private cocoon within the urban transit infrastructure. All eight of the Los Angeles participants reported listening to radio or music in their car. They all also reported that they used their drive time to catch up on voice calls. Unlike the case of public transit commuters, car commuters work to optimize their audio rather than visual input. For example, one of our Los Angeles participants describes how he tries to leave the house near the top of the hour, at 8:28 for example, so he can be sure to catch the news on National Public Radio. Another Los Angeles participant describes how he takes his iPod with him wherever he goes. "If I go to fill up my car with gas, which is five minutes away, I bring it just to have it." He describes his complicated process of plugging and unplugging his iPod from car and body as he moves from car to gym and other environments, but that does not deter him for carrying it with him everywhere. This transition from inside and outside of the car was a constant struggle for people with digital music players. The five LA participants with MP3 players tried with varying degrees of success to use them in their car. Discussion with participants about the personalization of their audio environment in their car brought up numerous areas of frustration. Participants in LA ended up relying largely on radio because of these difficulties.

Although the dynamics of media cocooning differ depending on whether people are walking, driving, or using public transportation, there are common characteristics. In all cases, people are mobilizing private media infrastructures within public infrastructures to momentarily claim them for personal space. People shut out involvements with the auditory and social environment that is physically local to them in environments that they have only a passing relationship to them. In other words, they see their relationship to environments that they pass through on their way to different destinations as temporary and limited. People generally make efforts to maintain the boundary of their cocoon, shielding their micro, personal space from the broader shared context. Readers or mobile phone users on the train posture so their texts are not readable to others. Headphones shelter individuals from the ambient audio as well as sheltering others from the personal audio. The leakage between personal sound and public sound in the case of mobile phone talk has continued to be a site of social tension because it fails to adhere to the norm of cocooning of personal media (Ling, 2002; Okabe and Ito, 2005). Although some people might shoulder boom boxes or leave their car windows open to broadcast their music, among those we studied the norm was clearly to maintain a boundary between personal audio and the ambient environment.

Camping

Another category of hybrid and person-centered place making that we observed among our participants was the process of constructing personal work space "encampments" by bringing portable media to public places of choice. The most common form of encampment involved using cafés and other spaces like libraries or public parks as places to camp out and work. This is not a ubiquitous practice like we see with media cocoons, but something that we only saw with a small subset of our participants, primarily those who did not rely exclusively on office-based infrastructures for their work. Although this was a minority of the population in our study, it was a thread that ran across the three different cities. Two participants each in Los Angeles and in Tokyo, and four participants in London engaged in this form of place-making. These participants were all engaged in freelance work or personal hobbies, suggesting there are commonalities of practice for this category of activity, regardless of the specific city or national context. Unlike the case of media cocoons, where people do not have a specific personal investment or interest in the places they are passing through, in the case of encampments, people appropriate places where they feel some affinity. They put down roots that have temporal limits, but are more extended than commuters who are simply passing through. Rather than "killing time" in incidental and in-between places, encampments involved "spending time" and "scheduling time" in desirable locations outside of home and office. The location is a specific destination that people seek out and have a personal relationship with. They will often have a mobile kit that is specifically tailored for setting up camp, including bulkier devices like laptops or scanners that are not part of their more stripped down mobile kit.

In Los Angeles, "Bob" works as a freelance writer and likes to work at his favorite café on the west side. His use of a neighborhood café epitomizes the hybrid place that we call an encampment. He uses the café as an office where he focuses on writing, unlike his home office that he uses to connect to the Internet to surf and blog. For Bob, the space of the café is a social space where he has developed relationships and put down roots. He is a regular who is known by the café staff and other patrons and he uses the café as a space to meet with his collaborators. He feels comfortable enough there that he will even have food delivered to the café from other restaurants. When he sits down to write, however, he faces his laptop and cocoons with the use of his MP3 player. He says, "I need something to tune out, that I like to write with. I can't write in silence." When going to the café, his mobile kit always includes reading material, his laptop, and his MP3 player. He does not connect to the Internet while he is there because his goal is to focus on writing screenplays. In other words, the space of a neighborhood café provides personalized social resources, food, and a distinctive ambience that makes it an attractive destination for Bob to camp out in with his gear.

A graphic artist in LA, "Cara," similarly describes how she will carry her laptop and a scanner with her to libraries and cafés to work outside of her home office. She generally travels by bike with a very stripped down mobile kit that fits in her pockets, but when she is going to camp out somewhere she uses her backpack with her larger media devices. She utilizes resources in the library, so there is a practical reason for her to camp out at that location, but her choice to work in cafés is based on ambience and the pleasure of working outside of the home. Encampments are created by people who are engaged in freelance work as well as people who have hobbies or educational pursuits that they engage in outside of the home and office. "Gai" in Tokyo describes how he uses his local library and Starbucks as a space of retreat that differs from his weekday worker identity. He has a separate purple bag that contains a different mobile kit from his weekday briefcase, which he takes to the library to read and study on the weekend. Gai also makes an effort to have a more personal relationship with his local Starbucks where he also likes to encamp. He leaves a personal mug there that marks him as a regular. Another participant in Tokyo, who likes to write on his PDA in family restaurants and other semi-public places, describes how his "brain feels more lively" when he is in places occupied by others.

Most participants did not specifically seek out Internet infrastructures when they worked in cafés or public places, but for three of our London participants this was an important factor. For example, "Lacey" generally carries her laptop with her, and regularly uses public access WiFi. She worked her way through a series of wireless access cards, and she carried two at the time that she participated in our study. Her husband provided her with ones that gave her free time for thirty days. Between those and free WiFi locations she could usually get a connection. There used to be more free wireless around London, she explained, but over the past year, places that were once free were now charging through some new wireless companies. Her most frequently used one was called "The Cloud," which worked at her favorite coffee shop.

In some cases, the boundaries between a cocoon and an encampment are somewhat indistinct. A more subtle example of seeking out public space to camp out comes from one of our Tokyo participants, who on occasion rides a bus rather than a train even though it takes more time. He says he prefers the ambience of the bus: "I enjoy the scenery from inside the bus . . . I like looking out at the town. The inside of a bus has a relaxed feeling." Presence in a vibrant public space is central to cocooning as well as camping out in urban space. In the case of cocooning, however, people generally experienced it as a practice of shutting out a hostile or undesirable environment, but in the case of encampments, people saw value in residing for a period of time in a desirable location. Just as people seek out beautiful campsites to set out their gear and reside for short periods of time, urbanites find attractive public places to temporarily set up camp with the help of their information technologies. The attraction of working in a specific "camping site" can include the personal relationships fostered there, food and drink, infrastructures (tables, electricity, WiFi) and, most importantly, diffuse social ambience. With the current crop of technologies such as laptops and MP3 players, people can enjoy having both rich personal media and workspaces as well as the benefits of an ambient public or service-oriented space.

Footprints

Portable information devices provide opportunities for personalization of public and semi-public spaces in the form of cocooning and encampments, but also in the form of individualized relationships to commercial establishments. In the case of cafés, we've seen how people develop personal relationships over time that make certain locations desirable campsites. In the cities we studied, a more typical way of establishing and maintaining relationships to restaurants, shops, and transit infra-structures is through the mediation of various member, reward, stamp, and access cards. In all three of the cities we examined, we were struck by the proliferation of different cards within the wallets of our research participants. As we investigated this category of "information object" further, we came to realize that people are increasingly relying on these relatively systematic and information-based systems for managing their relationships with urban services. The cards that we find in people's wallets perform a wide variety of financial and social functions, but here we are specifically interested in how cards mediate and personalize people's relationships to various establishments in urban space.

The process of maintaining records of customer transactions can be considered a process of "footprinting," or leaving traces in a particular location. Unlike the case of cocooning and encampments, customer foot-printing is a process that is largely driven by the particular location-based establishment rather than by the individual. Footprinting is the process of integrating an individual's trajectory into the transactional history of a particular establishment, and customer cards are the mediating devices. In the case of large global cities that often are populated by transplanted and transient populations, individuals and businesses are increasingly relying on these more systemic ways of tracking the relation between people and location-specific services, rather than on more interpersonal modes of recognizing who a "regular" is at a particular establishment. The stacks of reward and stamp cards that people find in their wallets are traces of their movement through urban space and, in turn, become tracers for businesses to track customer loyalty.

Almost all participants described the difficulties they had in managing the proliferation of different reward and loyalty cards. Paper-based stamp cards were present in all three cities. Electronic discount cards, used in grocery stores in all three cities and in large electronic stores in Japan, are a more technically sophisticated version of paper stamp cards. By swiping a member card, the store can keep track of purchases and give a discount of points based on a percentage of purchases. The last type of reward system is credit card systems where points are banked towards airline mileage or other rewards. In LA and London, certain retailers had credit cards that were specific to their stores. In Japan, there is some experimentation with coupon and reward systems that were accessed via mobile phone. For example, certain search sites offer discount coupons or point systems that are accessed through the mobile web, through web searches or by photographing a Quick Response (QR) code with a camera phone. We saw only a handful of instances where people tried to use these systems.

The overall proliferation of these cards in people's wallets was notable, and many, particularly in Tokyo, kept stacks of these cards at home. A typical stack in a Tokyo-ite's wallet would include five to fifteen point and reward cards, and double that number or more in a stack at home. In Tokyo, point and stamp cards were issued for almost every type of service and retail establishment, including bakeries, electronics shops, clothing stores, and bars. In London and Los Angeles, those numbers were fewer, and were generally restricted to grocery store and coffee cards. Most people were fairly offhanded in what prompted them to get a card. Usually it was offered by the salesperson and they decided to take it. In the US, reward credit cards are often offered at the sales counter, and they offer to take 10 percent off the current purchase. This can be a motivation for someone who is otherwise relatively indifferent to these schemes to pick up a new card. For example, "Joan" has credit cards for Target, Banana Republic, and Victoria's Secret because she got 10 percent off on the day of purchases. "It was like ten percent on whatever I bought that day if I got the card so like, fine. Okay. I'll just never use it."

Participants varied in the degree of attention they paid to different reward and loyalty schemes. Individual variation was greater than regional variation; in every city we found people who worked hard to maximize the benefits of different reward schemes, and others who preferred to largely ignore them or found them too much of a hassle or a violation of privacy. Those who were attentive to these schemes tended to have a general awareness of how much they were getting from them and knew how different rewards were calculated, but many people only had a vague idea of how the electronic systems calculated rewards and how they were redeemed. Consider, for example, contrasting examples in London. "Susan" has seven different point cards. She uses mostly her Sainsbury grocery card and her Boots drugstore card. The others were for a grocery store she virtually never goes to, two coffee shops, one bakery, one video store, and one massage service. Each had different point systems. Despite the relatively large number of cards she uses, she is not terribly attentive to the details of how the points are used. For the Sainsbury card, she uses the reward points every time she purchases and does not realize that she can save and keep track of the points for larger rewards. For her Boots card, she doesn't know how many points she has or how she can redeem them. "You've got to use some machine or something to figure out your points. I'm not actually sure."

"Judy," on the other hand, has a similar array of cards, but she is somewhat more attentive to how rewards are banked and redeemed. She has figured out how to use the complicated system at Boots. "Normally, I collect points until it gets to thirty or forty pounds and then I'll buy myself a present like a hair dryer or perfume or makeup. Saving up the points until they mean something. Kind of a reward to myself then."

A handful of participants resisted in different degrees the process of footprinting through these types of reward schemes. One concern was over a bulky wallet. Many participants in Tokyo voiced concern over the expanding wallet, but everyone still carried around a relatively large array of stamp and point cards. "Cathy" in Los Angeles hates carrying around different cards and prefers a minimalist wallet. She carries around stamp cards for the coffee shops she frequents because they have to exist in paper. For the grocery stores, she prefers to give them her phone number rather than have to carry another card around.

Other participants had a more explicitly critical stance to the proliferation of information-based reward schemes. "Susan" in London has the most critical stance among the people we interviewed, though she still uses reward cards:

A: I think you have to spend about a million pounds to get anything much for free. But because I buy contact lens solution and things like that, quite expensive things, then it does gradually mount up. I kind of object to the whole idea really . . . So, now all those people will take your card and you get your money. You have to spend like—you have to spend a pound, and then you get two points. Once you've got five hundred points, you get two pound fifty off for shopping. I wrote that out one day. So you have to spend two hundred and fifty quid to get two quid. It's not really worth shopping.
Q: And do you use the card? Why do you carry it?
A: Yeah. You know Michael Moore? I went to a Michael Moore thing where he told everybody they had to cut them up because they were evil.
Q: Oh, he did? How are they evil?
A: Well, because you shouldn't have loyalty toward the company. You should have loyalty towards your friends and the family and things like that. It's just a real scam to try and make you shop in the same place.

In Tokyo, Gai has a cautious stance toward different reward and customer footprinting schemes that center around privacy concerns. He is careful not to use his credit card for any transactions that he would not want others to know about. He's nervous about digital cash schemes that keep detailed footprint information. "It would be convenient if all cars had ETC [Electric Toll Collection] installed to begin with but I'm a little uncomfortable with the idea that it identifies the driver."

Others resisted the depersonalization of customer loyalty by engaging in alternative ways of being recognized and leaving a footprint at favorite establishments. For example, one of our female participants in our Tokyo study has a fixed "ant path" for shopping at an upscale mall. During our shadowing session with her, she describes the stores she regularly frequents, and some of the employees know her by name. Though she may have reward cards for different boutiques, she also develops a personal relationship through regular routes through the mall. The ways in which people develop relationships to "camp sites" are also evidence of a more person-centered relationship to establishments.

In Tokyo, Taka makes use of the usual array of reward cards and frequents fashionable franchises like Starbucks where he uses his coffee bean card. At the same time, he also likes to develop personal relationships with people who work at the cafés and stores he frequents. While shadowing Taka, we see him strike up a conversation with the woman behind the Starbucks counter. "I like to speak to the clerk when I am buying something," he explains. Among our research participants in all three cities, however, this mode of developing personal relationships to urban services or establishments was rare. In contrast to the large number of point, reward, and transactions cards in people's wallets, people had personal relationships to very few services and only a few individuals were known "regulars" at cafés, stores, and restaurants.

For the most part, point, stamp, and reward cards are relatively unimportant technologies for people as they go about their day-to-day life. A majority of people use them if they are not inconvenient. A minority of people actively work to maximize the benefits of these systems. Most find these systems mildly annoying and impersonal and a few try to actively resist them in both direct and subtle ways. Although establishments see them as ways of tying customers into particular places and developing a sense of identification, presence, and loyalty with their service, people in our study did not experience these reward schemes in this way. Although electronic footprinting has the advantage of ease of use, they have an even more depersonalizing effect on people's interfacing with urban infrastructures and raise privacy concerns. With the move towards franchising and chain stores, reward schemes are increasingly delocalized as well as depersonalized. They automate the more messy human systems that have traditionally been in play, where shop owners and workers recognize regulars and reward them with discounts, free drinks, or coffee. Unlike the sedimentation of human relations when people are known regulars, card-based footprinting seems to most often foster an effect of interchangeability unless the establishment is a local one that is used frequently in an individual's ant path. People are also resistant to leaving personal traces in locations where they do not have a personal relationship. People's attempt to retain a personal relationship with particular service people or local establishments is a small effort to resist this trend towards technology mediation and depersonalizing in our relationship to urban services.

Information Objects and the Mediation of Urban Settings

In this chapter, we have described ways in which portable information objects and devices mediate people's relationships to urban infrastructures, locations, and services in three global cities. Although there is much variability in the specifics of infrastructures and services in the different cities we have studied, there are many shared practices, activities, and trends. The basic mobile kit of phone, wallet, and keys are a constant in all three cities, as are the items in the second-order mobile kit that often includes a music player and reading material. These are the basic technological building blocks for access, interfacing, and footprinting as people move about the city. One of the most striking findings of our study was the degree to which the contents of the mobile kit and related practices were similar in the three global cities. The major differences we identified were the prevalence of car-based cocoons in Los Angeles and the greater reliance on card-based footprinting in Tokyo. In all three cities however, we saw individual-driven efforts and maximizing process of cocooning and camping and business-driven efforts to mobilize footprinting.

The overall trend is toward increased reliance on information-based, automated, and impersonal systems for managing relationships with urban infrastructures and services. As people carry increasingly rich and immersive media, even crowded locations such as public transportation become spaces of private media consumption. With the advent of digital music, mobile communications, and other forms of portable media, these cocoons are increasingly personalized and customized. A related tendency is in play for technologies that manage our access and interfacing with private and semi-private locations and infrastructures. While keys and ID cards have always been highly individualized access technologies, now transit infrastructures and communications infrastructures are also becoming more customized. Digital cash cards for micro-transactions enable people to keep track of each train or bus ride, and, in contrast to payphones, mobile phones are information-age technologies that enable careful tracking of each call, packet, and text message.

Conclusion

The trend toward automating and systematizing interactions with urban locations is perhaps most pronounced in the proliferation of different reward and point schemes, particularly digital ones attached to large chains and franchises. Although the activities of customers and staff are tracked more than ever with these new schemes, they are also interchangeable. It is not the personal characteristics of an individual that matter as much as their information identity, an identity that can be transferred to another by sharing point cards or member numbers. Just as cocooning and portable digital technologies reduce the frequency of serendipitous encounters with people's personal identities in public space, these automated reward and point schemes reduce the practices of personal management of customer loyalty. In other words, more and more of our articulation of personal and social relations to urban space is being delegated to different technologically embodied infrastructures, accessed with portable technologies of various kinds.

A study of the everyday, mundane activities of interfacing with urban space reveals shifts in urban experience that are low key but pervasive and have subtle effects in a wide range of social, cultural, and technical domains. Urbanites travel through the city carrying a broadening array of information devices and tools for manifesting their identity in public space. Our focus has been on these information devices, so in some ways our claims towards the informatting of urban experience may be overstated. At the same time, however, our research in a range of urban locations reveals a resilient set of practices and trends that are gradually entering the information age. The social outcomes of people engaging in private, mobile phone talk in public spaces is just one element in a much larger array of technosocial practices that mold public space to accommodate and trace personal identity and experience. Embedded infrastructures of location-based services are by nature slow to change, in contrast to the ease with which people have adopted personal technologies like the mobile phone or personal computer. As more and more functions of cocooning, interfacing, and footprinting become embedded in information devices that are converging with mobile phones and handheld computers, we are seeing an evolution of urban infrastructures and services with informational devices and infrastructures. In this chapter, we have tried to identify the underlying social practices that drive interfacing with urban locations, as well as the technological shifts that are reshaping these practices in subtle ways.

Acknowledgments

This study was a conducted as a collaborative fieldwork project between Intel Research's People and Practices group and Keio University's Docomo House Design Cottage and was supported by Intel Research. In addition to the authors of this chapter, fieldwork for this project was conducted by Michele Chang, Rachel Cody, Heidi Cooley, Katrina Jungnickel, and Scott Mainwaring.

Bibliography

Cooper, Lee, Graham Johnson, and Chris Baber. "A Run on Sterling–Personal Finance on the Move." Paper delivered at the Third International Symposium on Wearable Computers (ISWC). 18-19 October 1999, San Francisco, California.

Dourish, Paul. *Where the Action Is: The Foundations of Embodied Interaction.* Cambridge, MA: MIT Press, 2001.

Dourish, Paul, and Genevieve Bell. "The Infrastructure of Experience and the Experience of Infrastructure: Meaning and Structure in Everyday Encounters With Space." *Environment and Planning B: Planning and Design,* 34 (March 2007): 414-430.

Jackson, Steven J., Paul N. Edwards, Geoffrey C. Bowker, and Cory P. Knobel. "Understanding Infrastructure: History, Heuristics, and Cyberinfrastructure Policy." *First Monday* 12 (June 2007), http://firstmonday.org/issues/issue12_6/jackson/index.html.

Goffman, Erving. *Behavior in Public Places: Notes on the Social Organization of Gatherings.* New York, NY: Free Press, 1963.

Grinter, Rebecca E. and Margery A. Eldridge. "y do tngrs luv 2 txt msg?" In the *Proceedings of the Seventh European Conference on Computer-Supported Cooperative Work,* edited by Wolfgang Prinz, Matthias Jarke, Yvonne Rogers, Kjeld Schmidt, and Volker Wulf, 219-238. Bonn, Germany: Kluwer Academic Publishers, 2001.

Habuchi, Ichiyo. "Accelerating Reflexivity." In *Personal, Portable, Pedestrian: Mobile Phones in Japanese* Life, edited by Mizuko Ito, Daisuke Okabe, and Misa Matsuda, 165-182. Cambridge, MA: MIT Press, 2005.

Ito, Mizuko, and Daisuke Okabe. "Technosocial Situations: Emergent Structurings of Mobile Email Use." In *Personal, Portable, Pedestrian: Mobile Phones in Japanese Life,* edited by Mizuko Ito, Daisuke Okabe, and Misa Matsuda, 257-273. Cambridge, MA: MIT Press, 2005.

Ito, Mizuko, Daisuke Okabe, and Misa Matsuda, Eds. *Personal, Portable, Pedestrian: Mobile Phones in Japanese Life.* Cambridge, MA: MIT Press, 2005.

Kindberg, Tim, Mirjana Spasojevic, Rowanne Fleck, and Abigail Sellen. "How and Why People Use Camera Phones." HP Laboratories Technical Report, *HPL-2004-216.* Sussex, UK: University of Sussex, November 2004, http://www.hpl.hp.com/techreports/2004/HPL-2004-216.html

Koskinen, Ilpo. "Pervasive Image Capture and Sharing: Methodological Remarks." Paper delivered at the Pervasive Image Capture and Sharing Workshop, Ubiquitous Computing Conference. 11-14 September 2005, Tokyo, Japan.

Licoppe, Christian, and Yoriko Inada. "Emergent Ues of a Multiplayer Location-aware Game: The Interactional Consequences of Mediated Encounters." *Mobilities*, 1 (March 2006): 39-61.

Ling, Richard S. "The Social Juxtaposition of Mobile Telephone Conversations and Public Spaces." Paper delivered at the Conference on the Social Consequence of Mobile Telephones. July 2002, Chunchon, Korea.

Ling, Richard S. *The Mobile Connection: The Cell Phone's Impact on Society*. San Francisco, CA: Elsevier, 2004.

Ling, Richard S., and Tom Julsrud. "Grounded Genres in Multimedia Messaging." In *A Sense of Place: the Global and the Local in Mobile Communication*, edited by Kristóf Nyíri, 329-338. Vienna, Austria: Passagen Verlag, 2005.

Mainwaring, Scott D., Ken Anderson, and Michele F. Chang. "What's in Your Walllet? Implications for Global E-Wallet Design." Paper delivered at the Conference on Human Factors in Computing Systems (CHI). 6 April 2005, Portland, OR.

McGonigal, Jane. "The Puppet Master Problem: Design for Real-World, Mission-Based Gaming." In *Second Person: Role-Paying and Story in Games and Play,* edited by Pat Harrigan and Noah Wardrip-Fruin. Cambridge, MA: MIT Press, 2006.

Murtagh, Ged M. "Seeing the 'Rules': Preliminary Observations of Action, Interaction and Mobile Phone Use." In *Wireless World: Social and International Aspects of the Mobile Age*, edited by Barry Brown, Nicola Green, and Richard Harper, 81-91. London, UK: Springer-Verlag, 2002.

Okabe, Daisuke. 2004. "Emergent Social Practices, Situations and Relations through Everyday Camera Phone Use. Paper delivered at the 2004 International Conference on Mobile Communication. 18-19 October 2004, Seoul, Korea.

Okabe, Daisuke and Mizuko Ito. "Keitai and Public Transportation." In *Personal, Portable, Pedestrian: Mobile Phones in Japanese Life*, edited by Mizuko Ito, Daisuke Okabe, and Misa Matsuda, 205-218. Cambridge, MA: MIT Press, 2005.

Okabe, Daisuke and Mizuko Ito. "Everyday Contexts of Camera Phone Use: Steps Toward Technosocial Ethnographic Frameworks." In *Mobile Communication in Everyday Life: Ethnographic Views, Observations and Reflections*, edited by Joachim R. Höflich and Maren Hartmann, 79-102. Berlin, Germany: Franks and Timme, 2006.

Plant, Sadie. *On the Mobile: The Effects of Mobile Telephones on Social and Individual Life*. Motorola.

Rivière, Carole. "Mobile Camera Phones: A New Form of 'Being Together' in Daily Interpersonal Communication." In *Mobile Communications: Renegotiation of the Social Sphere,* edited by Richard S. Ling and Per E. Pederson, 167-185. London, UK: Springer-Verlag, 2005.

Star, Susan Leigh. "The Ethnography of Infrastructure." *The American Behavioral Scientist, 43* (Nov-Dec 1999): 377-391.

Van House, Nancy A., M.arc Davis, Yuri Takhteyev, Morgan Ames, and Megan Finn. "The Social Uses of Personal Photography: Methods for Projecting Future Imaging Applications." September 2004: http://www.sims.berkeley.edu/~vanhouse/pubs.htm [accessed December 3, 2005].

Van House, Nancy A., Marc Davis, Morgan Ames, Megan Finn, and Vijay Viswanathan. "The Uses of Personal Networked Digital Imaging: An Empirical Study of Cameraphone Photos and Sharing." Paper delivered at the Conference on Human Factors in Computing Systems (CHI). 6 April 2005, Portland, OR.

Weilenmann, Alexandra. "'I Can't Talk Now, I'm in a Fitting Room': Formulating Availability and Location in Mobile Phone Conversations." *Environment and Planning A*, 35.9 (2003): 1589-1605.

Wellman, Barry. *Networks in the Global Village: Life in Contemporary Communities*. Boulder, CO: Westview Press, 1999.

Yoshii, H., M. Matsuda, C. Habuchi, S. Dobashi, K. Iwata, and N. Kin. *Keitai Denwa Riyou no Shinka to sono Eikyou*. Tokyo, Japan: Mobile Communications Kenkyuukai, 2002.

4

New Reasons for Mobile Communication: Intensification of Time-Space Geography in the Mobile Era

Ilkka Arminen
University of Tampere

At the millennium, when I became involved with research on the social dimensions and consequences of mobile technologies, I was struck by a paradox. An air of enthusiasm surrounded the mobile world. Both ordinary people and industries were thrilled by the new mobile possibilities. The relatively reliable statistics of mobile operators, however, showed that people were using mobile phones just five minutes a day on average in Finland (one of the mobile technology forerunners at that point) mainly talking to each other, sending some text messages, and not really much more (Nurmela, 2001). As the enthusiasm seemed sincere, I had to ask what was so revolutionary about these five minutes a day. I have been asking this question ever since.

Mobile technologies and the cultural patterns of their usage have evolved at a tremendous speed, but the elementary characteristics of usage of mobile communication technologies have remained stable. Communication, time-saving, and time-killing have turned out to be the elementary functions of mobile and smart phones. Large segments of consumers seem eager to purchase the newest and trendiest mobile handset with plenty of multimedia capacity, but the usage of multimedia or broadband mobile services has remained low, a negligible fraction of mobile operators' revenues (Foggin, 2005).[1]

Despite partially failed hopes on mobile broadband, mobile communication has become ubiquitous. It alters existing communication patterns, enables new kinds of contact between people, and yet remains embedded in the prevailing social relations and practices. Many of the new mobile communication practices entail small, subtle changes in the patterns of communication.[2] On the whole, relatively small alterations in communication practices amount to broader changes in ways of life and in the organizing principles of society (McNeill and McNeill, 2003).

As Ling (2004) and others have suggested, perhaps the greatest consequence of mobile communication technologies is their impact on the experience of space and time and the coordination of social affairs (Castells, et al., 2007; Katz, 2005; Arminen, 2005b). In this chapter, I will locate the transformation of time-space experience on the level of actual mobile phone usage. I will discuss new interrelated communicative practices relevant to time-space experience with the help of actual mobile phone calls and SMS messages. I address three new communicative practices that are central aspects of mobile phone usage: mobile real-time coordination of social action, extended seamless accountability of mobile actors, and distant, mobile co-presence. Together these entail an intensified time-space geography that engenders optimism, fear, and criticism (Rheingold, 2002; Katz, 2005; Hassan, 2003).[3]

Collecting Data from Users

To analyze the actual mobile telephone usage, a set of Finnish mobile phone conversations was recorded in summer 2002, including seventy-four complete calls and eight partial recordings. The mobile phone used had an inbuilt recording device. The mobile calls of two women and two men (aged twenty-three to thirty-eight) were taped within about a week with the permission of all communicating parties. The participants could select the calls to be submitted to research, and the anonymity of the participants was guaranteed. The data consist of about forty dyads when the communications partners are taken into account.

With few deletions, the set covers almost all calls from the subjects, consisting of about four hours of speaking time. It covers mobile-to-mobile and landline-to-mobile or mobile-to-landline conversations. Most of the calls were between friends and relatives, but some were work-related. The calls were transcribed and analyzed in detail by using conversation analytical (CA) methods (see the Appendix to this chapter for the transcription conventions). Minna Leinonen transcribed the mobile data.

This amount of data is sufficient for the analysis of elementary structures of social action that is accomplished at the level of social interaction (Sacks, 1992). Mobile communication is as orderly as any other type of social action (Atkinson and Heritage, 1984) and this analytical approach is able to cover the fundamental forms of social action among those who were included in this study. It is worth noting that the sample is limited in terms of age range. There were only few teenagers and elderly people among the forty dyads. For the distinctive communication patterns of teenagers, the extended literature should be consulted (Laursen, 2005; Weilenmann and Larsson, 2002). Further, the data were collected in Finland. However, the elementary forms of social action are not strongly culturally bound. People make meeting arrangements, warn each other about (traffic) hazards, and participate in group celebrations. On that level, nothing is tied to Finland. Similar communicative exchanges take place world around (for further methodological discussion, see Arminen, 2005b; 2006).

For historical comparisons, 107 Finnish landline-to-landline telephone calls from the 1980s and 90s were obtained.[4] The landline call data set enables empirical comparisons to see the actual differences between landline and mobile calls (see Arminen and Leinonen, 2006). In addition, a set of 206 SMS messages was collected in 2005, of more than forty pairs. This includes plenty of sequences of messages (message-reply chains) and allows for the explication of the communicative structure of text messaging.

CA methodology offers a strict analysis of sequential aspects of social actions in real time and real settings (Hutchby and Wooffitt, 1998; Arminen, 2005a). It identifies, specifies, and compares interactional patterns that constitute or contribute to establishing the social world as perceived. The aim is to catch the characteristic features of mundane activities that mold them into what they are. Whatever humans do can be examined to discover and describe the way their actions are carried out. This methodology can be applied to open up the real-time coordination of social action mediated by mobile technologies. The aim is to explore the new forms of sociability and the distinctive features of new social practices. The idea is not just to show that mobile communication is a form of interaction, but to find out what more there is, to inform us about the emergence of new social realities. The final goal is to elaborate the ways in which new technologies are consequential for the social practices they afford. The findings inform us about possibilities, conditions, and limits for new applications (Dourish, 2001; Dourish and Button, 1998).

Social Consequences of Mobile Telephony

A lot has been written about the social consequences of mobile telephony in recent years (e.g., Ling, 2004; Castells, et al., 2007; Geser,

2005). Castells and his colleagues assert that mobile telephony's contribution to the growth of autonomy and the unity of peer groups are among the strongest trends (Castells, et al., 2007: 247-249). They point out that both individual and collective autonomy increase vis-à-vis space, time, and normative constraints. At the same time, the extended communication capability strengthens the peer groups. At this point a critical reader may wonder, "strengthens *individual* and *collective* autonomy, and *peer groups*. Is this possible? Is this not a contradiction?" Geser (2005) maintains that cell phones allow us to escape into self-controlled social relationships with family and friends, thus tending to revive a pre-modern worldview and hinder individual development of character (24-26). At the outset, Geser's portrait is at odds with Ling's emphasis (2004) on the role of mobile telephony in the swift coordination of social action. Mobile telephony enables more flexible social coordination of work and everyday activity. There is no reason to believe that the improved coordination of social action as such would undermine modernity. In contrast, mobile telephony may increase productivity and accelerate modernization (Green, 2002a).

Is it possible to make sense of these contradictory accounts of the consequences? First, mobile communication technology involves the Lazarus effect, breathing life into "wasted," "dead" moments (Perry, et al., 2001). It allows the time "in-between," "on the road," to become useful. This rationalization of time usage produces paradoxes. As the "empty" time is made available, the mobile-networked actor has "more" time (to be used). The mobile actor may thus afford both more individual freedom and more ties to social contacts. Further, the rationalization of time usage does not determine the way in which the "extra" time will be used, since it depends on the type(s) of mobile network(s) the actor is part of. There is no deterministic relationship between technology and social configuration.

Through her extended ethnographic fieldwork in rural West Bengal, Tenhunen (2006) found that the impact of mobile phones showed a peculiar duality in that it both traversed and stabilized village life. Mobile phones enabled a direct communicative access to wider society; they allowed access to enhanced market information on agricultural goods, etc.; they enabled maintenance of contact with family and kinship networks, enhancing traditional values; and they also undermined the authority of traditional village chiefs by providing access to information that used to be mediated by chiefs. The appropriation of mobile ICT in rural communities did not have any single, overarching consequence, but rather a plethora of consequences. It seemed to be too early to say whether mobile ICT would strengthen traditionalism, modernization, or both. The mobile ICT adapts to a societal configuration that mediates socio-technical development that, in turn, affects culture, politics, and society. The ties between science, technology, and society are pervasive and reciprocal (see McNeill and McNeill, 2003).

The rationalization of time usage and the evolving new communication patterns are the directly observable aspects of mobile communication. In all, the adoption of mobile communication is a small step in the evolution of the communicative matrix of humankind that heads toward a growing complexity (McNeill and McNeill 2003). It is a part of the development that binds the network of people closer together. This is felt as an intensification of time-space geography. We become a part of a growing, diversifying, and accelerating mobile communication network. This entirety is characterized by ever-expanding complexity (Hulme and Truch, 2005). In the rest of this chapter, I will detail three new mobile social practices that contribute to the increasing complexity and the intensification of time-space geography.

Real-Time Coordination of Social Action

Although the role of mobile telephones for the coordination of ongoing distant social activities has already been discussed several times (e.g., Ling and Yttri, 2002; Ling, 2004; Cooper, et al., 2002), it is still worth attention as the dominant, most typical task of mobile communication. At least half and often more of the mobile calls and text messages seem to be related to coordination of social action (Hulme and Truch, 2005; Arminen, 2005c). Many of the mobile real-time coordination practices are unique to wireless ICT. Further, the coordination of activities is not external to everyday life, but an essential part of it. Hence, mobile communication is embedded in and intertwines with the constitution of everyday life and the ways of life. In all, the new coordination practices contribute to the shifting time-space experience.

The content of calls and text messages shows that communication (such as requests, reminders, and announcements) tends to be related to other ongoing activities or events. Mobile communication supports other forms of social exchange and does not simply replace them. Making arrangements to meet seems to be the most common mobile practice.[5] Commuting, travel and other transition moments are typical and also a unique environment for mobile communication. Driving a car provides a specific, regular context for mobile communication. Sometimes communication is directly related to the ongoing task itself, such as driving. In Extract 1, the driver warns the car behind about a deer by the road. Communication is inseparable from the ongoing activity. Talk is produced economically to deliver rapid, real-time instructions for the activity (see Appendix for the transcription conventions):

Extract 1: 2002-07-06_23-29-48 (P= Pekka, caller; A= Ari, answerer)

1.   A: no morjes pekka,
        oh hello: pekka,

2.   P: kahteltiin tossa vasemmalla puolen tietä
        we saw there at left side of the road

3.   P: peuraa äsken että,
        deer a moment ago so that,

4.   A: ah[a,
        I [see,

5.   P: [että varo.
          [that watch out.

In Extract 1, a warning call from the car ahead is made to the car behind; mobile, real-time communication like this is unique to wireless ICT. Notably, the details of communication are reflexively linked to the type of action; among other things, the caller goes straight to the point by skipping the return of greeting. This departure from the normal canons of communication establishes the sense of urgency (Arminen and Leinonen, 2006). Note also the way in which the description is built in lines 2-3. The warning is achieved by first stating where to look before stating what to look for. The embodied, situated sense of social action is created through its interactional realization.

Mobile communication has established a new communication culture that has a distinct language and etiquette (Castells, et al., 2007). Both written and oral languages have new forms adapted to the situations of use. Mobile conversations have a number of distinct features, just like text messages (Laursen, 2005). In the second extract, Pekka makes a call about their meeting arrangements:

Extract 2: 2002-07-03_20-01-54.wav (P= Pekka, caller; J= Jouko, answerer)

1.   J: MORO,
        HI,

2. → P: MOI mis   meet,
        HI   where are you,

3. $(0.7)^6$

4. → J: mä oon täällä Ernestossa jo,
          I am here at Ernesto's already,

Here the caller both returns the greeting and initiates the topic through a singular prosodic unit: "HI where are you?" The greeting is not produced as an independent item, but is embedded into a part of the topic initiation. Here, as in the previous example, the reason for the call is uttered as early as the caller's first turn, thus radically reducing the opening from conventional landline call openings.[7] The reduction of rituals of landline calls is a part of the intensified time-space of mobile communication. Secondly, the location of parties becomes routinely relevant as the reason for the call is established through the location inquiry in an immediate presence. Here the recipient of the question orients to this immediacy through his temporal marker "jo" (already) at line 4. The mobile communication connects the parties' common action to their immediate presence. Parties to mobile communication do not necessarily orient to an external, objective time, but share their own immediate space-time. The communication is embedded in the time frame of common activity, establishing a shared space-time and overcoming the physical distance between them.

Mobile communication gets its specific sense through its reflexive linkage to the surrounding social world since it is an inseparable part of the real-time ongoing activities in which the parties are engaged. Wireless ICT not only revives "dead" moments, but also provides communicative access anytime, anywhere. This ubiquitous communication has both a practical side—smoothing the arrangements—as well as a socio-emotional, symbolic value. When people communicate about their whereabouts and availability for mutual actions, they do not just state precursors for practical arrangements, but also establish and maintain their social relationships. The availability of and hindrances to joint activities get caught up in symbolic qualities. The limits to joint action do not derive from material circumstances alone, but tend to index the limits of the social relationship. Mobile communication makes all mundane activities shareable, allowing them to be linked to the personalities and relationships involved. The call made or received on the beach has the potential for the connotations of "beach" to become a part of the message. A call made at a break in a business meeting is prone to provide cues identifying the caller in a particular way. Mobile communication does not "free" us from places, spaces, and practices, but makes them communicationally available to other mobile-networked parties; this leads to a new, enriched symbolic texture of everyday life.

Extended, Seamless Accountability of Social Action

Discussion of the consequences of mobile communication has emphasized the new flexibility of social arrangements and softening of schedules. The rationalization of time usage that ubiquitous communication affords also enables real-time monitoring of communicating parties. In fact, real-time monitoring is a logical aspect of the flexible, mobile coordination of social affairs. Mobile communication may allow us to inform others if we are late or, as a matter of fact, when we suppose we will not be on time. The mobile technologies make us also traceable and accountable. A person who is not there at the appointed time is likely to be reminded, unless she or he has already notified the other parties of being late. Mobile communication does not necessarily soften and relax the schedules (although it may), but it does enable continuing monitoring and accountability in mobile relations (Green, 2002b).

In Extract 3, both parties orient to the other party "missing" their appointment and both seem to hold the other party accountable. Again, the details of this interaction are rich in building up the situated sense of the action.

Extract 3: 2000-01-01_06-04-32.wav (C= Jarmo, caller; R= Sari, answerer)

1.   R: joo?
            yes?

2.   (0.2)[8]

3.   C: terve,
            hello,

4.   (.)

5. → C: no,
            huh,[9]

6.   (0.8)

7. → R: missä sä oot
            where are you,)

8.   (.)

9.   C: täälä <ruokalassa, > h
            here <in the cafeteria,> h

10. (0.2)

11. R: nii minäki,
         so am I:,

12. (0.2)

13. C: aha (h [yvä,)
         o:h (g [ood,)

14. R: [(-)

15. (0.4)

16. R: no nii mä nään sut. (h)e
         oh yeah I see you. (h)e

The molding of the situated sense of the action starts immediately. Instead of the canonical greeting, the call is opened with a blunt "*joo?*" (yes?). That allocates the turn to the caller, making him accountable for the initiation of the interaction. At the next turn, the caller seems to try to normalize the interaction by his greeting, but after no response he produces the response token "no" (huh) inviting the other to move on to the reason of the call. Through her inquiry about the whereabouts of the caller, the answerer reveals her understanding that the other party is not at the agreed place. At line 9, the caller states that he is where he is supposed to be. The trouble is then resolved in the next turn. Here both parties orient to the accountability of the other; both seem to have held the other responsible for not showing up where they were supposed to. The cautiousness in opening the topic builds up a sense of delicacy. The reason for call is delayed beyond its canonical place (c.f. (1) and (2)). Both parties seem to have avoided accusing the other, although they both seem to have assumed the other being late. The "blindness" of both parties is revealed in a comic fashion, as it turned out that both had been at the right place but not seen each other.

Mobile communication anytime, anywhere, increases social accountability. The revival of "dead" moments not only gives us extra time, but also makes us open to real-time monitoring and control. Mobile communication etiquette seems to involve the norms of "being always available" and "reciprocating messages/calls you get" (Laursen, 2005). The normative pressure for availability also allows an increase in accountability, a continuing monitoring of communicative parties. Through mobile ICT, parties to social action may extend the accountability to the very accomplishment of the action (i.e., the accountability permeates the ongoing coordination of action and does not simply follow it). In this way, the revival of empty time is not without its other side.

The emergence of extended, seamless accountability of social action sharpens the depiction of mobile society. It does not appear that mobile communication relieves us from the ever-growing time pressures of modern societies (Hassan, 2003; Ylijoki and Mäntylä, 2003). The flexible, mobile coordination may smooth and soften some social affairs, but the shared mobile time-scapes are prone to accelerated, non-stop pressures and increased possibilities for control. The mobile network time may be more unpredictable, volatile, and chaotic, but not necessarily softer.

Distant Mobile Co-Presence

James Katz (2005) has pointed out that mobile communication does not discriminate between religious callings. Jewish worshippers at the Wailing Wall are seen to hold mobile phones aloft to allow their distant co-religionist have their prayers heard and made audible to others. Katz tells us that comparable scenes have taken place among Hindus, Islamists, and Catholics. The ubiquity of mobile phones does not differentiate between religions or secular and sacred contexts, enabling intimate connection to any moment of social life. Mobile communication through various media—text, talk, images—may become frequent and multiplex "up to the point where copresent interactions and mediated distant exchanges seem woven into a single, seamless web" (Licoppe, 2004: 135).

Mobile telephony may revive dead, empty moments, but it may also accentuate and build up significant occasions. Much of the mobile communication may be distanced from the immediate context, but it also has the potential of being immersed in the situation to allow the heat of the moment to be communicated (Raudaskoski, forthcoming). Both the frequency of communication and the intimate connection to ongoing activities may increase the emotional intensity of social relationship. The frequent contact in and through dead moments may express intimacy and allow for knowledge about the other anywhere, at any time, rather than just in purposefully selected, auspicious moments of public show. On the other hand, the intimate communication allows callers to share affects and emotions, allowing their non-present partners access to the experience on the spot.

In speech Extract 4, the details of the interaction are again salient in molding the real-time sense of the activity taking place. The caller appears to have made arrangements (number blocking) before the call to achieve a suitable mode for the interaction. Through his joke-identification, he designs his call from the outset in a festive mood. In this way, the caller displays the immanent relevance of the context for the call. Both the caller and the called have stayed overnight in some camping areas around the big annual Hot Rod show.[10] The call is made in the morning, at 10:30 a.m. on the second day of the event.

Extract 4: 2002-07-07_10-30-41.wav (R= Pekka, answerer; C= Rauno, caller)

1.   R: Pekka?,

2.   (0.8)

3. → C: hannes johannes vihannes jorolainen virolainen,
         ((a word play based on the name of a famous Finnish
         politician, Johannes Virolainen—impossible to translate))
4.   (.)

5. → C: päi:vää,
         goo:d afternoon,

6. → R: päi:vä[ä.
         goo:d afterno[on.

7. → C: [(h)(h)e (h)e (h)e (h)e (h)e

8. → C: anteeks että herätän   vahing[oss.
         sorry that I'm waking you up by [accident.

9. → R: [se pitkähiuksinen
                                      [the longhaired

10. →   kaveri j [oka
         guy   w [ho

11. → C: [(h)e (h)e (h)e

12. C: noh mitäs
         so what's

This mobile call is interesting both in its details and in its reflexive tie to its context. First, a humorous tone is established in a number of ways starting from the mock-identification, and continuing with the prolonged intonation of a slightly misplaced greeting ("good afternoon"), imitated by the recipient (lines 5-6), a mock apology (8), and also a joking identification of the caller (9-10). It appears that at lines 9-10, the recipient of the call identifies the caller for the other co-present people, thereby making him relevant for the group of people sharing the same social event. The utterance identifying the caller is pointedly left unfinished ("The long-haired guy who . . ."). Without access to the answerer's proximate situation, neither the caller nor we can know whether the utterance was completed by others present or if it was left open to be returned after the call.[11] In any case, the mock identification topicalizes the caller and makes him socially and virtually present for the co-present others. The call is adopted as a part of the texture of shared celebration at the festival the parties attend together, albeit not all face-to-face all the time. In this way, the mobile communication augments the limits of face-to-face communication. Further, it allows the caller to share the same social moment and mood, affording a call right on the spot and enabling an elaborate context and recipient design. Already, the beginning of the call hints at the possibilities the mobile media have for parties to establish social presence without physical presence. At a later part of the call—not shown here because of the space restrictions—the parties tell each other dirty stories about last evening, thereby mutually reinforcing the symbolic texture of the event experienced together. Mobile communication enables a new, augmented sociability, creating a new, intimate co-presence at moments of joy and celebration that transgress physical boundaries.

Mobile ICT does not afford distant co-presence simply in the context of joy and emotional intensity, but also in other contexts and institutional environments. Phrases such as mobile office, mobile parenting, and mobile learning show that mobile ICT is providing new forms of distant social practice.[12] These practices are hybrids—Latour's immutable mobiles—that move around but retain their shape. Mobile technologies melt down solid practices, maintaining recognizable shapes in a liquid form. For example, mobile learning refers just to usage of mobile technologies such as mobile and smart phones to enhance learning. Characteristically, it concerns knowledge bound to a location or a situation. Its organizing principles arise from situated tasks; it builds on multimodal activities and practices; and it draws not only on texts, but also diagrams, pictures, and maps. It uses the affordances of mobile media to connect separate contexts, thereby challenging the paradigm of traditional pedagogy (Nyíri, 2002). Likewise, the mobile office and mobile parenting are debatable hybrids. The new social practices meet always resistance. There is a misunderstanding and a fear that old practices should be given up because of the new ones. Perhaps it is best to see these new hybrids as complements to old practices, not their replacements. It is unlikely that distant co-presence can ever substitute for physical presence, but it may allow the formation of practices applicable when there is no face-to-face presence.[13]

The Affordance of Social Action

Mobile communication affords new types of social action (Raudaskoski, forthcoming). Activities, objects, spaces, and places do not have any "natural" meaning; their meaning is achieved in action in interaction. Distant mobile communicative actions create new contexts for action, amounting to new types of activity. This emergent new reality is still largely unexplored.

People routinely use mobile media to communicate where they are, where they are going, and to arrange meetings. This real-time coordination of social action is the most pervasive mobile communicative action. Commuting and travel impose many communicative tasks that mobile communication can perform, such as asking directions, negotiating meeting times and places, and reporting delays. Emergencies and hazardous situations are a particular class of real-time, location-sensitive activity that is also time critical. In all, while flexible mobile coordination complements modern, calculated time-based coordination of action, mobile schedules are not necessarily softer, but may be more hectic and unpredictable.

The coordination of social action interacts with emerging socio-emotional and symbolic values. Communication of whereabouts and availability makes available social rankings and subjective evaluations, demanding that the subject prioritize alternatives. Much of social communication concerns preliminaries. For example, when a person is asked whether she is doing anything special, the inquiry may be a preliminary to the goal of communicative action; it may have been done to get to know whether the answerer would be available for some joint activity (Schegloff, 1980). The answers to preliminaries visibly build up social hierarchies and display the person's preferences. Chains of connotative meanings are established in this manner, and the coordination of social action intertwines with the symbolic organization of everyday life establishing the actor's habits, which signifies a chosen way of life. In the ubiquitous mobile presence, the settings and activities may be symbolically embellished. Seamless communication not only rationalizes time usage, but also intensifies social presence.

Extended accountability is a natural corollary of this ubiquitous communication. The accountability of action extends both to the timing and social dimension of activities. Instead of accountability afterwards, the perpetual contact extends to the very moment that the activity is accomplished. Intimate connection to everyday life also enables social accountability of actions and choices through seamless communication. Depending on the social configuration, this extended accountability may strengthen external, purely goal-rational control as well as social responsibility.

Both accountability and other aspects of mobile communication may turn out to be mixed blessings. Although it is uncertain whether mobile communication might corrupt character, as has been suggested, it is certainly intrusive at times (see Ling, 2004). Mobile communication may intrude on the party called and the proximate people of mobile communicators. There are increasing pressures to set health, safety, and social limits to mobile communication. It remains to be seen how these efforts influence the development of mobile communication.

Large-scale consequences of mobile communication include rationalization of time usage and the improvement of communicative access within social networks—changes which amount to an increase in communicative time and increasing frequency of communication. The improved communications access to networked mobile actors increases the amount of available people in the network at any single moment, and the increase in person-to-person communication boosts the matrix of social contacts. The consequences may be paradoxical. On the one hand, the increasing frequency of communication enables closer ties with the people in the network; on the other hand, it also allows new flexibility, an increased individual autonomy that is at odds with a communal way of life. To sum up, mobile communication is another step toward the growing complexity of social realities. Social networks may become both closer and more fragile in the era of mobile telephony.

Conclusion

Mobile communication is reshaping person-to-person communication: there will be more contacts, shorter exchanges, and new multi-modal, real-time communicative practices. The new affordances of mobility that mobile phones enable are readily available for analysis through the recordings of mobile conversations and messages, as they are indexical to embodied practices. As a whole, the adoption of new ways of communicating shows how people orient themselves to and make use of the new affordances offered by technologies.

The novelties of mobile communication concern the sequential properties of the ways in which communication and action are joined in interaction. The emerging contingencies of communication are inseparable from the embodied action when somebody phones to ask for directions while driving a car, or answers a mobile phone while in the toilet of a train. The changes in the communication are intertwined with changes in the sequential organization of communication, activity contexts, and discursive identities in person-to-person communication. Although communication as such retains many traditional norms, social actions themselves have become mobile. These changes together contribute to what can be called the intensification of time-space geography, which appears to be a relevant component of new communication patterns in the mobile era.

Appendix: Transcription Conventions

In the transcripts, the speakers' names, and possibly some other details, have usually been changed in order to secure the anonymity of the people involved. Transcription symbols and conventions of conversation analysis are used throughout the extracts (see Atkinson and Heritage, 1984: ix-xvi).

[ ]	Simultaneous speech and voices, its start and end
=	Immediately continuous talk, no interval
(0.6)	Pause and its length in seconds
(.)	Micro pause, shorter than 0.2 seconds
.h	In-breath
hh	Out-breath
__	Emphasis
:	Stretch
YES	Loud
.	Falling intonation
,	Continuing intonation
?	Rising inflection, not necessarily a question
?,	Weak rise in intonation
↑	Marked rise in pitch
↓	Marked fall in pitch
da-	Production of word is cut off
word<	Abruptly finished, but not cut off
> <	Pronounced faster than the surrounding speech
< >	Pronounced slower than the surrounding speech
$	Laughter in the voice
@ @	Animated voice

○ ○	Diminishing voice
# #	Shivering voice
hah	Laughter
(word)	Heard indistinctly
(( ))	Researcher's comment
→	Target line; crucial instance for the analyzed speech

Notes

1. In this respect, Japan and Korea, at the forefront of current mobile technology development, do not actually differ critically from the rest of the world. Except "Keitai e-mail," which combines SMS and mobile e-mail, the adoption of mobile broadband and multimedia in Japan does not seem to be crucially more advanced than in Western countries (Ito, et al., 2005). This is not to say that mobile multimedia is entirely unused; pictures are taken, music and videos are downloaded, but multimedia has not (yet) become a part of everyday communication. It has mainly been used for catch and store (Kindberg, et al., 2004).

2. Indeed, some researchers have claimed on good grounds that mobile communication has led only to a superficial transformation in communication (see Arminen, 2005a).

3. Initially, the notion of time-space geography is influenced by Bakhtin's (1981) discussion on points in the geography of a community where time and space intersect and fuse. I observed that for mobile actors time and space are recurrently and systematically interwoven and inseparable (Arminen, 2005b). Places are spoken and texted as minutes from X. Mobile communication builds a time-space geography of its own.

4. I gratefully acknowledge the generosity of the Department of Finnish Language at Helsinki University, which has made a large set of recorded landline telephone calls (most with transcripts) from its data archive available for this research. The set was a random selection of the archive of hundreds of calls from different callers.

5. I avoid exact percentages on purpose. Several studies have presented slightly different numbers. The categories, such as "meeting arrangements," are open to different operationalizations. Further, sub-populations of mobile users vary in their communication type frequencies. Here I discuss the general properties, not the characteristics of a particular population.

6. (0.7) stands for a pause of seven tenths of a second. The notation (.) is used for shorter micro-pauses (see the Appendix for the transcription conventions).

7. For example, in American canonical landline call openings, the reason for call is uttered in the caller's fourth turn, after greetings, identifications, and "how-are-you"s (Schegloff, 1986; Arminen and Leinonen, 2006).

8. It is no coincidence that number of pauses happens in this opening. The delayed production of utterances is a way to convey the sense of "uneasiness" in the production of undesirable actions, or actions that are less preferred than their paradigmatic alternatives. Here "*joo?*" produces an expectation, which is not quite met with "*terve.*"

9. Here the independent "no" works as a "go ahead," and can be translated as "huh" (Sorjonen, 2002).

10. No separate ethnography has been collected for this part of the study, but the series of calls themselves offer plenty of contextual information, and a rich picture of the life of the people involved emerges. In fact, extracts 1 and 4 are from the same

set (on the way to the Hot Rod Show, the next morning, etc.). Mobile calls and messages build a virtual presence of the people communicating to the researcher too. Naturally, "real" ethnography also has many benefits (see Weilenmann and Larsson, 2002).

11. For prospective indexicals that make relevant their subsequent explication, see Goodwin, 1996; Arminen, 2005c.

12. I do not suggest that all proposed "mobile applications" are successful, but rather that we have affinity with mobile social practices, not all of which are yet realized.

13. A reviewer suggested that mobile communication establishes a "co-location" beyond face-to-face situations. Indeed, mobile communication enables parties to be involved in the same practice without being in the same spot. This is the idea of the distant co-presence.

Bibliography

Arminen, Ilkka. "Ethnomethodology and conversation analysis." In vol. 2 of *21st Century Sociology: A Reference Handbook*, edited by. Clifton D. Bryant and Dennis L. Peck. Thousand Oaks, CA: Sage, 2006.

Arminen, Ilkka. *Institutional Interaction: Studies of Talk at Work*. Aldershot, UK: Ashgate, 2005a.

Arminen, Ilkka. "Sequential Order and Sequence Structure: The Case of Incommensurable Studies of Mobile Talk." *Discourse Studies* 7 (December 2005a): 649-662.

Arminen, Ilkka. "Social Functions of Location in Mobile Telephony." *Personal and Ubiquitous Computing* 10.5, 2005:319-323. http://www.personal-complement*ubicomp.com/ (accessed November 10, 2005c).

Arminen, Ilkka and Minna Leinonen. "Mobile Phone Call Openings: Tailoring Answers to Personalized Summons." *Discourse Studies*, 8 (June 2006): 339-368.

Atkinson, J. Maxwell and John Heritage, Eds. *Structures of Social Action: Studies in Conversation Analysis*. Cambridge, UK: Cambridge University Press, 1984.

Bakhtin, Mikhail M. *The Dialogic Imagination: Four Essays*. Translated by Caryl Emerson and Michael Holquist. Austin, TX: University of Texas Press, 1981.

Castells, Manuel, Mireia Fernandez-Ardevol, Jack Linchuan Qiu, and Araba Sey. *Mobile Communication and Society: A Global Perspective*. Cambridge, MA: MIT Press, 2007.

Cooper, Geoff, Nicola Green, Richard Harper, and Ged Murtagh. "Mobile society? Technology, Distance and Presence." In *Virtual Society*, edited by Steve Woolgar, 286-301. Oxford, UK: Oxford University Press, 2002.

Dourish, Paul. *Where the Action Is: The Foundations of Embodied Interaction*. Cambridge, MA: MIT Press, 2001.

Dourish, Paul and Graham Button. "On "Technomethodology": Foundational Relationships between Ethnomethodology and System Design." *Human-Computer Interaction*, 13 (1998): 395-432.

Foggin, Nick. "Mythology and Mobile Data." In *Thumb Culture: The Meaning of Mobile Phones for Society,* edited by Peter Glotz, Stefan Bertschi, and Chris Locke, 251-258. New Brunswick, NJ: Transaction Publishers, 2005.

Geser, Hans. "Is the Cell Phone Undermining the Social Order? Understanding Mobile Technology from a Sociological Perspective." In *Thumb Culture: The Meaning of Mobile Phones for Society*, edited by Peter Glotz, Stefan Bertschi, and Chris Locke, 23-36. New Brunswick, NJ: Transaction Publishers, 2005.

Goodwin, Charles. "Transparent Vision." In *Interaction and Grammar*, edited by Elinor Ochs, Emanuel A. Schegloff, and Sandra A. Thompson, 370-404. Cambridge, UK: Cambridge University Press, 1996.

Green, Nicola. "On the Move: Technology, Mobility, and the Mediation of Social Time and Space." *The Information Society,* 18.4 (2002): 281-292.

Green, Nicola. "Who's Watching Whom? Monitoring, Regulation and Accountability in Mobile Relations." In *Wireless World: Social, Cultural and Interactive Aspects of the Mobile Age*, edited by Barry Brown, Nicola Green, and Richard Harper. London, UK: Springer-Verlag, 2002.

Hassan, Robert. "Network Time and the New Knowledge Epoch." *Time & Society,* 12 (September 2003): 225-241.

Hulme, Michael and Anna Truch. "The Role of Interspace in Sustaining Identity." In *Thumb Culture: The Meaning of Mobile Phones for Society*, edited by Peter Glotz, Stefan Bertschi, and Chris Locke, 137-148. New Brunswick, NJ: Transaction Publishers, 2005.

Hutchby, Ian and Robin Wooffitt. *Conversation Analysis: Principles, Practices and Applications*. Oxford, UK: Polity Press, 1998.

Ito, Mizuko, Daisuke Okabe, and Misa Matsuda, Eds. *Personal, Portable, Pedestrian: Mobile Phones in Japanese Life*. Cambridge, MA: MIT Press, 2005.

Katz, James E. "Mobile Communication and the Transformation of Daily Life: The Next Phase of Research on Mobiles." In *Thumb Culture: The Meaning of Mobile Phones for Society*, edited by Peter Glotz, Stefan Bertschi, and Chris Locke, 171-184. New Brunswick, NJ: Transaction Publishers, 2005.

Kindberg, Tim, Mirjana Spasojevic, Rowanne Fleck, and Abigail Sellen. "How and Why People Use Camera Phones." Bristol, UK: HP Laboratories, November 26, 2004. http://www.hpl.hp.com/techreports/2004/HPL-2004-216.pdf

Laursen, Ditte. "Please Reply! The Replying Norm in Adolescent SMS Communication." In *The Inside Text: Social, Cultural and Design Perspectives on SMS*, edited by Richard Harper, Leysia Palen, and Alex Taylor, 53-74. Dordrecht, Netherlands: Springer, 2005.

Licoppe, Christian. "'Connected' Presence: The Emergence of a New Repertoire for Managing Social Relationships in a Changing Communication Technoscape." *Environment and Planning D: Society and Space,* 22.1 (2004): 135-156.

Ling, Richard S. *The Mobile Connection: The Cell Phone's Impact on Society*. San Francisco, CA: Morgan Kaufmann, 2004.

Ling, Richard S. and Birgitte Yttri. "Hyper-Coordination via Mobile Phones in Norway." In *Perpetual Contact: Mobile Communication, Private Talk,*

Public Performance, edited by James E. Katz and Mark Aakhus, 139-169. Cambridge, UK: Cambridge University Press, 2002.

McNeill, John R. and William H. McNeill. *The Human Web: A Bird's-Eye View of World History.* New York, NY: W.W. Norton & Company, Inc., 2003.

Nyíri, Kristóf. "Towards a Philosophy of M-Learning." Paper delivered at the IEEE International Workshop. 29-30 August 2002, Växjö, Sweden.

Perry, Mark, Kenton O'Hara, Abigail Sellen, Barry Brown, and Richard Harper. "Dealing with Mobility: Understanding Access Anytime, Anywhere." *ACM Transactions on Computer-Human Interaction,* 8 (December 2001), 323-347.

Raudaskoski, Sanna. "Affordances of Mobile Phones." Ph.D. dissertation, University of Tampere, forthcoming.

Rheingold, Howard. *Smart Mobs: The Next Social Revolution.* Cambridge, MA: Perseus Publishing Group, 2002.

Sacks, Howard. *Lectures on Conversation.* Oxford, UK: Blackwell Publishing, 1995.

Schegloff, Emanuel A. "The Routine as Achievement." *Human Studies* 9 (June 1986): 111-151.

Schegloff, Emanuel A. "Preliminaries to Preliminaries: 'Can I ask you a question?'" *Sociological Inquiry,* 50 (July 1980): 104-52.

Sorjonen, Marja-Leena. "Recipient Activities: The Particle *No* as a Go-Ahead Response in Finnish Conversations." In *The Language of Turn and Sequence,* edited by Celia E. Ford, Barbara A. Fox and Sandra A. Thompson, 165-95. New York, NY: Oxford University Press, 2002.

Tenhunen, Sirpa. "Mobile Technology in the Village: ICTs, Culture, and Social Change in India." Paper delivered at the ISA World Conference. 22-29 July, 2006. Durban, South Africa.

Weilenmann, Alexandra and Catrine Larsson. "Local Use and Sharing of Mobile Phones." In *Wireless World: Social and Interactional Aspects of the Mobile Age,* edited by Barry Brown, Nicola Green, and Richard Harper, 92-107. London: Springer Verlag, 2002.

Ylijoki, Oili-Helena and Hans Mäntylä. "Conflicting Time Perspectives in Academic Work." *Time & Society,* 12 (March 2003): 55-78.

5

Nonverbal Cues in Mobile Phone Text Messages: The Effects of Chronemics and Proxemics

Nicola Döring
Ilmenau University of Technology

Sandra Pöschl
Ilmenau University of Technology

Interpersonal communication between mobile phone users seems at the point of departure to have no temporal or spatial boundaries. Indeed, the telecommunication industry enthusiastically dubs it *anytime, anywhere communication*. However, mobile phones undeniably have increased temporal and spatial flexibility in social interactions. Time and space have not become obsolete. On the contrary, more degrees of freedom in the relational management of time and space demand for more reflection, negotiation, and rule setting, both in the private and public sphere. Actually using a mobile phone "anytime, anywhere" is widely regarded as *poor cell phone etiquette* as it is disruptive for bystanders (Haddon, 1998: 7; Haddon, 2000: 5; Ling, 2002; Murtagh, 2002).

Another reason to examine time and space vis-à-vis mobile phone communication is the communicative *common ground* (Clark and Brennan, 1991) of the participants. Often, upon answering the phone, mobile interlocutors let each other know where they are and shape their conversation accordingly (e.g., cut it short if the callee is momentarily stranded in a traffic jam and cannot allocate his or her full attention to the mobile phone call; avoid intimate topics if the callee is in the company of other people, etc.).

From a communication psychology perspective the interpersonal management of time (*chronemics*; DeVito, 1988: 201) and the interpersonal management of space (*proxemics*; DeVito, 1988: 109) also generate meaningful *nonverbal cues* in formal and informal relationships (Burgoon, et al., 1995). To let someone wait or to approach someone closely can be powerful ways to affirm certain qualitative aspects of the mutual relationship (for instance, in terms of dominance or intimacy).

SMS is a textual and mobile form of computer-mediated communication (CMC). However, text-based computer-mediated communication is not seen as including non-verbal cues. This said, email messages and mobile phone text messages (SMS messages), for instance, include automatic time stamps displaying the point in time when the message was sent out. The sending time of a digital message can be interpreted as a non-verbal cue in the chronemics (interpersonal management of time) code system.

In an experimental study of the chronemics of email messages, Walther and Tidwell (1995), demonstrated that people perceive the same message content quite differently in terms of dimensions describing intimacy/liking and dominance/submissiveness depending on the time stamp (e.g., a private message is perceived as more intimate if sent out at night as opposed to daytime). Following up on the chronemics paradigm of Walther and Tidwell (1995), this chapter presents the design and results of an experimental study on SMS chronemics. German subjects perceived the same SMS message sent from a supervisor to his subordinate as more intimate and less dominant when sent out during the night as opposed to in the daytime, when the message was perceived as less intimate but more dominant. A further experiment also was conducted with reference to a proxemics (interpersonal management of space) code system. The automatic localization of mobile phone users is already possible via cellular networks or satellite positioning systems: automatic time stamps but also location stamps can be added to the out-going messages. We argue that people perceive SMS content differently according to the physical distance or proximity of the SMS sender. Different send locations did not change the perception of the message content, however. The chapter describes the experimental paradigms and new results, and also summarizes the current state of research on CMC chronemics and proxemics.

Theoretical Approach

SMS (short message service) communication as one form of computer-mediated communication (CMC) is first and foremost text-based or verbal communication. Therefore, many CMC theories are potentially applicable to SMS communication.

Reduced Social Cues Theory

The reduced social cues theory, also dubbed the cues-filtered-out theory (see Kiesler, et al., 1984; Culnan and Markus, 1987) argues that textual CMC lacks nonverbal social cues (e.g., clothing, facial expressions, posture, gestures) and para-verbal social cues (e.g., voice pitch, talking speed). The interlocutors do not share a common environment and cannot see, hear, smell, or touch each other. There is no gazing, smiling, blushing, stuttering, frowning, twinkling, back patting, hand-holding, kissing, shrugging, or any other kind of nonverbal communication. According to the reduced social cues theory, CMC is therefore emotionally and socially impoverished.

Social Information Processing Theory

The social information processing theory abandons the filtered cues approach and states that CMC does indeed include social cues (Lea and Spears, 1992; Walther, 1992; Walther and Parks, 2002). Content analyses of digital text messages reveal that people make an effort to actively include nonverbal cues. They use emoticons or smileys to symbolize their smiles, :-), kisses :-*, or frowns :-(, and they include a variety of expressive disclaimers like *shrug*, LOL, *sigh*, *stutter*, <irony on>, etc. to fine-tune their verbal messages (for an overview see Walther and D'Addario, 2001). Hugs can be expressed via brackets, (((((Denis))))), with the amount of brackets indicating the degree of enthusiasm. A significant part of online and mobile users indulge themselves in the computer-mediated exchange of sexual gestures and—in conflict with the cues-filtered-out approach—report high levels of emotional arousal and satisfaction (Döring, 2000: 881). Response latencies in email or SMS communication are further examples of nonverbal cues. Extended response times can be perceived as creating an uneasy silence, while short response times might nonverbally communicate thoughtfulness, eagerness, or closeness. According to the social information processing theory, people are able to provide enough social cues during computer-mediated communication in order to create social presence. CMC, therefore, can be as emotional as face-to-face communication. Moreover, CMC can reduce shyness and social inhibitions, can foster self-disclosure (e.g., revelation of intimate and delicate emotions) and thus lead to hyper-emotionality (Walther, 1996).

Self-Presentation Theory

Nonverbal communication is often believed to be especially truthful since people are more trained to control their words than their body language (e.g., avoidance of eye contact as a nonverbal cue can lead to the detection of a verbal lie). The self-presentation theory (Goffman, 1959) can be interpreted as an extension of the social information processing theory, because it differentiates expressions or *cues given* (consciously and intentionally controlled) from cues given-off (expressed unconsciously and unintentionally). While the social information processing theory focuses on controlled nonverbal cues (e.g., explicitly including a twinkling smiley to clarify irony) the self-presentation perspective raises the question of cues given off in computer-mediated communication. Freudian slips can occur in CMC or SMS communication, both as verbal slips (e.g., dubious misspellings) and nonverbal slips (e.g., forgetting to reply or replying to the wrong person). Additionally, the sending time of a message can be a cue given off or a cue given. Some people adjust their computer clock before sending an e-mail to bring the sending time in line with certain impression formation tactics (e.g., to give the impression of working overtime or being an early riser). Other people deliberately postpone sending an already completed message to tactically provide a specific responsiveness image (e.g., to avoid the impression of over-involvement in a fresh dating relationship). In CMC more expressions of self are "given" rather than "given off," meaning that greater control over self-presentational behavior in CMC allows individuals to manage their online interactions more strategically (Ellison, et al., 2006; for chronemic or temporal impression formation strategies in CMC see Liu and Ginther, 2001: 52).

Nonverbal Skills

The meaning of nonverbal cues in CMC is highly context-dependent. For example, temporal patterns in dyadic communication might differ from group communication. Nonverbal computer-mediated communication demands respective nonverbal coding and decoding skills in the telecommunication participants. General nonverbal skills are mostly investigated in the context of face-to-face-communication (Burgoon and Bacue, 2003) and thus need to be specified for CMC contexts.

Literature Review

The role of chronemic and proxemic cues in online and mobile computer-mediated textual communication has been addressed by only a small number of studies. It is interesting to note that most of these studies implicitly or explicitly rely on the social information processing theory.

CMC Chronemics Studies

The chronemic dimension can be divided into at least five relevant sub-dimensions. In all these sub-dimensions, the temporal communication patterns can be interpreted as cues that are given or given off.

One chronemics sub-dimension is the response time or response latency. Short response times can be interpreted as nonverbal cues of interpersonal closeness, immediacy, care, presence, and even submissiveness (e.g., when a subordinate is supposed to answer promptly to messages of his or her boss; see Walther and Tidwell, 1995). Although email technically is an asynchronous medium, content analyses of emails and their time stamps reveal that people usually answer emails within twenty-four hours. Belated email replies often contain apologies and explanations to compensate for the negative nonverbal cue of an extended response time (Kalman and Rafaeli, 2005; Kalman, et al., 2006). By the same token, SMS communication is not technically synchronous; however, response times of only a few minutes are typical, fostering even more interpersonal immediacy.

Response times are shortest in synchronous computer-mediated communication (e.g., online or mobile instant messaging, online or mobile chat services). Experimental studies show that people evaluate synchronous or real-time CMC more positively than asynchronous CMC. Synchronicity is associated with higher involvement and a more positive impression of the communication partner (Burgoon, et al., 2002; Ng and Detenber, 2005; Nowak, et al., 2005). Being able to communicate in real time seems to improve the impression of closeness and communication efficiency.

Two further chronemics sub-dimensions are communication frequency (e.g., how many messages are exchanged per week) and communication duration (e.g., how long or wordy the messages are). People observing small online discussion groups as part of an experimental study reported that they developed a fuller impression of the discussion participants more quickly if they sent longer messages and sent messages more often, despite identical message content in the high/low frequency and long/short duration experimental conditions (Liu, et al., 2002). There are two plausible psychological explanations of this effect. *Writing* more and longer messages might be a meta-communicative signal of greater involvement on part of the sender, who is therefore evaluated more positively. *Reading* more and longer messages expands the time the receiver is exposed to the sender's textual presence. In accordance with the psychological mere exposure effect (Zajonc, 1968), the receiver experiences increased familiarity and sympathy towards the sender. Text messages are technically restricted to 160 characters and, therefore, not particularly wordy. A frequent exchange of text messages is typical, though, and might foster interpersonal closeness.

The sending time of a computer-mediated message is usually logged in the time and date stamp or imprint of the message header in emails or SMS messages. The same message content can be perceived differently depending on the sending time. The nonverbal meaning of the sending time seems to interact with the message content. An experimental study revealed that the same task-related email message was perceived as more dominant when sent at night as opposed to daytime (Walther and Tidwell, 1995). On the other hand, a social email message sent at night was, under certain conditions, perceived as more intimate. This effect can be interpreted in relation to cultural time norms. Task-related or formal conversations are usually restricted to office hours; overstepping these boundaries with nightly task messages might appear pushy and bossy. Nighttime social conversations usually take place between intimate friends or family, therefore, nightly private emails might be associated with high intimacy.

CMC Proxemics Studies

Physical proximity and physical distance are powerful nonverbal cues in interpersonal communication. "Physical closeness fosters psychological closeness and mutuality—a sense of connection, similarity, solidarity, openness, and understanding. Physical distance creates detachment, perceived dissimilarity and lack of receptivity to others' communication and viewpoints" (Burgoon, et al., 2002). When using mobile communication channels, such as mobile telephony or text messages, participants often provide information about their where-abouts ("location telling"). The information has mainly three functions (Arminen, 2006):

- It is used to ensure interactional availability (are the communication partners at places where they can communicate via mobile phone without being disturbed?).
- It has a praxiological function (practical relevance of the whereabouts for specific activities, e.g., arranging a meeting point or ordering something from a supermarket).
- It also has a socio-emotional function (e.g., in socio-emotionally meaningful places, like tourist attractions or places of biographical importance, like a birthplace).

Therefore, socially meaningful location information does not equal geographical locations (Weilenman and Leuchovious, 2004). The proxemics dimension is multi-dimensional as well, but has not been explored much in the field of online and mobile communication up to this point.

Physical proximity or co-presence describes, of course, the case when those using ICT are physically co-located during computer-mediated communication. Experimental studies with computer-mediated group decision support systems (GDSS) proved no significant differences between a same-place and a different-place condition. There are no differences in the quality and efficiency of task completion between small groups who are physically co-located (same room) and physically dispersed (different rooms) when using GDSS for a brainstorming task. The asynchronous computer-mediated communication was equivalent in each case (Valacich, et al., 1993; Valacich, et al., 1994). However, another experiment that focused on pairs of participants communicating synchronously via online chat revealed significant differences between the same-room and different-rooms conditions. Those who were co-located while conducting the online task felt a greater sense of connection with one another, were more involved in the task, and judged their partners as more competent, dependable, reliable, sociable, and attractive. Clearly in this case, physical proximity conferred significant advantages in terms of the computer-mediated communication process itself and the social judgments emanating from it (Burgoon, et al., 2002). Turning the tables once again, another experiment revealed the opposite effect. The task-related synchronous computer-mediated communication quality was better in physically distributed groups, with half of the group in one room and the other half of the group in another room, than in co-located groups, with the whole group in one room (Burgoon, et al., 2002). In this case, the authors posit that this is possibly because the nonverbal cues of physical co-presence can be distracting or irritating, especially in a group context. The mixed results (no difference, physical proximity advantage, and physical proximity disadvantage) indicate that there are interaction effects: the power and meaning of physical co-presence as a nonverbal cue *during* computer-mediated communication might depend on different factors like the type of communication task, the number of communication partners, or the type of asynchronous or synchronous online or mobile medium. On the whole, the examination of physical co-presence while engaging in CMC is not a common scenario since computer-mediated communication usually takes place between physically dispersed participants. We must strain to think of situations where this is a natural way of interacting. However, ecologically valid exceptions might be found in mobile communication scenarios (e.g., people sitting in the same meeting room are exchanging SMS messages as a second private communication channel during their oral conversations).

Although proxemic cues in communication are often the focus of research, there are few empirical studies that focus on proxemic behavior such as situational arrangements, body language, or arrangements of personal space in regard to mobile communication (see Ling, 2002; Murtagh, 2002; Höflich, 2003). Ling (2002) for example, conducted observational and experimental studies to gain insight into the use of mobile telephony in public spaces. The studies revealed that when people take a call on their mobile phones in public spaces, they usually create some sort of private space to disengage themselves from the actual situation at hand. They can do this by walking away from co-present others, or by closing their body form (turning their body or head away, or looking down). Ling purposefully disturbed this disengagement by moving into the phone users' personal sphere in order to observe their reactions to his presence. In a store, for example, he feigned interest in the display of products immediately beside them. The result was that phone users yielded the space to him and wandered off to another less populated area. This experiment points to the importance and awareness of personal space and distance during mobile communication.

Instead of contrasting physical co-present and dispersed computer-mediated communication partners it seems to be more relevant to differentiate physical dispersed communication participants in terms of different *geographical distances* and *types of geographical locations*. A computer-mediated message like an email or an SMS message might be interpreted differently if sent out from a location very close (within a few hundred meters) or very far away (from another country) from the actual location of the receiver (in geographical distance). The identical message might also have different connotations if sent out from a location familiar or unfamiliar, attractive or unattractive to the receiver (in terms of the type of location). These proxemic sub-dimensions have been neglected in previous online and mobile communication research.

This seems rather surprising, as the investigation of nonverbal cues such as chronemic and proxemic cues in mobile communication also has implications for media design. Whereas time stamps are already automatically inserted in SMS messages when sent, services and applications that provide the users with proxemic cues have also been developed recently. So-called *location-based services* integrate location telling to make its functions (interactional availability, praxiological function, and socio-emotional function) utilizable for the users (see Arminen, 2006).

Amin, et al. (2005), for example, developed *SenseMS,* a prototype of a mobile service that can be implemented on PDAs and conducted a field trial with six teenagers. With SenseMS, text messages can be enhanced with different colors and sizes. Furthermore, a stamp with a background image of the current whereabouts of the sender can be added. This service provides a graphical form of location telling by the sender; an automatic logging of the location via the radio cell is not carried out.

In general, location-based services in mobile communication serve to locate subscribers automatically, for instance via cell IDs in a mobile network or via access points in a Wireless Local Area Network (W-LAN) environment (Chen, et al., 2005). This possibility of automatic localization and tracking of users brings up the question of data privacy. User studies show that the willingness to automatically disclose one's own whereabouts to other people or services depends on who requires the information, why the information is requested and how detailed it is supposed to be (Consolvo, et al., 2005).

In other sectors, such as tourism and marketing, location-based services for mobile phones are used to point customers to places of interest or restaurants, or for couponing purposes. They are also being developed for Personal Information Management (PIM) applications. PIM enables users to manage shopping lists or to-do lists on mobile phones, which can activate location-based memo functions (Ludford, et al., 2006).

Finally, there are location-based services that support social contacts, networking, and community formation. The automatic localization of communication partners facilitates spontaneous contacts, be it with unknown people or acquaintances. The following services already exist:

- Jung, Persson, and Blom (2005) developed the *Defined Delivery System* (DeDe), a prototype for Nokia cell phones that was tested on seven teenagers in Finland. When sending text or multimedia messages, context variables can be defined that have to be fulfilled before the message is delivered to the addressee. Variables include (a) the time of day, (b) before or after a call to a certain number, (c) closeness to a Bluetooth device, and (d) location in a specific radio cell. The radio cells can be saved on the devices and given names like "home" or "work." With the DeDe system, the pupils were able to wish a friend good luck with an exam on the evening before—the message was delivered only when the addressee arrived at school. Field tests proved that the "location" variable was used most often, followed by "delivery time." To fix the delivery of a message to a certain place can increase the efficiency of communication but, at the same time, more forward planning is required.
- Kjeldskov and Paay (2005) developed the *Just-for-Us* system, another prototype that underwent evaluation by experts. A field trial in Australia is planned. The system maps a large square in Melbourne, Australia, including all local restaurants and venues. In addition, a small map shows people from the user's contact list who are close to the square. The system provides users with background information on the square and enables spontaneously arranged meetings with others who are close by.
- *Reno,* an interactive prototype of a location disclosure application, and *Boise,* a paper prototype of a map-based service, were developed in the US by Iachello, et al. (2005). Reno was tested in a field trial with eight adults. It can be used to request the whereabouts of a contact partner. The location is labeled (e.g., "at home," "in the gym") and reported via text message, provided the localized person releases this information. To protect their privacy, senders can suppress the notification, but can also make vague or even false statements in answer of the request. Boise has the same functions as Reno, but the whereabouts are displayed on a map. Even tracking will be possible. Field studies to test this prototype are planned.
- *FriendZone,* a commercial localization service by Swiss Comm, was offered by Vodafone from 2003 to 2005 in Germany. It is a mobile community service that shows the whereabouts of community members on a map. It additionally provides an instant messenger, mobile chatting with people in the vicinity, and also an anonymous instant messenger that does not transmit the user's number. Members with a certain profile deposited in a database can be contacted for a face-to-face meeting (Burak and Sharon, 2004). However, this service has been suspended.
- In the EU project *Youngster,* a context-sensitive mobile service was developed for use by European teenagers (Ling and Sollund, 2002). The service was available on traditional mobile phones, PDAs, and the Internet. It included a buddy list, free messaging to buddies who

also used Youngster, and a localization function. It is important to note that the teenagers themselves were able to control who was on their buddy list and to what degree others in the trial could locate them. The Youngster service was tested in a field trial with approximately sixty teenagers in Grimstad, Norway. The results of the field study show that there were two main groups of users. The adopters used the Youngster system to communicate with other Youngster users and took advantage of context-sensitive functions like locating their buddies. In contrast to them, the rejecters lacked interest in using the system. After trying out various functions, they decided that text messages better suited their needs, for example, for contacting friends who didn't use Youngster. The advanced functions like map-based locating services were not fully exploited.

Further, spatial cues are not restricted to the physical world but can also be generated in immersive virtual environments. Virtual proximity addresses the spatial positions of characters in a virtual or computer-generated, shared environment. In visual two-dimensional online game or chat environments (e.g., depicting a bar or a beach or, for example, in online games such as World of Warcraft) the participants are represented by small images such as humanoid, fantasy cartoon figures, or portrait photographs (so-called online characters or avatars). During their textual online conversations, people can navigate their graphical avatars around the virtual environment, moving closer to other avatars or moving away from them. Krikorian, et al. (2000) could demonstrate that the proximity of avatars in a graphical chat environment correlates with the interpersonal attraction and relationship building between the communication participants navigating the avatars. Therefore, the virtual proximity of avatars can be interpreted as a nonverbal social cue. Virtual proximity or tele-proximity (Kreijns, et al., 2002) as well as other forms of avatars' virtual body language (e.g., clothing, body postures, hand gestures, or facial expressions; compare Salem and Earle, 2000; Kujanpää and Manninen, 2003) are restricted to avatar worlds often realized in PC based online but hardly realized in mobile communication so far.

Rationale and Hypotheses

In SMS communication—one of the mobile "killer applications"—chronemic and proxemic cues are relevant. As noted above, mobile phone text messages include automatic time stamps; therefore, they provide a non-verbal cue in the chronemics code system. Further, the automatic localization of mobile phone users is possible, though not commonly used, via the cellular network or satellite positioning systems. Therefore, not only automatic time stamps but also location stamps can be added to sent-out messages. In order to better understand the communicative effects of these cues two experimental studies were conducted to answer the following research questions:

1. Do people think of SMS content differently according to the time stamp indicating when the message was sent out by the sender?
2. Do people think of SMS content differently according to the location stamp indicating from which location the message was sent out by the sender?

Chronemics Hypotheses

Following up on the email chronemics experiment of Walther and Tidwell (1995) we provided our participants with SMS messages that had either a daytime or a nighttime time stamp. Like Walther and Tidwell, we used both a social message (airport pickup and gossip using informal language) and a task-related message (preparation of a business meeting using formal language) sent by a male supervisor to one of his female subordinates. The participants had to rate the SMS messages in terms of perceived intimacy and dominance. In line with the e-mail chronemics hypotheses of Walther and Tidwell (1995: 464) we formulated the following one-sided hypotheses considering the interaction between SMS content and chronemics:

-   Hypothesis C1: The time stamp interacts with the perception of SMS content such that a social message sent at night is perceived as more intimate than a social message sent during the day, while a task message sent at night is perceived as less intimate than a task message sent during day.
-   Hypothesis C2: The time stamp interacts with the perception of SMS content such that a task message sent at night is perceived as more dominant than a task message sent during the day, while a social message sent at night is perceived as less dominant than a social message sent during the day.

Proxemics Hypotheses

A second experimental study was conducted to address SMS *proxemics*. In this study, we used the same experimental design as in the first study but kept the messages' time stamps constant to daytime and added locations stamps in the format "radio cell 4545 [London Greenwich]." Three different location stamps of varying geographic distances between the SMS sender and the receiver were used (same town as receiver, ca. 5 kilometers; big city in the same country, ca. 350 kilometers; big city in a neighboring country, ca. 1000 kilometers). Due to lack of previous research on proxemic cues in CMC, only very global two-sided hypotheses can be formulated.

- Hypothesis P1: The location stamp influences the dominance perception of SMS messages, be it as a main or interaction effect.
- Hypothesis P2: The location stamp influences the intimacy perception of SMS messages, be it as a main or interaction effect.

Study 1: SMS Chronemics[1]

The Approach

Our media psychological SMS chronemics study was carried out as a paper and pencil questionnaire experiment. We used different questionnaire versions in order to create the experimental conditions. Subjects were recruited during university lectures and randomly assigned to the different experimental groups.[2] The study included two independent variables and followed a 2x2 (daytime/nighttime time stamp x social/ task message content) design. The two main dependent measures were intimacy and dominance ratings of the SMS messages.

Instruments were standardized paper-pencil questionnaires divided into four parts. First, the questionnaire started with an instruction and second respondents were presented with the stimulus SMS message of the respective experimental groups. Third, items from Burgoon and Hale's (1987) Relational Communication Questionnaire were used to measure the intimacy ("creates a feeling of closeness"/"shows affection") and dominance ("is dominating the conversation"/"is patronizing") impressions of the message on five-point Likert scales. Finally, the questionnaire presented the respondents with questions covering *mobile communication experience* and *demographic variables*.

All subjects were students of a middle-sized German university. Convenience sampling was used in various lectures of different disciplines where subjects were asked to volunteer. Each cell of the 2x2 design was randomly filled with 90 subjects (50 percent female, 50 percent male) resulting in a total sample size of $N = 360$ (50 percent female, 50 percent male). Demographic statistics indicated an age range from 18 to 44 years with a mean age of M 22.3 ($SD = 2.3$) years. The vast majority of the student subjects already had work-life experience (e.g., summer jobs, trainee programs, internships, etc.). Nearly every subject (99 percent) owned and used a mobile phone and, among the users, they had used the device at least five years. According to the data collected, the most popular mobile phone functions were alarm clock, mobile telephony, and SMS messaging.

Findings

The data were analyzed with fixed factors analysis of variance. The descriptive statistics for intimacy and dominance in relation to social and task-oriented content and sending time are presented in Table 5.1.

SMS message content effect. Perhaps it is not surprising that the social SMS message was rated significantly higher on intimacy than the task-related message ($p < .001$; $\eta^2 = .32$). The task-related SMS message on the other hand was perceived as significantly higher on dominance than the social message ($p < .01$; $\eta^2 = .02$), compare Table 5.1.

SMS sending time effect. As Table 5.2 shows, all messages sent during nighttime—social as well as task-oriented—were perceived as significantly higher on intimacy than daytime messages ($p < .01$, $\eta^2 = .03$). At the same time, social and task-oriented daytime messages were evaluated as more dominant ($p = .05$, $\eta^2 = .01$) than messages with a time stamp from the night. Intimacy and dominance perceptions were independent ($r = .09$, $p = .10$).

SMS content x sending time interaction non-effect. In contrast to our interaction hypotheses C1 and C2, the sending time did not have a *content-specific* influence. Rather, the results show that the time stamp played out in terms of the respondents' perception of intimacy/dominance. Neither the social message content ($p = .75$) nor the task-related content ($p = .68$) interacted with the sending time.

Discussion

Our experiment confirms the social information processing stance on chronemic cues in mobile computer-mediated communication. The material shows that 54 percent of the subjects reported that they pay attention to the time stamps in their everyday SMS communication. The experimental data revealed a significant main effect of the sending time. Daytime SMS messages were rated as significantly more dominant and less intimate, while nighttime SMS messages were rated as more intimate and less dominant.

The stimulus SMS message was embedded in a supervisor-subordinate relationship shaping the respective time norms and chronemic cues. A nighttime SMS message from the supervisor obviously signaled more intimacy—both with socio-emotional and task-related message content. At the same time, nighttime SMS messages from the supervisor were

Table 5.1
Descriptive statistics for intimacy and dominance in relation to message content and time

Message Content	Social			Task		
Time	Total	Daytime	Nighttime	Total	Daytime	Nighttime
Intimacy						
M	3.12	2.08	3.06	2.19	2.30	3.32
SD	.79	.75	.83	.69	.61	.73
N	175	86	89	182	87	95
Dominance						
M	2.86	2.95	3.14	3.10	2.76	3.02
SD	.67	.62	.82	.81	.70	.81
N	175	86	89	182	87	95

Note: Intimacy and Dominance were measured using a five-point Likert scale ranging from 1 (totally disagree) to 5 (totally agree).

Table 5.2
Descriptive statistics for intimacy and dominance in relation to day and nighttime

Time	Daytime	Nighttime
Intimacy		
M	2.57	2.83
SD	.92	.85
n	173	184
Dominance		
M	3.01	2.89
SD	.73	.77
n	173	184

Note: Intimacy and Dominance were measured using a five-point Likert scale ranging from 1 (totally disagree) to 5 (totally agree).

evaluated as less dominant, probably because the respondents assumed that a nighttime message would not be read and reacted upon until the next day, while perhaps a supervisor might expect an immediate response when sending a daytime message. Thus, the daytime message has an immediacy that will exert more influence over the message receiver.

The experiment showed no gender effects. Female and male subjects reacted equally.[3] An additional experimental variation that left open if the male supervisor addressed a female or a male subordinate did not generate different results than the gender-specific stimulus material.

Study 2: SMS Proxemics[4]

The Approach

The procedure of our media psychological SMS proxemics study resembled the procedure of the chronemics study (see above). The study included two independent variables and followed a 3x2 design. That is, we contrasted three different distances (same town/big city same country/ big city foreign country location stamp) by two different message types (social/task message content). The two main dependent measures were the intimacy and dominance ratings of the SMS messages. We decided on the described location stamps for the following reasons: in our study, we concentrated on situations where face-to-face communication was not possible because of the distance between sender and addressee. The location stamp indicating the same town differs from the location stamp from the big city in the same country insofar as a face-to-face meeting might be possible in the first case. Hence, we expected different reactions to the message concerning intimacy and dominance. It could be that addressees show more appreciation for using SMS as a means of contact if personal contact is not feasible, and therefore differ in their estimation of intimacy and dominance. The third location stamp was introduced because Germans do not generally use their mobile phones during stays abroad, as the fees charged for using services in a foreign country are relatively high. Receiving a text message from abroad is rather special, so we expected differences in the estimation of the message concerning intimacy and dominance.

As with the previous experiment, instruments were standardized paper-pencil questionnaires divided into four parts. The questionnaire started with an instruction and then in the second portion presented the appropriate stimulus SMS message for the particular experimental group. The third section gathered the respondents' answers for Burgoon and Hale's (1987) Relational Communication Questionnaire that were used to measure intimacy and dominance impressions of the message on five-point Likert scales. Finally, the last part of the questionnaire covered mobile communication experience and demographic variables.

Again, the subjects for the second experiment were students of a middle-sized German university. Convenience sampling was used in various lectures of different disciplines, where subjects were asked to volunteer. Each cell of the 3x2 design was randomly filled with 90 subjects (50 percent female, 50 percent male) resulting in a total sample size of N = 540 (50 percent female, 50 percent male). Demographic statistics indicated an age range from 18 to 40 years with a mean age of $M = 21.49$ ($SD = 2.10$) years. The vast majority of the subjects already had experience in the working world. Nearly every subject (98 percent) owned a mobile phone and had used it for at least five years. In a confirmation of the data gathered in the previous experiment, the most popular mobile phone functions again were the alarm clock, mobile telephony, and SMS messaging functions.

Findings

SMS message content effect. As with the previous experiment, the social SMS message was rated significantly higher on intimacy than the task-related message ($p < .001$; $\eta^2 = .30$, for descriptive statistics compare Table 5.3). The task-related SMS message on the other hand was perceived as significantly higher on dominance than the social message ($p < .01$; $\eta^2 = .02$).

SMS message sending location non-effect. The sending location or physical distance of the SMS sender—varying between same town as the receiver (close distance), big city in the same country (middle distance), and big city in a foreign country (foreign country)—did not influence the perceived intimacy of the messages ($p = .72$), as Table 5.4 shows. Likewise the sending location did not affect the perceived dominance of the messages ($p = .45$).

SMS message content x sending location interaction non-effect. The sending location also did not have a content-specific influence on intimacy or dominance perceptions. Neither the social message content ($p = .40$) nor the task-related content ($p = .93$) interacted with the sending location.

Discussion

The experiment failed to demonstrate either a sending location main effect or a sending location interaction effect. Unlike time stamps, loca-

Table 5.3
Descriptive statistics for intimacy and dominance in relation to
message content and distance

Message Content	Total	Social			Total	Task		
		Close Distance	Middle Distance	Foreign Country		Close Distance	Middle Distance	Foreign Country
Intimacy								
M	4.00	3.94	3.97	4.07	3.20	3.20	3.20	3.17
SD	.61	.60	.61	.61	.64	.68	.68	.55
n	262	87	86	89	273	96	91	86
Dominance								
M	2.66	2.61	2.70	2.65	2.80	2.76	2.82	2.82
SD	.57	.59	.60	.53	.55	.54	.59	.54
n	262	87	86	89	273	96	91	86

Note: Intimacy and Dominance were measured using a five-point Likert scale ranging from 1 (totally disagree) to 5 (totally agree).

Table 5.4
Descriptive statistics for intimacy and dominance in relation
the sender's distance

Distance	Close Distance	Middle Distance	Foreign Country
Intimacy			
M	3.55	3.58	3.62
SD	.74	.75	.74
N	183	177	175
Dominance			
M	2.70	2.76	2.74
SD	.56	.59	.54
N	183	177	175

Note: Intimacy and Dominance were measured using a five-point Likert scale ranging from 1 (totally disagree) to 5 (totally agree).

tion stamps are not an established feature of SMS. The majority of our German subjects (55 percent) said they would not like to have location stamps included in SMS communication, while 23 percent were undecided, and 22 percent were in favor of location stamps. Probably the unfamiliarity of location stamps hindered a consistent interpretation of this nonverbal cue. In addition, the introduction of location stamps has the potential of telling the recipient of an SMS where the sender is at any particular moment. While in some cases this information might be of some use (for example, when people are trying to coordinate a meeting), it can also be too revealing (when a teen wants to evade his/her parents' questions).

Conclusion

Nowadays, when it is possible to reach people even if they are on the move and maybe even outside "calling hours," the handling of time and space is a vital part of using mobile telephony and short message service (compare Katz and Aakhus, 2002; Ling, 2004; Nyiri, 2005). For example, sending an SMS is often used outside "calling hours" to find out whether the communication partner is available for calling. Furthermore, one of the questions often asked in communications via the mobile phone, be it telephony or SMS, is "Where are you?" This question serves to estimate the communication partner's context and situation. It does make a difference whether someone is at home, in a train, or in a meeting. Even if we are available everywhere thanks to our mobile phones, we cannot communicate as easily in every situation. Whereas using SMS or telephony on public transport usually does not lead to problems, doing the same during an important business meeting might have negative consequences. Further, the sender's actions (sending an SMS to see if someone is available for phone calls or the question "Where are you?") lead to certain interpretations by the addressee. An SMS sent at night might be interpreted as more urgent or more intimate than an SMS sent during the day. The answer to the question, "Where are you?" might be different if peers or parents want to know our whereabouts. Receiving an SMS from a foreign country might be an equivalent to a post card and something special. For a complete understanding of textual online and mobile communication, nonverbal temporal and spatial cues that are given and interpreted should not be ignored. Previous research on chronemic and proxemic cues in CMC is sparse in terms of both theoretical elaboration and empirical foundation. Still, several chronemic as well as proxemic sub-dimensions can be distinguished and illustrated with anecdotic examples and first studies.

Our SMS chronemics experiment confirmed that the time stamp of an SMS message affects how people see its intimacy and dominance, even if the time stamp's effect size was small in our experiment. The location stamp showed a tendency to be interpreted as more intimate with growing distance between sender and addressee, but did not prove to have a significant effect. This is rather surprising, as mobile communication as such is not a location-free communication, as described above. Furthermore, it seems unlikely that proxemic cues that are so powerful in face-to-face communication would not affect mobile communication.

However, our findings showed that SMS messages do not lack paraverbal and nonverbal cues as understood from the Reduced Social Cues Theory (see Kiesler, et al., 1984; Culnan and Markus, 1987). We did find a content effect on dominance and intimacy ratings, which can be used to characterize a relationship and therefore are social cues. In the case of proxemics, the manipulated contents had even stronger effects than the selected location stamps. Therefore, according to the Social Information Processing Theory (compare Lea and Spears, 1992; Walther, 1992; Walther and Parks, 2002), our results show that people seem to actively include and interpret social cues in SMS messages, thereby clarifying their relationship, expressing intimacy or distance, and dominance. As SMS services are mostly used between people who know each other, it is easier to establish closeness, since relevant background information on the communication partners is known.

The time and location stamps we used were "cues given off," according to the Self-Presentation Theory (Goffman, 1959), because they were automatically added to the text messages used as stimulus material. While automatic time stamps are mundane in SMS, subjects were very reluctant to accept automatic location stamps. Other studies, however, revealed that location-based services are more accepted by users if they can control to whom they reveal their whereabouts (compare Iachello, et al., 2005; Lehikoinen and Kaikkonen, 2006; Oulasvirta, et al., 2005). Thus, location stamps seem to be accepted as user-controlled "cues given," but not as "cues given off."

One drawback of our study was the rather specific context formulated in the stimulus material. We only examined supervisor-subordinate relationships. Our line of research seems expandable; apart from the relationships studied here, other types of formal and informal interpersonal relationship contexts and message contents could be investigated, for example, relationships between parents and children, romantic relationships, and peer group interaction. In addition, the chronemic sub-dimensions not examined in our study should be analyzed. Response time as well as communication frequency and duration might prove beneficial for the understanding of SMS use. It could be that addressees deliberately manipulate their response time in order to create a specific impression on the sender; for example, a too immediate answer to an SMS in a romantic relationship just after getting to know each other could be regarded as over-commitment, or a subordinate could manipulate send times in order to give the impression of working overtime. Frequency and duration of messages could be regarded—dependent on the content, e.g., in social contacts—as measures relationship quality. It may also be interesting to investigate not only single SMS messages, but also SMS interactions. Focusing on this aspect, response time becomes evident as a social cue, as a long waiting time for an answer can be interpreted as an uncomfortable silence by one of the communication partners. Furthermore, in addition to intimacy and dominance ratings, other dimensions of message and sender impressions should be considered, again both theoretically and empirically. It seems promising to include more open questions in research instruments to further explore the respondents' assumptions and interpretations of different send times and send locations.

Including such open research questions in the experimental paradigm also serves to override certain disadvantages. The reduction of complexity of the studied phenomena can be moderated if the experimental design allows for the open exploration of the subjects' assessments and interpretations. In this way, the research benefits from the methodological advantages provided by experimental studies. With experiments, causal effects of systematic variation of experimental conditions on dependent variables can be demonstrated.

The investigation of nonverbal cues such as chronemic and proxemic cues in mobile communication also has implications for media design. Whereas time stamps are already automatically inserted in SMS messages when sent, services and applications that provide the users with proxemic cues have also been developed recently. As the literature review given above could show (compare Burak and Sharon, 2004; Iachello, et al., 2005; Jung, et al., 2005; Kjeldskov and Paay, 2005; Ling and Sollund, 2002) most of these location-based services are still prototypes that are currently evaluated in field studies. Most of the prototypes are developed to provide applications that support social contacts as well as network and community formation. The automatic localization of communication partners facilitates spontaneous contacts.

However, the use of time stamps and location stamps as cues "given" or "given off" raises further questions in connection with Communication Skills Theory (Verderber and Verderber, 2003). The theory states that interpersonal communication demands specific verbal and nonverbal communication skills. The meaning of nonverbal cues in SMS communication as well as in other communication modes is highly context-dependent, with interpersonal relationships and even cultural backgrounds being examples for relevant contexts (compare Katz and Aakhus, 2002; Campbell, 2006). Therefore, time and location cues can only contribute positively to communication efficiency and quality if the sender and addressee are able and willing to integrate and interpret these cues in the same spirit.

The effort and competence to use and interpret those cues, especially with the new services provided, must not be underestimated. Since the emergence of mobile phones we have had—and still have—to learn to restructure time and space: when to be available or not, when to expect others to be available for communication and when to accept that they are not. In order to use mobile communication appropriately and purposefully, specific competencies—mobile phone competencies—have to be learned. For example, there are situations where it is not appropriate to make calls with a mobile phone, for instance, during school lessons or in an exclusive restaurant (see Ling, 1997; Katz, 2005). Although parents provide mobile phones to their teenage children for using them as a "long leash," they can also be used to control the teenagers and seen as a burden (Haddon, 2000).

Conclusion

With the implementation of more and more complex services and applications, the challenges in this field of conflict reach a new dimension. The effort to use nonverbal cues will rise, just as the effort to interpret them will be greater with increasing complexity of received messages. Yet, one of the factors that made SMS services a killer application surely was that they reduce complexity. With the restriction to a fixed number of characters, messages are written to the point. Also, messages can be sent without a specific cause, just to contact someone. Besides, sending text messages helps shy people address others, because they do not have to get into closer contact as in a phone call. Especially with awkward messages, texts avoid a more direct communication. This leads to the question whether more complex SMS services are wanted, and under what conditions subscribers will accept and use them. It could well be that the effort will be too much, or that the avoidance of face-to-face meeting will be made more difficult with location-based services. Revealing one's whereabouts, and those of one's peers, to others might engender problematic situations.

This leads us to further challenges, namely, the correct interpretation of the numerous cues. What do users feel if their partner is merely two hundred meters away but chooses to write a text message instead of coming over? What reasons will be attributed to this behavior; will it be seen as positive, neutral, or negative? Besides, there is the possibility of manipulation, both with time and location stamps. It could be difficult to decide if the transmitted information is correct or untrue. It can be assumed that the integration of those services into our everyday life will further dissolve our notion of space and time, just as changed behavior to master these challenges will be observable. Therefore, it is of importance to further investigate the use, usage conditions, and the interpretation of nonverbal cues—such as proxemic and chronemic cues—in mobile communication services.

Notes

1. The authors would like to thank Dennis Brüntje, Dominik Haug, Christin Prasmo, Kerstin Ringel, Imke Rühle, and Mario Ziemkendorf for their help with the organization and implementation of the study.
2. The subjects' participation in both studies was voluntary and based on informed consent. Anonymity was guaranteed and data analysis restricted to aggregated values. The whole experimental procedure was in accordance with the ethical research guidelines of the German Psychological Association.
3. To examine a gender effect, an additional experimental variation was introduced: in one condition of the variation, a male supervisor addressed a female subordinate. In the other condition, the presented stimulus material was ambiguous as to whether a male supervisor addressed a female or a male subordinate. This variation did not generate different results.
4. The authors would like to thank Annemarie Bütow, Stefan Lindner, Anne Looks, Christin Loose, Ingmar Steinicke, and Daniel Urbich for their help with the organization and implementation of the study.

Bibliography

Amin, Alia K, Bram Kersten, Olga Kulyk, Elly Pelgrim, Chih-Ming Wang, and Panos Markopolous. "SenseMS: A User-centered Approach to Enrich the Messaging Experience for Teens by Non-verbal Means." Paper delivered at the 7th International Conference on Human Computer Interaction with Mobile Devices and Services. 21 September 2005, Salzburg, Austria.

Arminen, Ilkka. "Social Functions of Location in Mobile Telephony." *Personal and Ubiquitous Computing*, 10 (August 2006): 319-323.

Burak, Asaf and Taly Sharon. "Usage Patterns of FriendZone: Mobile Location-Based Community Services." Paper delivered at the 3rd international conference on Mobile and Ubiquitous Multimedia. 29 October, 2004, College Park, Maryland.

Burgoon, Judee K. and Aaron E. Bacue. "Nonverbal Communication Skills." In *Handbook of Communication and Social Interaction Skills,* edited by Brant R. Burleson and John O. Greene, 79-219. Mahwah, NJ: Erlbaum, 2003.

Burgoon, Judee K., Joseph A. Bonito, Artemio Ramirez, Jr., Norah E. Dunbar, Karadeen Kam, and Jenna Fischer. "Testing the Interactivity Principle: Effects of Mediation, Propinquity, and Verbal and Nonverbal Modalities in Interpersonal Interaction." *Journal of Communication,* 52 (September 2002): 657-677.

Burgoon, Judee K. and Jerold L. Hale. "Validation and Measurement of the Fundamental Themes of Relational Communication." *Communication Monographs,* 54 (March 1987): 19-41.

Burgoon, Judee K., David B. Buller, and W. Gill Woodall. *Nonverbal Communications: The Unspoken Dialogue.* London, UK: McGraw-Hill, 1995.

Burgoon, Judee K., Michael Burgoon, Kathy Broneck, Eusebio Alvaro, and Jay F. Nunamaker. "Effects of Synchronicity and Proximity on Group Communication." Paper delivered at the annual conference of the National Communication Association. November 2002, New Orleans, Louisiana.

Campbell, Scott. "A Cross-Cultural Comparison of Perceptions and Uses of Mobile Telephony." Paper delivered at the annual conference of the International Communications Association. 22 June 2006, Dresden, Germany.

Chen, Yen-Cheng., Yao-Jung Chan, and Cheung-Wo She. "Enabling Location-Based Services in Wireless LAN Hotspots." *International Journal of Network Management,* 15 (May 2005): 163-175.

Clark, Herbert H. and Susan E. Brennan. "Grounding in Communication." In *Perspectives on Socially Shared Cognition, edited by* Lauren B. Reskick, John M. Levine, and Stephanie D. Teasley, 127-149. Washington, DC: American Psychological Association, 1991.

Consolvo, Sunny, Ian E. Smith, Tara Matthews, Anthony LaMarca, Jason Tabert, and Pauline Powledge. "Location Disclosure to Social Relations: Why, When, and What People Want to Share." Paper delivered at the Conference on Human Factors in Computing Systems, 5 April 2005, Portland, Oregon.

Culnan, Mary J., and M. Lynne Markus. "Information Technologies." In *Handbook of Organizational Communication: An Interdisciplinary Perspective, edited by Frederic* M. Jablin, Linda L. Putnam, Karlene H. Roberts, and Lyman Porter, 420-444. London, UK: Sage, 1987.

DeVito, Joesph A. *The Nonverbal Communication Workbook.* Prospect Heights, IL: Waveland Press, 1988.

Döring, Nicola. "Feminist Views of Cybersex: Victimization, Liberation, and Empowerment." *CyberPsychology and Behavior,* 3 (October 2000): 863-884.

Ellison, Nicole, Rebecca Heino, and Jennifer Gibbs. "Managing Impressions Online: Self-Presentation Processes in the Online Dating Environment."

Journal of Computer-Mediated Communication, 11 (January 2006): 415-441.

Goffman, Erving. *The Presentation of Self in Everyday Life*. New York, NY: Anchor, 1959.

Haddon, Leslie. "The Experience of the Mobile Phone." Paper delivered at the XIV World Congress of Sociology. 26 July - 1 August 1998, Montreal, Canada.

Haddon, Leslie. "The Social Consequences of Mobile Telephony: Framing Questions." Paper delivered at the Sosiale Konskvenser av Mobiltelefoni, 16 June 2000, Oslo, Norway.

Höflich, Joachim. "Part of Two Frames: Mobile Communication and the Situational Arrangement of Communicative Behaviour." In *Mobile Democracy: Essays on Society, Self and Politics*, edited by Kristóf Nyíri, 33-53. Vienna, Austria: Passagen Verlag, 2003.

Iachello, Giovanni, Ian Smith, Sunny Consolvo, Mike Chen, and Gregory D. Abowd. "Developing Privacy Guidelines for Social Location Disclosure Applications and Services." *Paper delivered at the Symposium on Usable Privacy and Security. 7 July 2005, Pittsburgh, Pennsylvania.*

Jung, Younghee, Per Persson, and Jan Blom. "DeDe: Design and Evaluation of a Context-Enhanced Mobile Messaging System." Paper delivered at the Conference on Human Factors in Computing Systems. 6 April, 2005, Portland, Oregon.

Kalman, Yoram M. and Sheizaf Rafaeli. "Email Chronemics: Unobtrusive Profiling of Response Time." Paper delivered at the 38th Hawaii International Conference on System Sciences. 2005, Big Island, Hawaii.

Kalman, Yoram M., Gilad Ravid, Daphne R. Raban, and Sheizaf Rafaeli. "Speak Now or Forever Hold Your Peace: Power Law Chronemics of Turn-taking and Response in Asynchronous CMC." Paper delivered at the annual conference of the International Communication Association. 20 June 2006, Dresden, Germany.

Katz, James E. and Mark Aakhus, Eds. *Perpetual Contact: Mobile Communication,Private Talk, Public Performance*. Cambridge, UK: Cambridge University Press, 2002.

Katz, James E. "Mobile Phones in Educational Settings." In *A Sense of Place: The Global and the Local in Mobile Communication*, edited by Kristóf Nyíri, 305-319. Vienna, Austria: Passagen Verlag, 2005.

Kiesler, Sara, Jane Siegel, and Timothy W. McGuire. "Social Psychological Aspects of Computer-Mediated Communication." *American Psychologist, 39* (October 1984): 1123-1134.

Kjeldskov, Jesper and Jeni Paay. "Just-for-us: A Context-Aware Mobile Information System Facilitating Sociality." Paper delivered at the 7th International Conference on Human Computer Interaction with Mobile Devices and Services. 20 September 2005, Salzburg, Austria.

Kreijns, Karel, Paul A. Kirschner, and Wim Jochems. "The Sociability of Computer-Supported Collaborative Learning Environments." *Journal of Education Technology & Society* 5 (January 2002): 8-22.

Krikorian, Dean H., Jae-Shin Lee, T. Makana Chock, and Chad Harms. "Isn't that Spatial? Distance and Communication in a 2-D Virtual Environment." *Journal of Computer-Mediated Communication,* 5 (June 2000), http://jcmc.indiana.edu/vol5/issue4/krikorian.html.

Kujanpää, T. and T. Manninen. "Supporting Visual Elements of Non-Verbal Communication in Computer Game Avatars." In *Proceedings of Level Up: Digital Games Research,* edited by Marinka Copier and Joost Raessens, 220-233. Utrecht, Netherlands: Universiteit Utrecht, 2003.

Lea, Martin and Russell Spears. "Paralanguage and Social Perception in Computer-Mediated Communication." *Journal of Organizational Computing,* 2.3 (1992): 321-341.

Lehikoinen, Jaakko T. and Anne Kaikkonen. "PePe Field study: Constructing Meanings for Locations in the Context of Mobile Presence." Paper delivered at the 8th International Conference on Human-Computer Interaction with Mobile Devices and Services. 13 September 2006, Espoo, Finland.

Ling, Richard S. *The Mobile Connection: The Cell Phone's Impact on Society.* San Francisco, CA: Elsevier, 2004.

Ling, Richard S. "The Social Juxtaposition of MobileTelephone Conversations and Public Spaces." Paper delivered at the Conference on the Social Consequences of Mobile Telephones. July 2002, Chunchon, Korea.

Ling, Richard S. "'One Can Talk About Common Manners!' The Use of Mobile Telephones in Inappropriate Situations." In *Themes in Mobile Telephony: Final rReport of the COST 248 Home and Work group,* edited by Leslie Haddon. Farsta, Sweden: Telia, 1997.

Ling, Richard S. and Alf Sollund, eds. *Deliverable 13: Planning, Operation and Evaluation of the Field Trials.* EU Youngster Project, 2002.

Liu, Yuliang and Dean Ginther. "Managing Impression Formation in Computer-Mediated Communication." *Educause Quarterly,* 3 (2001): 50-54.

Liu, Yuliang, Dean Ginther, and Paul Zelhart. "An Exploratory Study of the Effects of Frequency and Duration of Messaging on Impression Development in Computer-Mediated Communication." *Social Science Computer Review* 20 (February 2002): 73-80.

Ludford, Paemla J., Dan Frankowski, Ken Relly, Kurt Wilms, and Loren Terveen. "Because I Carry My Cell Phone Anyway: Functional Location-Based Reminder Applications." Paper delivered at the Conference on Human Factors in Computing Systems. 26 April 2006, Montreal, Canada.

Murtagh, Ged M. "Seeing the 'Rules': Preliminary Observations of Action, Interaction and Mobile Phone Use." In *Wireless World: Social and International Aspects of the Mobile Age,* edited by Barry Brown, Nicola Green, and Richard Harper, 81-91. London, UK: Springer-Verlag, 2002.

Ng, Elaine W.J., and Benjamin H. Detenber. "The Impact of Synchronicity and Civility in Online Political Discussions on Perceptions and Intentions to Participate." *Journal of Computer-Mediated Communication,* 10 (April 2005): http://jcmc.indiana.edu/vol10/issue3/ng.html.

Nowak, Kristine, James H. Watt, and Joseph B. Walther. "The Influence of Synchrony and Sensory Modality on the Person Perception Process in Computer Mediated Groups." *Journal of Computer-Mediated Communication* 10 (3 2005), http://jcmc.indiana.edu/vol10/issue3/nowak.html.

Nyíri, Kristóf. Ed. *A Sense of Place: The Global and the Local in Mobile Communication*. Vienna, Austria: Passagen Verlag, 2005.

Oulasvirta, Antti, Mika Raento, and Sauli Tiitta. "ContextContacts: Re-Designing SmartPhone's Contact Book too Support Mobile Awareness and Collaboration." Paper delivered at the 7th International Conference on Human Computer Interaction with Mobile Devices and Services. 20 September 2005. Salzburg, Austria.

Salem, Ben and Nic Earle. "Designing a non-verbal language for expressive avatars." Paper delivered at the 3rd International Conference on Collaborative Virtual Environments. 12 September 2000, San Francisco, California.

Valacich, Joseph S., David Paranka, Joey F. George, and J.F. Nunamaker, Jr. "Communication Concurrency and the New Media: A New Dimension for Media Richness." *Communication Research*, 20 (April 1993): 249-276

Valacich, Joseph S, Joey F. George, J.F. Nunamaker, Jr., and Douglas R. Vogel. "Physical Proximity Effects on Computer-Mediated Group Idea Generation." *Small Group Research* 25 (February 1994): 83-104.

Verderber, Rudolph F. and Kathleen S. Verderber. *Inter-Act: Interpersonal Communication Concepts, Skills, and Contexts*. Oxford, UK: Oxford University Press, 2003.

Walther, Joseph B. "Computer-Mediated Communication: Impersonal, Interpersonal, and Hyperpersonal Interaction." *Communication Research, 23* (February 1996): 3-43.

Walther, Joseph B. "Interpersonal Effects in Computer-Mediated Interaction: A Relational Perspective." *Communication Research, 19* (February 1992): 52-90.

Walther, Joseph B. and Kyle.P. D'Addario. "The Impacts of Emoticons on Message Interpretation in Computer-Mediated Communication." *Social Science Computer Review*, 19 (August 2001): 324-347.

Walther, Joseph B. and Malcolm R. Parks. "Cues Filtered Out, Cues Filtered In: Computer-Mediated Communication and Relationships." In *The Handbook of Interpersonal Communication, edited by* Mark L. Knapp, John A. Daly, and Gerald R. Miller, 529-563. 2nd ed. Thousand Oaks, CA: Sage, 2002.

Walther, Joseph B. and Lisa C. Tidwell. "Nonverbal Cues in Computer-Mediated Communication, and the Effect of Chronemics on Relational Communication." *Journal of Organizational Computing*, 5 (1995): 355-378.

Weilenman, Alexandra H. and Peter Leuchovius. "'I'm Waiting Where We Met Last Time': Exploring Everyday Positioning Practices to Inform Design." Paper delivered at the 3rd Nordic Conference on Human-Computer Interaction. 23-27 October 2004, Tampere, Finland.

Zajonc, Robert B. "Attitudinal Effects of Mere Exposure." *Journal of Personality and Social Psychology Monographs*, 9 (June 1968): 1-27.

6

Mobile Phones: Transforming the Everyday Social Communication Practice of Urban Youth

Eva Thulin
Göteborg University

Bertil Vilhelmson
Göteborg University

The massive use of the mobile telephones, or "mobiles," has added a new dimension of virtual mobility to a continuing trend toward geographically flexible, faster, and more personalized social interaction. Together with other information and communication technologies (ICTs), the technical ability to provide individuals with instant access to anybody and anything, anywhere, and anytime has increased enormously. This has prompted much theoretical interest in the consequences of mobile technology in terms of how movement, space, place, and time are constructed in an increasingly informational and networked society (see Adams, 2005; Castells, 2001; Graham, 2000; Green, 2002; Sheller and Urry, 2006). There is also a need to consider the empirically explicit everyday social practices through which time and space are framed when ICT devices and services are commonly adopted and used (Haythornthwaite and Wellman, 2002; Haddon, 2004; Ling, 2004). Commonly used and experienced, mobile technology may work to reorganize certain social and physical structures of society, just as the automobile, telephone, television, and other space-transcending technologies did in the past. We will, therefore, focus on the evolving implications of mobiles in shaping the everyday lives of young people—a group of particular interest from a dynamic perspective.

It is no overstatement to say that the mobile phone has been taken for granted by young people for quite a few years. According to survey estimates, virtually all young people in Sweden have access to a mobile (Bolin, 2006; Thulin and Vilhelmson, 2007). Young people are among the major consumers of mobile phone technology and are often considered to be forerunners in its adoption and evolution. They were among the first to "domesticate" mobile applications, such as text messaging, using the short message service (SMS) as a means of social communication (Oksman and Turtiainen, 2004). It is, therefore, reasonable to believe that this group is the most suitable object of study when considering the developing and lasting consequences of mobile use for everyday life: the formation of new habits and contact patterns, the evolution of how time and place are used for various activities, and the effects of mobile use on other means of communication. Though the period of youth is in many ways a period of specific needs and demands particularly concerning education, leisure activities, friends, and social networks, it has also been claimed that the values, routines, and contacts established during these years tend to remain stable as a cohort ages (Inglehart, 1997; Inglehart and Welzel, 2005; Robinson and Godbey, 1997).

However, such focused approaches concentrating on early adopters or high-consuming groups risk exaggerating the distinctive impact and role of a smart technology that is most likely integrated into people's everyday practices in varied and complex ways (Valentine and Holloway, 2002). The need for and use of a mobile should therefore be examined in relation to other in-home and out-of-home everyday activities, as well as the need for other means of communication and the use of physical transport for social interaction. Over the years in which the mobile has become generally accepted and adopted, new means of Internet-based communication have also been introduced—for example, email, instant messaging, and chat rooms—creating opportunities for socio-spatial interaction that are both competitive and complementary (see Thulin and Vilhelmson, 2005, 2006).

This study attempts to place the use of mobile phones in the broader context of the change of everyday life and communication. Our research framework emphasizes social relations, contact and activity patterns, and time use when studying the relationships between ICTs on the one hand and human activity and society on the other (as proposed by Bakardjieva and Smith, 2001; Haddon, 2004; Lie and Sörensen, 1996; Thulin, 2004; Haythornthwaite and Wellman, 2002). The concept of everyday life here denotes a stable pattern of daily activities that have become habits and routines—the people with whom an individual interacts, the activities he or she spends time doing, and where that time is spent—and that might be affected by mobile technology.

The explicit and principal aim of the article is to explore how young people's everyday patterns of social communication, contacts, and time use have been affected by the increased use of mobiles. Social communication is defined as private, interpersonal contact, excluding work-related communication and the non-communicative use of mobiles. Empirically, we rely on an intensive panel study of a group of Swedish urban youth. On three occasions—in 2000 when they were eighteen years old, two years later when they were twenty, and finally in 2005 when they were twenty-three—each person used a time diary to record his or her daily use of time, place, and ICT use over one week. These self-reports were followed by in-depth interviews. Using information regarding people's actual activities from the diaries as well as opinions from the interviews, we will focus on the following issues regarding the panel's social practice of mobile phone use: (a) the changing levels and distributions of mobile communication; (b) the implications for other means of communication and spatial mobility; (c) the change of people's use of time for face-to-face contact and social interaction; and (d) the perception of, and means of coping with, increased flexibility and dependency associated with permanent access and instant reach.

In the next section we will briefly review current research in order to recognize central processes and implications associated so far with the increased use of mobiles among young people. Then, we further describe our empirical data and the panel, diaries, and interviews used to gather them. This is followed by the presentation and analysis of our findings regarding changing social practice, which leads us to our main conclusions.

Everyday Implications: Processes of Intensification, Complementarity, Flexibility, and Fragmentation

The mobile phone has the capacity to alter social patterns and community organization (Green, 2002; Janelle and Gillespie, 2004; Ling, 2004). Like other transportation and communication technologies, such as automobiles, fixed-line telephones, and the Internet, it has the potential to transform people's patterns of mobility, activity, and contact in time and space. History tells that the spread of the car, for example, prompted a general transformation of physical mobility from slower to faster interaction, an extension of people's daily activity space, a fragmentation of their time use, and ensuing urban sprawl (Couclelis, 2000; Schroeder, 2002; Vilhelmson, 2005, 2007). The spread of the ordinary fixed-line telephone largely reinforced these trends; it mainly became a complement, rather than a substitute, for physical travel and face-to-face meetings (Fischer, 1992; Lacohée and Anderson, 2001). Social practice transformed as telephone use intensified contacts with family and friends, and became a tool for planning and coordinating joint activities and appointments. Furthermore, spontaneous or unplanned visits became less common. The combined and long-term effects of these technologies were intensified interaction, a spatial extension of social networks, and more time spent communicating. These effects also had repercussions for the local community, though there is controversy over whether these technologies liberated local communities (Wellman, 1999) or eroded them (Putnam, 2000).

Even though the fixed-line telephone meant (and still means) a radical widening of people's access to others, personal use of it is constrained by time and space. Availability is fixed to certain locations, such as the home or the work place, and to times when the phone (or line) is not occupied by someone else. The mobile erases these constraints by making the phone a device entirely connected to the individual, rather than being a shared household utility. An individual and unique telephone number provides a connection to a personal network of instant and global reach (equivalent to the Internet), and the act of making contact becomes largely decoupled from the moorings of place and time. A basic question of both theoretical and practical concern, then, is that of the implications for everyday life. Here we recognize three areas of expected effects on everyday practice that can be found in the literature: (a) social impact, or changes in contact patterns and face-to-face interaction; (b) consequences regarding spatial mobility, that is, physical travel or virtual contacts made via the Internet; and (c) implications for individual planning, coordination, and use of time.

In the area of social impact, several studies show that the mobile intensifies and partly transforms the practice of social communication (e.g., Ling and Haddon, 2001; Smoreda and Thomas, 2001; Madell and Muncer, 2005). Among young people, the mobile is perceived and used as an always-open personal link to a largely local network of friends. Through this personal network, young people easily make contact from almost any place, at almost any time, and for nearly any reason. It stimulates additional contact, yet this contact is more impulsive, short, fragmented, and dispersed in time and space; it is contact that would otherwise not have occurred. Text messaging adds another dimension to this: it enables young people to keep each other informed and to comment and express their feelings when other means of communication are inconvenient, for example, late at night or in class at school (Ling, 2004). Some studies also show that frequent use of the mobile is associated with more frequent face-to-face interaction (Ling and Haddon, 2001). So far, an increased and high level of mobile use appears to have led to an intensification of social contact and an increase in the time spent on social communication. In other cases, however, the mobile has simply replaced the conventional telephone.

The second set of implications concerns the physical mobility of people; that is, how travel behaviors and patterns have been affected. Kopomaa (2000) described the mobile as a nomadic artifact and a "moving force" behind more mobile lifestyles. He predicted that the increased use of mobile communication and wireless applications would produce more travel, and that young people would begin to spend more time in urban public ("third") spaces, such as restaurants, bars, and cafés, instead of at home. The mobile thus reduces the time-space constraints of everyday life, and promotes more out-of-home activities and travel—one does not have to stay at home waiting for the telephone to ring or for a friend to drop by. This is reminiscent of the continuing debate over whether or not the virtual mobility provided by computers and the Internet will replace, complement, or even generate physical mobility and transportation in various contexts (see Thulin and Vilhelmson, 2006). Some argue that mobile technologies will transform the intrinsic meaning and experience of physical travel (Lyons and Urry, 2005; Mokhtarian, 2005). Instead of being an activity mainly arising from the need to carry out (stationary) activities at other places, travel will also become, with the rise of various mobile and wireless communications, a more pleasant end in itself. Travel time will metamorphose from rather useless "waiting time" into creative time, used for virtual communication with other people or for sheer entertainment (watching TV, films, listening to music or the radio, etc.), in which the mobile may play a central role (Okabe and Ito, 2005). All in all, this strongly predicts that the mobile phone will complement, and not replace, physical travel, face-to-face contact, and socializing in real life.

The increased use of mobiles creates a third category of implications concerning people's everyday scheduling, coordination, and actual use of time for social activities and interaction. A far-reaching change—observed and commented on by several researchers—appears to have occurred here (see Cooper, et al., 2002; Ling, 2004; Ling and Haddon, 2001; Townsend, 2000). Before the mobile became common, the clock was the main instrument for scheduling and coordinating everyday activities. The mobile now makes it possible to constantly negotiate and renegotiate agreements for meetings and joint activities in real time as circumstances change. Plans for the day become more flexible and schedules become less fixed in time and space, allowing for more spontaneous or impulsive decision making—at least among young people (Ling and Haddon, 2001; Ling and Yttri, 2002). For example, an appointment may be initiated by a person arriving at a meeting place, such as a café or restaurant, and calling to see if any friends happen to be around. The mobile thus promotes a flexible lifestyle of instant exchange and constant updates. The space, time, and content thresholds for communicative action are thus reduced. A more impulsive practice of decision making evolves, and people become more careless about timekeeping. Any discussion of increased flexibility and instant access also encompasses notions of the negative impacts of mobile use at the individual level: the increased fragmentation of everyday activities in time and space (Couclelis, 2000; Sullivan and Gershuny, 2001) and the increased tempo, time pressures, and demands of instant access among young people (Green, 2002). Non-communicative periods of the day become shorter, split up by incoming phone calls and a stream of text messages and emails that must be managed and answered (Ling, 2004). Travel time and other periods of downtime are used for virtual communication, allowing more activities to be combined and compressed, resulting in a seemingly more "efficient" way of using time in daily life (Haddon, 2004).

The discussion thus far has discerned certain interrelated tendencies fueled by the widespread use of mobile phones—processes of intensification, complementarity, flexibility, and fragmentation of contacts in time and space. These seem vital for any thorough understanding of how ICTs affect everyday practices and lifestyles in contemporary society and lend urgency to the further empirical exploration of the changing use of mobiles.

Research Approach for Exploring Communication Patterns

To achieve our aim of investigating how young people's everyday patterns of social communication and contacts are affected by the increased use of mobile phones, we concentrate on four interrelated research questions. The first concerns the changing levels and differences between groups (e.g., gender) in the use of mobile communication. The second concerns whether people's use of time for face-to-face contact and social interaction is intensified as mobile use increases. The third relates to complementarity, namely, what mobile use implies for other means of communication (e.g., the Internet) spatial mobility (transportation) and the use of place (e.g., in-home vs. out-of-home activities). A fourth question deals with young people's changing perceptions of, and means of coping with, an increased flexibility and fragmentation of everyday activities associated with the permanent access and instant reach offered by mobiles.

As these questions are dynamic in character, we draw on longitudinal information. We make use of data from a three-wave panel study of 43 high-school students living in Göteborg, a medium-sized city of about 500,000 inhabitants (750,000 in the extended urban region) located in western Sweden. Students from one specific high school were recruited in order to obtain a reasonably homogeneous panel across socio-economic status (middle class), life course stage, and geographic location (living in the central or semi-central parts of the city). Students from both a natural science and a social science class were selected and there were an even number of males and females. No other attempts were made to control the selection (e.g., in terms of ICT access or mobile use).

Personal time-use diaries and in-depth interviews were used to capture individual changes and habit-formation processes in relation to the use of computers, mobile phones, and physical transportation. Data collection first occurred in the autumn of 2000 when the respondents were eighteen years old, was repeated two years later, in the autumn of 2002, and then completed with a final wave, in the autumn of 2005. During this period, the research subjects not only became older and more used to mobile phones, but also entered a new stage in the course of their lives: finishing school, leaving home, entering working life or higher education, etc. Such shifts are likely to cause changes in time use (e.g., the amount of free time available) that are difficult to distinguish from age-related ones—something that is important to bear in mind when interpreting the findings of this study. The attrition was six people between the first and the second waves and nine people between the second and third, with the final panel consisting of twenty-eight research subjects (fifteen women and thirteen men).

In order to deal with the first three empirical questions introduced above, data were collected using time-use diaries covering one ordinary week. A small notebook with five generic questions in the form of headings was handed out (Figure 6.1). The respondents were instructed in how to carry and regularly update their notebook/diary during the week. Emails and phone calls were used to remind the respondents to maintain these diaries. The diary reports included detailed information about real and virtual contacts: contact modes, purposes, locations, and duration. Reliable time-use estimates for mobile use could not be obtained, although the frequency and timing of contacts were included.

Our fourth research question aimed to capture the respondents' changing perceptions and attitudes towards the mobile phone. In order to achieve this, the diary study was followed by in-depth interviews conducted by one of the authors. The interview was partly structured by the content of each respondent's diary depicting actual mobile use. Questions were asked regarding how routines were established and the perceived role of mobile phone use in everyday life. A particular theme was the extent to which interviewees felt that their flexibility and freedom had been enhanced or if, conversely, they felt that they had become more dependent on or constrained by their mobiles. In this chapter, we use the interviews to analyze how the respondents manage the mobile phone's ability to provide individuals with instant access to other people and activities almost anywhere and anytime.

Outcomes of the Study

The Use of the Mobile Phone Increased and Became Less Gender Dependent

Data aggregated from the one-week time use and contact diaries of our panel captured the daily patterns of social communication during a

Figure 6.1
An example of the study's diary

Time?	What am I doing?	Where am I?	With whom?	Am I using ICT/media?
11:20	waking up	at home	alone	no
11:30	taking a shower	at home	alone	no
11:50	eating breakfast	at home	alone	newspaper
12:20	studying	at home	alone	no
13:00	calling a friend	at home	alone	home telephone
13:10	studying	at home	alone	no
14:00	getting textmessage	at home	alone	mobile
14:01	continue studying	at home	alone	no
16:00	chatting with friend	at home	alone	Internet
17:00	eating lunch	at home	family	no
18:00	walking to the bus	walking to the bus	alone	no
18:05	sending textmessage	on the bus	alone	mobile
18:06	on the bus	on the bus	alone	no
18:15	visiting a friend	at Anders house	Anders	no
18:30	watching TV	at Anders house	Anders	TV

Figure 6.2
Daily mobile phone use in the panel of urban young people, Göteborg Sweden,
autumn 2000, 2002, and 2005

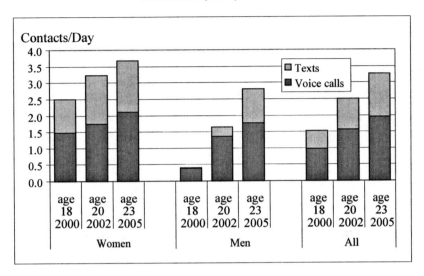

period when information and communication technologies spread rapidly in the Swedish population. The use of the mobile increased considerably over the five years of the study (Figure 6.2). The average contact frequency doubled, from 1.5 to more than 3 contacts per day.[1] Overall, the young women used their mobiles much more frequently than did the young men, especially for sending text messages, although these differences declined over the study period and as the respondents grew older.[2] It should also be noted that the observed levels of, and changes in, mobile phone use frequencies correspond with estimates based on national data (Bolin, 2006).

New/Recent Applications are Not Commonly Used

Although the use of voice calls and text messages has become more popular over the years, the use of more recent applications remains very low. In the third wave of the study, there were only a few instances of respondents browsing the Internet and sending emails or MMS messages, despite the fact that many of them now had access to technically more advanced mobiles. When asked about these and other upcoming applications, most interviewees displayed rather shallow interest.

Increased Use of Mobile Phones is Not Associated with a Decline in Time Spent on Other Means of Communication

Mobile phone use affects the respondents' daily use of time and place. The time diaries revealed that an increased and more intensive use of mobiles went hand in hand with an increase in time spent on other forms of virtual contact—internet, email, and IM/chatting—and with no reduction in travel time (Table 6.1).

This suggests that contacts via mobile phone mainly complement "real" interaction, physical mobility, and computer-based communication. However, fixed-line telephones are an important exception, as they are increasingly replaced by mobiles. This is probably due to a reduction in mobile operational costs during the final years of the study (2002-2005), which made the mobile competitive even for longer phone calls. We further observed that a considerable amount of mobile communication (about 40 percent of all calls and 50 percent of all SMS messages) was done from the home, which demonstrates that young people increasingly employ the mobile as a central node of communication, not only when "on the move" or when the fixed-line telephone is out of reach (Thulin and Vilhelmson, 2007).

The Mobile Phone is Integrated Into a Process of Intensified Everyday Contact and Social Interaction

Interpersonal virtual contacts have in general been intensified, and more time was spent on various forms of social interaction during the study period (see Table 6.1). The panel study covers a period of great change in the respondents' lives, when many of them entered a new life course stage—finishing school, leaving home, entering working life or higher education. Such changes certainly affected the need and (available) time for daily social interaction, with increases in leisure time or the expansion of social networks. It is difficult to distinguish the changes arising from mobile use from those arising from such life-course changes, which highlights the importance of not isolating or exaggerating the role of new technology and of keeping in mind that other factors could also explain changes in social behavior.

High Levels of Access to Mobiles Phones do Not Always Equal High Levels of Use

That daily patterns of social communication are shaped by other factors than simply technological ones becomes apparent when groups of

Table 6.1

Time spent on various forms of social communication and contact in the panel of young people, Göteborg, Sweden, autumn 2000, 2002, and 2005 ($n = 28$)

	2000 (age 18)	2002 (age 20)	2005 (age 23)	2005- 2000[a]
Contact frequency (contacts/day)				
Mobile phone	1.6	2.6	3.4	0.002
Fixed line phone	1.9	2.0	0.8	0.000
Contacts—time use (minutes/day)				
Fixed line phone	24	24	13	0.013
Internet use	36	35	70	0.004
IM/chat	7	8	31	0.001
E-mail	2	6	14	0.053
Travel	98	92	97	0.665
Places—time use (minutes/day)				
In home	421	382	385	0.305
Out of home	492	516	536	0.223
At work	39	174	132	0.029
At school	200	56	104	0.001
At "third places"	252	285	299	0.158
"Third places" socialising	174	192	199	0.374
"Free" time activities (minutes/day)	584	649	659	0.009

[a] Difference presented in p-values; Wilcoxon signed ranks test

Figure 6.3

Daily frequency of mobile phone use in the panel of young people, Sweden, autumn 2000, 2002, and 2005

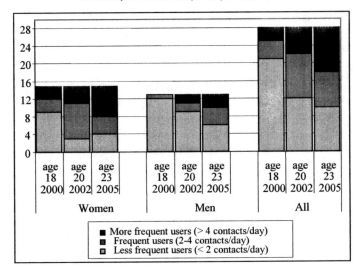

users are compared. The diaries indicate large individual variation in daily mobile phone use, and, from an empirical point of view, only a rather small group really fits the common stereotype of young people on the move "constantly" using their mobiles. Only one-third of the group used their mobiles for more than four contacts per day, including both text messages and voice calls (Figure 6.3). The marked individual variation in use persisted throughout the period, though at higher overall levels.

Frequent Use of the Mobile Phones is Associated with More Time Spent Socializing Face-to-Face, More Time Traveling, and Less Time Using the Internet

Differences in the use of mobiles are mirrored in other means of social communication; people who used their mobiles more frequently also spent more time on face-to-face interaction and travel (Table 6.2). This reveals the underlying detail of the complementary relationship noted above: for those who spend more time outside the house and use the mobile most, the mobile seems to reinforce total social contact, communication, and interaction outside the home. At the same time, these more frequent users spent less time using the Internet, which is predominantly a home-based means of communication (Vilhelmson and Thulin, 2008). The opposite relationship appears to hold for less frequent users of the mobile: they spent comparatively less time traveling and interacting with other people face-to-face, and more time making use of Internet-based communication at home, particularly to email or chat with friends. Our interviews reveal that more frequent Internet users often left various channels for instant messaging open when the computer was being used for other purposes, on or off line—an aspect often difficult to capture by time use diary method.

Though it may appear that the mobile phone and the Internet are competing technologies, and can be used as substitutes for each other, their use seems to attract different segments of the youth population. Rather than being determined solely by access to technology, actual choices between the two technologies depend on individual characteristics (e.g., personality, values, and attitudes) and on changes in the respondents' social lives and use of time and place. This is emphasized by the dynamics of mobile use, by the fact that eleven of the respondents decreased while seventeen increased their mobile use between 2002 and 2005.

Increased Use of the Mobile Phone is Associated with Increased Social Interaction

A distinction between "increasers" and "decreasers" was used to tentatively trace certain changes in time spent on communication and out-of-home social interaction. The longitudinal analysis (see Table 6.3) separates those who, between the ages of twenty and twenty-three, increased their mobile phone use and those who reduced it. It is observed that the increasers also increased their time traveling and also spent more time outside the home, especially at "third" places, socializing face-to-face. Arguably, the opposite relationship holds for respondents who, during the period, decreased their mobile phone use. Although the statistical significance is weak, it is indicated that they began to spend more time at home online and less time on trips. Longitudinal analysis thus indicates that increased mobile phone use is associated with increased out-of-home social interaction. These dynamic observations chiefly agree with the results of the cross-sectional comparison made above, indicating that more frequent mobile phone users spend more time socializing than other groups do (an equivalence that by no means follows automatically).

Mobile Phone Use Enables Flexibility and Freedom of Action

In the interviews, each research subject was asked to reflect on how mobile use had affected his or her everyday life. In general, their opinions confirm previous research findings concerning: (a) an intensified social interaction and rise of immediate and permanent access; (b) reduced thresholds and frictions for communicative action as to message content, as well as when and where communication takes place; (c) the evolution of more impulsive and flexible ways of coordinating social activity; and (d) a greater ease of meeting others spontaneously in daily life. These brief conclusions are largely based on interviews from the second wave of the panel study.[3] They are associated with predominantly positive attitudes towards the mobile and its repercussions for individual flexibility and freedom of action. Results of the third wave of the panel study somewhat modify this picture.

Immediate and Permanent Access, Social Pressures, Constraints, and Dependence

Interviews from the third wave (2005) indicate interesting changes concerning the panel's attitudes towards mobile phone use and coping

Table 6.2
Mobile phone use and time spent on various forms of social communication and contact in the panel of urban young people, Göteborg, Sweden (autumn 2005)

	Most frequent users[a]	Frequent users[b]	Less frequent users[c]	Difference (Most frequent-Less frequent)[d]
Contact frequency (contacts/day)				
Mobile phone	6,3	3,0	0,9	0.000
Fixed line phone	0,9	0,9	0,6	0.101
Contacts— time use (minutes/day)				
Fixed line phone	13	15	11	0.165
Internet	51	63	95	0.035
IM/chat	22	26	44	0.395
E-mail	6	6	27	0.011
Travel	118	94	77	0.026
Places— time use (minutes/day)				
In home	326	344	476	0.023
Out of home	622	566	425	0.008
Out of home socialising at "third places"	254	205	139	0.035

[a] 4+ contacts a day; n = 10
[b] 2-4 contacts a day; n = 8
[c] 0-2 contacts a day; n = 10
[d] differences reported using p values, Mann-Whitney U test

Table 6.3
Changes in mobile phone use and time spent on other forms of social communication in the panel of urban young people, Göteborg, Sweden, autumn 2002 and 2005

	Increasers[a]	p-value	Decreasers[b]	p-value[c]
Contact frequency (contacts/day)				
Mobile phone	3.9	0.012	-2.3	0.012
Fixed line phone	-2.3	0.028	-0.9	0.068
Contacts - time use (min/day)				
Fixed line phone	-31	0.011	2	0.779
Internet	26	0.314	40	0.028
Travel	28	0.051	-18	0.161
Places—time use (min/day)				
In home	-41	0.441	66	0.161
Out of home	77	0.260	-34	0.674
Out of home at "third" places	114	0.038	-55	0.263

[a] Increasers = increased mobile phone contacts > 2 contacts per day (n = 9)
[b] Decreasers = decreased mobile phone contacts > 0.5 contacts per day (n = 8)
[c] p-values from Wilcoxon Signed Ranks test

with issues of immediate and permanent access. In the first wave (2000), the strategies for managing access were diverse. Some people carried their mobiles everywhere and never turned them off, thus, they were reachable day and night. Others tried to balance their use, carrying their mobiles intermittently, intentionally, and only when really needed and leaving them at home or switching them off at other times. A few did not even have a mobile phone of their own. The more "balanced" users were more often men than women. Five years later, in 2005, this variety of use and users had significantly shifted towards a uniform strategy of personal "access management." Now, everyone brings the mobile along wherever she or he goes, ostensibly reachable all the time. Hence, initial differences in contact frequencies and access management between the young men and women of the panel became less apparent over time. The latter is well illustrated by the opinions expressed by one of our research subjects in 2000 and 2005, respectively:

> I don't like the mobile phone. It is disturbing when people talk. There are only a lot of crap phone calls. It is one of the most unnecessary things in the world. As a social tool I don't think that it is needed. (Subject 17, 2000)

> It is more of a necessity. Nowadays everyone has to have a mobile, society demands it. At first I didn't like it, but now I do. It is a part of the regular survival kit, you always have it on you. It's like having clothes on to carry your mobile. It's the same thing, like taking your keys with you. (Subject 17, 2005)

Hand in hand, over the same period, a perceived and expressed dependency on the mobile became more intense. At the age of eighteen, some respondents thought that they could do rather well without the mobile (four of them did not even have one at the time). Five years later this had changed, as illustrated by these contrasting statements from one of the interviewees:

> I would manage [not having a mobile] pretty well. It is nice to have it sometimes, but you would do pretty well without it, I believe. The mobile is good, but it is no necessity. (Subject 15, 2000)

> Well, [without a mobile] then you feel great anxiety. Then it feels like you are missing out on some important phone call, so you feel very dependent, you definitely do. (Subject 15, 2005)

This intensified notion of mobile phone dependence is probably associated with changes in the ways young people plan and coordinate their social lives and activities. As fixed time schedules, set plans for the day, and time-keeping no longer serve as primary instruments for coordinating social activity, the instant access offered by the mobile is becoming increasingly difficult to turn down. These changes also affect those who did not want or thought they did not need a mobile when first surveyed in 2000.

So, although rather large individual variations in the actual use of mobiles for voice calls and SMS messaging were evident as the panel members aged, their attitudes towards how to manage access became more uniform, and a general awareness of mobile dependence evolved. Immediate and permanent access is not only an obvious advantage, as it eases the time and spatial constraints of everyday social activity and contact; for those young people, it is increasingly also becoming a hard-to-refuse necessity.

The perceived advantages of the mobile phone, such as increased flexibility and freedom of action, are still much more evident than its perceived disadvantages, such as the decreasing ability to spend time and attention to ongoing, more valuable activities due to a possibly stressful and annoying increased flow of calls and text messages. However, over the years, tensions and pressures regarding the mobile have become more frequently expressed, and the experience of interruptions and disturbances is now emphasized by many:

> Sometimes it feels like you are doing many things at the same time. Someone calls you and you get something on your mind while you are doing something else. And all the time you are thinking that perhaps I should call that person and I must take care of all these things. (Subject 29, 2005)

> It is expected that you always can be reached, and it can actually get you pretty stressed out sometimes . . . you always get interrupted, if you are spending time with someone or if you just want to be by yourself. (Subject 34, 2005)

Other emerging changes in attitudes towards the need for instant and permanent access have also been observed. In some cases, these echo thoughts concerning how to cope with the mobile in a more controlled manner, by temporally screening some of the incoming communication or simply turning off the mobile. For example, some respondents shared:

> I have been thinking that it can be rather nice to "forget" to bring the mobile. You are a little bit too dependent on it today, everyone expects you to bring your mobile along all the time. (Subject 19, 2005)

> I have sometimes thought that it is nice to feel . . . like now on Christmas Eve, I turned off the sound and it was rather nice and I have tried to start thinking about turning it off. You feel more relaxed, and then you don't have to, I don't know, you don't need to be that accessible all the time. (Subject 34, 2005)

> And sometimes if you were not home, for example, in the laundry room, people say "But where have you been?" and then you think that this is crazy. Sometimes it would be nice to be able to cut yourself from all the telephones or just turn them off. Perhaps you wouldn't feel as much stress then. (Subject 29, 2005)

Yet, the respondents experience strong social expectations, saying that people around them do not accept it, but get frustrated or irritated if a person is not reachable. Some respondents describe coming up with white lies to explain why they did not answer the phone in situations in which they really simply did not want to talk, by saying that they had forgotten the mobile at home, there was poor coverage, or the batteries were low:

> Perhaps that what's most stressful about it, is that you have to come up with a good excuse when you are not reachable—so it is. (Subject 34, 2005)

Conclusion

Though the results of our intensive panel study must be treated cautiously in terms of generalizability, they hint at some likely processes concerning the use and implications of the mobile in society.

First, our results confirm general tendencies pointed out in previous research; namely, the intensification, complementarity, and flexibility of the mobile, which shows that the mobile transforms young people's daily social communication practices. Our panel data indicate that increased mobile use led to an overall intensification of social contact in these young people's lives. Mobile phone use (voice calls and text messages) increased significantly over the five-year period of the study and also became less gender dependent. Furthermore, the increased use of the mobile went hand in hand with respondents spending more time on other forms of virtual contact and interaction while not reducing face-to-face meetings and travel. The mobile, thus, generally served to complement existing means of social interaction. Additionally, interviews with the respondents (see also Thulin and Vilhelmson, 2007) confirmed that mobile phone usage tends to reduce the time, place, and content thresholds and frictions for communicative action, encourages more impulsive and flexible ways of coordinating social activity, and enables people to meet up spontaneously in everyday life.

Second and most notably, however, our results also stress the importance of not exaggerating the homogeneous transformative power of new information and communication technologies. Daily communication patterns are not determined solely by access to technology, but are highly dependent on individual characteristics (e.g., personality, personal need for communication) and structural demands on individuals' use of time and place. Thus, relationships are not uniform; patterns of divergence are apparent in our findings. Among the group of young people who spent more time outside the home and used their mobiles more frequently, the mobile seemed to generate additional out-of-home social interaction. Many of them stressed the role of the mobile in making it much easier to socialize and meet friends more often—reinforcing face-to-face meetings and enabling spontaneous meetings in daily life. At the same time, this group spent less time on Internet-based communication than did less frequent mobile users. The group of less frequent users stayed at home more, spent less time socializing face-to-face, but spent more time socializing on the Internet. These divergent tendencies were evident from a cross-sectional comparative perspective, to some extent also confirmed from a longitudinal one considering the changing time-use patterns of mobile use "increasers" and "decreasers."

Third, it is also important to note that a majority (two-thirds) of the panel were not considered to be "more frequent" mobile users and one-third actually reduced their use between the second and third wave of the study. Arguably, only a rather small group fit the common image, or stereotype, of young people constantly on the move and constantly in touch.

A final conclusion concerns the perceived implications of increased flexibility and fragmentation of people's use of time and space due to the mobile. Although there were large individual variations in actual levels of use over the five-year period of the study, strategies of personal "access management" became more uniform and the perceived dependency on the mobile more intense. There was a reduction in the number of people actively striving to restrain their mobile connection, for example, by carrying it only intermittently, or switching it off for periods of time. The life of instant access offered by the mobile thus became increasingly difficult to avoid as fixed time schedules, set daily plans, and the clock no longer served as primary instruments for coordinating social activity during leisure time. A large proportion of mobile communications were made from home, also suggesting that young people are increasingly employing the mobile as their prime personal node of communication, even in locations where a fixed-line telephone is readily available.

While experiencing increased dependency on the mobile, most of the young people in our panel expressed a genuinely positive attitude towards the mobile and its implications for flexibility and freedom of action in everyday life. However, results of the third wave of our investigation indicate a new tendency: a change in the balance between positive and negative attitudes among regular users. The experience of disturbance and interruption of ongoing activities, more fragmented time use, and pressures related to social expectations and the need to be instantly accessible are now emphasized by many. In some cases, this has led to consideration of how to cope with the mobile in a more balanced and controlled manner, as the initially freeing and flexible communication has raised a social dilemma when it is practiced by many.

Acknowledgments

The research presented here is part of the research project "Time for mobility" supported by the Swedish Agency for Innovation Research (Vinnova).

Notes

1. Increases in use between 2000 and 2005: *Total contacts by mobile*, $p < 0.01$; *voice calls*, $p < 0.05$; *text messages*, $p < 0.01$ (Wilcoxon Signed Ranks tests).
2. Differences between men and women for total contacts by mobile: $p < 0.001$ in 2000; $p < 0.05$ in 2002; *n.s.* in 2005. For voice calls: $p < 0.001$ in 2000; *n.s.* in 2002 and 2005. For text messages: $p < 0.001$ in 2000; $p < 0.01$ in 2002; *n.s.* in 2005 (Mann-Whitney U test).
3. These are reported in Thulin and Vilhelmson, 2007.

Bibliography

Adams, Paul C. *The Boundless Self: Communication in Physical and Virtual Spaces.* Syracuse, NY: Syracuse University Press, 2005.

Bakardjieva, Maria and Richard Smith. "The Internet in Everyday Life: Computer Networking from the Standpoint of the Domestic User." *New Media & Society*, 3 (March 2001): 67-83.

Bolin, Göran. "Makten över Tekniken eller Teknikens Makt?" In *Du Stora Nya Värld: Trettiofyra Kapitel om Politik, Medier och Samhälle,* edited by Sören Holmberg and Lennart Weibull, 403-411. Göteborg, Sweden: SOM-institutet, 2006.

Castells, Manuel. *The Internet Galaxy: Reflections on the Internet, Business, and Society.* New York, NY: Oxford University Press, 2001.

Cooper, Geoff. Nicola Green, Ged M. Murtagh, and Richard Harper. "Mobile Society? Technology, Distance, and Presence." In *Virtual society? Technology, Cyberbole, Reality,* edited by Steve Woolgar, 286-301. Oxford, UK: Oxford University Press. 2002.

Couclelis, Helen. "From Sustainable Transportation to Sustainable Accessibility: Can We Avoid a New *Tragedy of the Commons*?" In *Information, Place, and Cyberspace: Issues in Accessibility,* edited by Donald G. Janelle and David C. Hodge, 341-356. Berlin, Germany: Springer-Verlag, 2000.

Fischer, Claude S. *America Calling: A Social History of the Telephone to 1940.* Berkeley, CA: University of California Press, 1992.

Graham, Stephen. "The End of Geography or the Explosion of Place? Conceptualizing Space, Place and Information Technology." In *Information*

Tectonics: Space, Place and Technology in an Electronic Age, edited by Mark I. Wilson and Kenneth E. Corey, 7-28. Chichester: John Wiley & Sons, 2000.

Green, Nicola. "On the Move: Technology, Mobility, and the Mediation of Social Time and Space." *The Information Society,* 18.4 (2002): 281-292.

Haddon, Leslie. *Information and Communication Technology in Everyday Life: A Concise Introduction and Research Guide.* Oxford, UK: Berg, 2004

Haythornthwaite, Caroline and Barry Wellman. "The Internet in Everyday Life: An Introduction." In *The Internet in Everyday Life,* edited by Barry Wellman and Caroline Haythornthwaite, 3-41. Malden, MA: Blackwell, 2002.

Inglehart, Ronald. *Modernization and Postmodernization: Cultural, Economic, and Political Change in 43 Societies.* Princeton, NJ: Princeton University Press, 1997.

Inglehart, Ronald and Christian Welzel. *Modernization, Cultural Change and Democracy: The Human Development Sequence.* New York, NY: Cambridge University Press, 2005.

Janelle, Donald G. and Andrew Gillespie. "Space-Time Constructs for Linking Information and Communication Technologies with Issues in Sustainable Transportation." *Transport Reviews,* 24 (6, 2004): 665-667.

Kopomaa, Timo. *The City in Your Pocket: Birth of the Mobile Information Society.* Helskinki: Gaudeamus, 2000.

Lacohée, Hazel and Ben. Anderson. "Interacting with the Telephone." *International Journal of Human-Computer Studies,* 54 (May 2001): 665-699.

Lie, Merete and Knute H. Sörensen, eds. *Making Technology Our Own?: Doesticating Technology into Everyday Life.* Oslo, Norway: Scandinavian University Press,1996.

Ling, Richard S. *The Mobile Connection: The Cell Phone's Impact on Society.* San Francisco, CA: Morgan Kaufmann, 2004.

Ling, Richard S. and Leslie Haddon. "Mobile Telephony, Mobility and the Coordination of Everyday Life." In *Machines That Become Us: The Social Context of Personal Communication Technology,* edited by James E. Katz, 245-266. New Brunswick, NJ: Transaction Publishers, 2003.

Ling, Richard S. and Birgitte Yttri. "Hyper-Coordination via Mobile Phones in Norway." In *Perpetual Contact: Mobile Communication, Private Talk, Public Performance,* edited by James E. Katz and Mark Aakhus, 139-169. Cambridge, UK: Cambridge University Press, 2002.

Lyons, Glenn and John Urry. "Travel Time Use in the Information Age." *Transportation Research Part A: Policy and Practice,* 39(February-March 2005): 257-276.

Madell, Dominic and Steven Muncer. "Are Internet and Mobile Phone Cmmunication Complementary Activities Amongst Young People? A Study from a 'Rational Actor' Perspective." *Information, Communication & Society,* 8 (March 2005): 64-80.

Mokhtarian, Patricia L. "Travel as a Desired End, Not Just a Means." *Transportation Research Part A: Policy and Practice,* 39 (February-March 2005): 93-96.

Okabe, Daisuke and Mizuko Ito. "Keitai and Public Transportation." In *Personal, Portable, Pedestrian: Mobile Phones in Japanese Life*, edited by Mizuko Ito, Daisuke Okabe, and Misa Matsuda, 205-218. Cambridge, MA: MIT Press, 2005.

Oksman, Virpi and Jussi Turtiainen. "Mobile Communication as a Social Stage: Meanings of Mobile Cmmunication in Everyday Life among Teenagers in Finland." *New Media & Society,* 6 (June 2004): 319-339.

Putnam, Robert D. *Bowling Alone: The Collapse and Revival of American Community.* New York, NY: Simon & Schuster, 2000.

Robinson, John P. and Geoffrey Godbey. *Time for Life: The Surprising Ways Americans Use Their Time.* University Park, PA: Pennsylvania State University Press, 1997.

Schroeder, Ralph. "The Consumption of Technology in Everyday Life: Car, Telephone, Television in Sweden and America in a Comparative-historical Perspective." *Sociological Research Online,* 7 (4, 2002): http://www.socresonline.org.uk/7/4/schroeder.html (29 August 2006).

Sheller, Mimi and John Urry. "The New Mobilities Paradigm." *Environment and Planning A,* 38.2 (2006): 207-226.

Smoreda, Zbigniew and Frank Thomas. "Social Networks and Residential ICT Adoption and Use." Paper delivered at the EURESCOM Summit: 3G Technologies and Applications. 12-15 November 2001, Heidelberg, Germany.

Sullivan, Oriel and Jonathan Gershuny. "Cross-national Changes in Time-use: Some Sociological (Hi)stories Re-examined." *The British Journal of Sociology,* 52 (June 2001): 331-347.

Thulin, Eva. "The Virtual Mobility of Young People: The Use of Computers, the Internet and Mobile Phones from a Geographical Perspective." Ph.D. dissertation, University of Göteborg, Sweden, 2004.

Thulin, Eva and Bertil Vilhelmson. "Virtual Mobility of Urban Youth: ICT-based Communication in Sweden." *Tijdschrift voor Economische en Sociale Geografie [Journal of Economic & Social Geography],* 96 (December 2005): 477-487.

Thulin, Eva and Bertil Vilhelmson. "Virtual Mobility and Processes of Displacement: Young People's Changing Use of ICT, Time, and Place." *NETCOM—Networks and Communication Studies,* 20 (2006): 27-39.

Thulin, Eva and Bertil Vilhelmson. "Mobiles Everywhere: Youth, the Mobile Phone, and Changes in Everyday Practice." *Young: Nordic Journal of Youth Research,* 15 (August 2007): 235-233.

Townsend, Anthony M. "Life in the Real-time City: Mobile Telephones and Urban Metabolism." *Journal of Urban Technology,* 7 (August 2000): 85-104.

Valentine, Gill and Sarah L. Holloway. "Cyberkids? Exploring Children's Identities and Social Networks in On-line and Off-line Worlds." *Annals of the Association of American Geographers,* 92 (June 2002): 302-319.

Wellman, Barry. "The Network Community: An Introduction." In *Networks in the Global Village: Life in Contemporary Communities,* 1-48. Boulder, CO: Westview Press, 1999.

Vilhelmson, Bertil. "Urbanisation and Everyday Mobility: Long-term Changes of Travel in Urban Areas of Sweden." *Cybergeo: Revue Europeénne de Geographie*, 302 (February 2005): http://www.cybergeo.eu/index3536. html#texte (accessed August 29, 2006).

Vilhelmson, Bertil. "The Use of the Car: Mobility Dependencies of Urban Everyday Life." In *Threats from Car Traffic to the Quality of Urban Life: Problems, Causes, Solutions,* edited by Tommy Gärling and Linda Steg, 145-164. Amsterdam, Netherlands: Elsevier Science, 2007.

Vilhelmson, Bertil and Eva Thulin. "ICT, Proximity, and the Place of the Home: A Time-use Perspective." *Tijdschrift voor Economische en Sociale Geografie [Journal of Economic & Social Geography],* (forthcoming December 2008).

7

Trust, Friendship, and Expertise: The Use of Email, Mobile Dialogues, and SMS to Develop and Sustain Social Relations in a Distributed Work Group

Tom Erik Julsrud
Norwegian University of Science and Technology

John Willy Bakke
Telenor Research and Innovation

A central issue in writings about modern and flexible organizations is how new information and communication technologies (ICT) affect organizations and intra-organizational communication. Related to the rapid increase of mobile communication technologies, concepts like "mobile workplaces" and "virtual teams" have been common among organizational developers and within organizational research (Castells, 1996; Kristoffersen and Ljungberg, 2000; Lipnack and Stamps, 2000; Urry, 2000; Quan-Haase and Wellman, 2006; Castells, et al., 2006). Workplaces are becoming less place-bound and increasingly dependent on collaboration across distance assisted by mobile communication tools as well as computer based collaboration tools.

On a very general level, it is acknowledged that information and communication technologies alter the geography of communication, where relations easily can be established between individuals who are situated in different locations. ICTs connect different locations, and their use implies that the boundaries of the respective locations become (re)negotiated: "Instead then, of thinking of places as areas with boundaries around, they can be imagined as articulated moments in networks of social relations and understandings" (Massey, 1994: 154).

Collaboration can take place through multiple mediated channels despite geographical distance. Such virtual and distributed groups provide opportunities for knowledge building based on expertise located at multiple sites; to the extent that these different participants represent different perspectives, knowledge types, or cultures, it allows for knowledge sharing and innovations in more heterogeneous environments (Hollingshead, et al., 2002; Cummings, 2004). Portable and individual technologies may ensure instant interaction and feedback ensuring high efficiency and closeness to customer and clients (Julsrud, 2005). The challenge, however, is to make sure that different groups and teams are working together without leading to organizational "balkanization," where groups interact densely without sufficient intermediate contact, or where the internal relations within the group erode altogether.

Mobile communication tools and services are important devices that can help share information and knowledge within distributed groups. Yet, mobile technologies are rarely introduced as the only available means for communication. In virtually all cases, the mobile device is part of a larger menu of available technologies, such as face-to-face interaction, emails, and others. Nevertheless, studies in this area tend to look for particular qualities of single technologies that determine their use in organizations.[1] We will go beyond this single-technology bias and explore how new mobile technologies find their form within a particular social context and within an existing environment of communication tools. Rather than focusing solely on individual technologies and their technical properties, we will look at the way three important media technologies worked in concert within a particular group of physically distributed mobile knowledge workers: two mobile services, telephone conversations and mobile text messages (SMS), and PC-based email messages.

Within the study, we adopt a social network perspective to explore how these communication tools were used to establish, support, or sustain various types of social and spatial relations. This perspective draws attention away from the technical qualities, towards an understanding of how the communication technology is used in the process of supporting a network of different social relations (Contractor and Eisenberg, 1990; Wellman, et al., 1996; Wellman, 2001; Licoppe and Smoreda, 2005). One of the benefits of this approach is that it exposes the multiplexity[2] of relations within a group, and recent studies have used this approach to capture the larger ecology of media used to support collaboration in distributed groups (Haythornthwaite and Wellman, 1998; Haythornthwaite, 2001).

The social network approach to media and ICT use has received increased attention during the last decade, and research on how new media affects social relations is starting to accumulate (Haythornthwaite and Wellman, 1998; Bryant, et al., 2006; Ishii, 2006; Yuan and Gay, 2006). Yet, there are few empirical studies investigating the role that mobile technologies play in supporting relations among professional users.[3] A central objective of this study is to contribute towards filling this gap in the literature and investigating how mobile technologies are applied in a group of professional knowledge workers collaborating across geographical distance. We will, in this chapter, look at various social relations within a distributed group of knowledge workers and analyze how these relations are related to the daily use of SMS, emails, and mobile phones. As such, we will both explore the geographical distance involved in distributed work, the psychological distance between the distant workers, and their mediated interaction patterns. This chapter is also anchored in the tradition called "domestication of technologies," where it is acknowledged that technologies do not determine their use; technologies are malleable, and there is a degree of adaptation and interpretation needed to make technologies "one's own" and to incorporate them into work practices after they have been acquired (Silverstone and Haddon, 1996).

We start the chapter by describing how a distributed work group can be studied as a social network, constituted by a range of formal and informal social relations. Following this approach a group of distributed workers can be described as inter-connected by a multitude of social relations. These relations constitute a structural social space that will often be of importance to the well-being of the individuals as well as the efficiency of the group. Next, we will propose a rough analytical framework drawing a distinction between subjectively perceived relations and interaction-based relations in groups. It is suggested that observed interactions in organizations can be seen as manifestations of perceived relations where trust and expertise are central dimensions but that these relations might operate in different ways. We will then go on to present findings from a case study of a group of distributed workers within a computer company, exploring how the relations were supported by SMS, emails, and mobile phone dialogues.

Distributed Work Groups as Networks of Relations

The Social Network Approach

Distributed groups and teams have been at the center of attention for researchers for several years, involving scholars from work sociology, organization studies, communication studies, and computer-supported collaborative work (CSCW). Studies in this area address the ways individuals work together despite geographical dispersions, and how they are making use of various communication technologies to support their collaboration (Lipnack and Stamps, 2000; Hinds and Kiesler, 2002; Duarte and Snyder, 2004).

The social network approach offers a novel way to understand such groups and how ICTs are adopted and used (Garton, Haythornwhaite, et al., 1997). Compared to approaches studying groups through characteristic traits of individuals, a social network approach focuses on the various relations within the group and the way technologies at hand are applied to support or sustain those relations. Instead of developing an aggregated index of workplace communication based, for example, on usage of emails and mobile phone dialogues, a network approach will try to survey the particular relations and structures that are supported by these tools and the different roles individuals display in such networks. Similarly, where traditional perspectives tend to categorize and analyze distributed groups by aggregated scores for trust, identification, and efficiency, the network approach would try to look for the relational structures that transmit trustfulness, identification, or efficient information flows. Thereby, the network approach shows greater sensibility for the internal working of the group.

Within the rapidly evolving field of network analysis, a number of concepts and techniques have been developed to capture important features and structures of networks and nodes within such networks. This includes network centrality, density, tie-strength, core/periphery structures, cohesive sub units, role analysis, and much more (Wasserman and Faust, 1994; Scott, 2000; Brehm and Gates, 2004; Breiger, 2004). For researchers interested in studying distributed work groups, social network methodologies offer important analytical tools. Yet, the network approach is more than just a way of analyzing the data; in a wider context, it is a theoretical perspective that draws attention to the relations and structures of relations in a group, not solely on characteristics at the level of the individual or the group (Wellman, 1988; Wasserman and Faust, 1994; Scott, 2000; Kilduff and Tsai, 2003).

During the last two decades social network studies of distributed work groups have developed along different paths. One path has been the study of the efficiency of information flow-structures in groups. These studies have focused on a limited number of relations over a large sample of cases in order to find significant differences between high and low performing groups, and they have concluded that groups that perform well tend to have a more hierarchical information structure (Ahuja and Carley, 1999; Cummings and Cross, 2003; Hinds and McGrath, 2006). [4] A second path has focused more on the detailed patterns of interaction within distributed groups and teams and the way ICT supports different ties and tasks. These studies have been analyzing individual cases in depth, usually also using more elaborated qualitative analyses. A central finding here has been that collaborators with stronger ties—such as friends and close colleagues—are communicating more frequently than those with weaker ties, and they also tend to use more media channels to support the ties (Koku and Wellman, 2004; Haythornthwaite, 2005). Analyses of students working in virtual teams have also shown that different media were used for supporting weak and strong ties (Haythorthwhaite, 2005).

This chapter will follow up on the latter path of research, focusing on the various network structures constituted by selected communication media. However, rather than using the traditional distinction between strong and weak ties, we will make a distinction between *perceived* and *interaction-based* ties. In line with cognitive oriented network theories (Krackhardt, 1987; Corman and Scott, 1994), we argue that relations based on trust and expertise may be seen as a different type of relations, compared to interaction-based ties.

Perceived and Interaction-Based Relations

The distinction between strong and weak ties has been much applied in social network analysis, and the distinction has been path breaking for much of the innovative theoretical and empirical work coming out of the field in the last decades (Granovetter, 1973; Granovetter, 1983; Wellman and Wortley, 1990; Burt, 2005). Yet, researchers have for a long period noted that the terms are often difficult to apply in empirical organizational network studies (Wenger, 1991; Krackhardt, 1999; Nardi, et al., 2000). First, because the definition of strong ties is at the same time very broad and very specific, it points to characteristics such as time spent together, emotional intensity, intimacy, and reciprocity (Granovetter, 1973). This seems to point directly at ties within, such as nuclear families, and groups of close friends. Yet, for practical inquiries, these key words are difficult to operationalize, and divergent strategies have been applied to estimate the strength of the ties between individuals. Second, in organizations many relations seem to fall somewhere in between strong and weak ties. In particular, intra-organizational ties tend to be stronger than "weak ties," yet weaker than "strong ties" (Wenger, 1991; Nardi, et al., 2000). And thirdly, although the terms are well known for network scholars, they are not widely applied in general organization studies or within the fields of CSCW and media studies. General terms like trustfulness, identification, or friendship are more commonly used to describe work-relations (Gersick, et al., 2000). Thus, the strong/weak tie dichotomy appears as an association-rich metaphor that may be difficult to use in detailed analyses of relations in organizations.[5]

Instead of relying on this dichotomy, we will apply the more generic terms *trust, friendship,* and *expertise.* Thereby, it is possible to circumvent some of the difficulties embedded in using the dichotomy based on tie-strength. Still, a central question remains about how relations like trust, friendship, and expertise should be seen in relation to interaction. Are friendship and trust results of frequent interaction or is it the other way around? Researchers working in the field tend to give divergent answers to these questions. For instance, some researchers emphasize that interaction is important to build trust (Shapiro, et al., 1992); others argue that a high degree of interaction should be seen as an indicator of *distrust*, because it may reflect high levels of surveillance and control (Buskens, 1998).

To clarify these issues, we propose to establish an analytical distinction between interaction-based patterns (based on face-to-face or mediated interaction) and subjective relations based on subjective feelings towards other persons. This perspective finds support in cognitive network theories focusing on individuals' or groups' subjectively perceived relations in contrast to objective and interaction-based relations (Krackhardt, 1987; Corman and Scott, 1994). Corman and Scott have applied elements from Giddens' structuration theory to clarify the connections between observable communication networks and the latent networks of perceived relationships (Giddens, 1984). They argue that different modalities explain the recursive relationships between cognitive social structure and interaction. Much in line with Giddens they explain:

> We define a communication system as a set of continually reproduced communicative interactions between individuals and collectives situated in time and space. The network is an abstract structure of rules and resources of communicative actors in a given social collective, instantiated in communication systems, but having only a "virtual existence." (Corman and Scott, 1994: 174)

The social network is here described as a cognitive resource embedded within a particular social community or culture, where spatial and temporal aspects are included in the analysis. Further, Corman and Scott propose that the cognitive network structures are activated through taking part in common activities (foci) or enacted through various triggering events.

The advantage of this perspective is that it helps to establish a clear distinction between a (cognitive) network structure and a system of observable communicative actions. These structures are clearly related, but they are not isomorphic. Instead, we argue that studies of the ways these structures are interrelated constitute an interesting and fertile area for empirical studies. In the empirical analysis in this chapter, we will study interaction-based relations and subjective closeness as separate relational ties, not assuming in advance that they are related. The interesting question of how ICTs are used to support different relational structures (or not) can then be investigated in more detail, compared to studies primarily based on the strong tie/weak tie dichotomy.

Prescribed Relations

According to the cognitive approach to social networks, all social relations are basically abstract structures existing mainly as memories

Figure 7.1
Interaction and latent relations

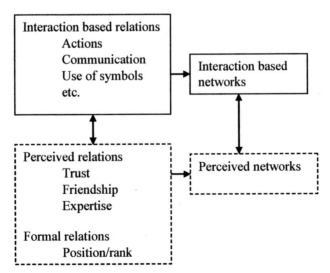

Note: Figure based on the work of Corman and Scott (1994).

or expectations in the minds of individuals. Yet, in organizations there is an important set of relations that is based on formal agreements and contracts, such as relations to subordinates. Informal relations in organizations and work places can be seen as imbedded within and partly constrained by a formal system involving a manager and sub-ordinates (Kadushin, 2005). Such formal relations in a distributed work group will usually be made explicit in job descriptions and in organizational charts. These relations are more formalized than trust, friendship, and expertise ties, even if they involve expectations that probably affect the interaction and communication patterns. For the purpose of this chapter, we label them "prescribed relations."

Trust, Friendship, and Expertise

In addition to interaction-based relations and formal or prescribed relations, we will in this chapter look at three different relational qualities—trust, friendship, and expertise. These are selected because they refer to important but different dimensions of working relationships; trust is an aspect of a social relations that can be seen as a "resource" that an individual has access to and may exploit in particular situations. In the last few years, trust has received increased recognition as a phenomenon worthy of closer examination in organizational studies, and several volumes provide reviews of theoretical positions and broad theoretical frameworks (Mayer, et al., 1995; McKnight, et al., 1998; Elsbach and Kramer, 1996; Tyler and Kramer, 1996; Rousseau, et al., 1998; Kramer and Cook, 2004). Trust may be defined as, "A willingness of a party to be vulnerable to actions of another party based on the expectations that the other will perform a particular action important to the trustor, irrespective of the ability to monitor or control that other party" (Mayer, et al., 1995: 2).

This definition emphasizes that trust is built on basically positive expectations regarding individuals' future behavior.[6] As a concept that is directly concerned with a relation between two individuals, it is a particularly relevant topic for a social network approach. From a social network point of view, trust is not primarily the property of an individual; rather, it is part of the relations between two or more individuals (McEvily, et al., 2003). Paying attention not only to dyadic ties but also to larger networks of indirect ties (i.e., between the egos' alters) may give an added value to the analysis of trust.

Friendship has mainly been studied in the context of individual personal social networks and among students (Wellman and Wortley,

1990; Haythornthwaite and Wellman, 1998; Wellman and Potter, 1999; McPherson, et al., 2001). In network terms, a friendship relation is usually described as reciprocal and durable (thereby incorporating temporal aspects) and it is closely related to trusting relations. Yet, in a work setting, close friends may have a relationship that is closer than regular workmates, indicating informal contact also in private settings.

Expertise refers to relations that are important for the conduct of everyday work tasks. This type of relations has been widely used to detect flows of information and knowledge in organizations and groups (Cross, et al., 2001; Cross and Prusak, 2002; Hollingshead, et al., 2002). However, we should note that it can also be seen as a more rational form of trustfulness, such as cognitive trust (Lewis and Weigert, 1985). To avoid confusion between the affective form of trust and the cognitive one, we will here stick to the term expertise. Although these qualities obviously also may be developed and maintained over distance—aided by ICTs—they are primarily explored in co-located settings.

NOMO and Omega[7]: Methods

The results presented here are based on a study of several work groups in a Nordic company, here called NOMO. NOMO is a Norwegian ICT provider with a fairly strong position in the Nordic markets. Approximately one year prior to our study, the company acquired and merged with a smaller Danish company to get an even stronger position in the Scandinavian market. This process was experienced as stressful for the employees in both companies. A major objective for the company after the acquisition was to integrate its operations across the national markets to create market synergies. This led to the setting up of a number of permanent work groups encompassing employees in different locations in Norway and Denmark. Since different functions now had to be coordinated across distances and national boundaries, distributed work was initiated and formalized in several different areas. The analysis in this chapter will focus on one such group, *Omega*. The core task of the Omega group was to manage and develop products for a particular segment of NOMO's customers. The group consisted of sixteen product managers; twelve in Norway and four in Denmark, with the manager located at the headquarters in Norway.[8] Virtually all respondents had previous employment within the respective organizations, and most of them made deliberate efforts to maintain relations with previous colleagues.

The work was divided between two main workplaces; one at the NOMO headquarters in Norway and one at the Danish department. At both sites, the employees had a mobile work style, where open offices were used in combination with portable PCs and mobile phones as their primary work phone. The company deployed a hot-desking strategy without fixed workplaces, ensuring a certain degree of internal physical mobility. Two of the Norwegian employees and one of the Danes were located outside the national hubs, making the group even more dispersed. Much of the work in the group also required traveling outside the city area, so the physical mobility was generally high. The work form implied that some of the employees had relatively frequent face-to-face interaction, while others met only when the group had their meetings.

The frequency of their meetings fluctuated in accordance with tasks and happenings in the organization. Yet, based on the estimates of the group members, we found that telephone conferences and regular (face-to-face) meetings were usually arranged bi-monthly (see Table 7.1). Videoconferences and PC-based conferences were, however, used relatively little in this group.

When our investigation started the group had worked together for twelve months. According to the interviews, the group had been involved in several critical discussions related to the consolidation of the former national product development groups. Now, most of the employees expressed that the group now moved in a positive direction where they were working together as a unified group.

General Methodological Design

The investigations followed the group from spring 2004 to the end of 2006. When we first got in contact with members of Omega, they had operated as a distributed work group for about fifteen months. The design of the study was based on a triangulation of different methodological

Table 7.1
Frequency of group-based communication in Omega,
based on averages of individual estimates (mean values)

	Estimated frequency (n = 15)	Mean std error
Telephone conferences	Bi-monthly	.291
Video conferences	Less than monthly	.215
PC-conferences	Less than monthly	.215
Physical meetings	Bi-monthly	.284

strategies, including qualitative interviews with individuals as well as quantitative studies of individual (ego-networks) and group-based social networks.[9]

The study started with an explorative qualitative study and was followed up with a quantitative study targeted at more specific issues evolving out of the explorative phase. Yet, in the initial phase, a general questionnaire was distributed to get baseline information about satisfaction, performance, and interaction patterns. In this chapter, we will mainly deploy the group-based network data and the data from the qualitative interviews.

The Qualitative Study

Before the main quantitative network study, semi-structured interviews were conducted with employees and managers to get a better picture of their work situation. The interviews followed an interview guide focusing on the respondents' main work tasks, social relations, identity in group/organization and trust issues, and lasted thirty to forty minutes. Fourteen of the sixteen employees in Omega were interviewed. Two of the employees in the group were not available for interviews due to shift in job assignments and sickness. In addition, we conducted interviews with individuals outside the group, including the leader's superior executive and other managers in the company. The rationale for this was to get a better understanding of the group's tasks and position in the company by including supplementary perspectives.

During the qualitative study intermediate reports and preliminary analyses were made. The interviews were coded as text files (using QSR NUD*IST software) and the main issues and topics from the interviews were classified. We used this coding as input for the subsequent social network module and for integrated analyses.

The Social Network Module

In the social network part of the study, interactions were registered through a web-based questionnaire and coded in a case-by-case social network matrix. We asked the persons to indicate interaction-based relations as well as perceived relations. A traditional "roster" design was used to the network study, where each group member received a list of the other members in the group (Wasserman and Faust, 1994). The informants were then asked to report the frequency of interaction with other members in the group as well as the type of media used in the interaction and the three perceived ties.

A critical issue of self-reported designs is that they often have poor reliability, as people are often bad at remembering and reporting their actual behavior (Bernard, et al., 1982). Nevertheless, self-reported data have been found to be fairly reliable when it comes to the individual ranking of different activities, and to compare interaction across different media (Hartley, et al., 1977). Thus, we treat them as indicative of the interaction within the group. The response to the survey was good, and after two reminders, all the employees in the groups save one had completed their questionnaire. The data were coded and analyzed through standard social network software (UCINET 6 and NetMinerII 2.5).

We used a single question to map the trust-based relationships: "If you decided to search for another job similar to the one you have today, but in another company; whom on the list would you most likely talk to about this?" The idea behind this formulation is that this type of discussion would imply trustfulness, as disclosure of such plans would be negative for the reputation of the individual in question.[10] Indirect questions are the most usual way to analyze trust-based relations in organizations. It should be noted, however, that such questions involve a risk for neglecting individuals that have a more introverted nature or simply prefer not to talk to anybody about such plans (even if they have trustful ties within the group).

The expertise relations were based on a question asking to whom the informant preferred speaking when facing problems in his/her work. Starting with the list of group members, we asked them to indicate whom on the list they would most likely turn to if they needed advice in their daily work. This expertise network does not address the affective aspect (like the trust ties), but the network with the most central professionals in the group.

The friendship relations were derived from our question whether there was someone on the list they considered as close friends in their group. Thus, we asked respondents specifically for close friends, not regular work mates.

Networks and Positions in Omega

In this section, we will present findings from the study, emphasizing results from the network analysis. We will start with a presentation of the formal structure of the group and the network structures indicating perceived and interaction-based relations. Next, we will discuss differences in general structures between these networks and variations in individuals' centrality within these networks.

Formal Structure

The formal structure of the group is presented in Figure 7.2. Torhild is the manager of the group. She started in this position just after the research project started, yet she is experienced and, in general, highly respected by the employees. One of her first decisions was to divide the group into three smaller sub-units, and she appointed Martin, Kari, and Knut as leaders of these units. In addition, she pointed out two other persons to be responsible for individual areas of product development in NOMO—Kai and Emil. It is worth noting that the four employees from the Danish unit (indicated by squares) were directed to different sub-units, and one was also appointed a sub-unit manager.

Yet, as noted above, the members did not work only within their units; much interaction and work took place in projects involving employees from groups other than Omega. This activity is however not included in the results displayed here.

Figure 7.2
Omega's formal structure

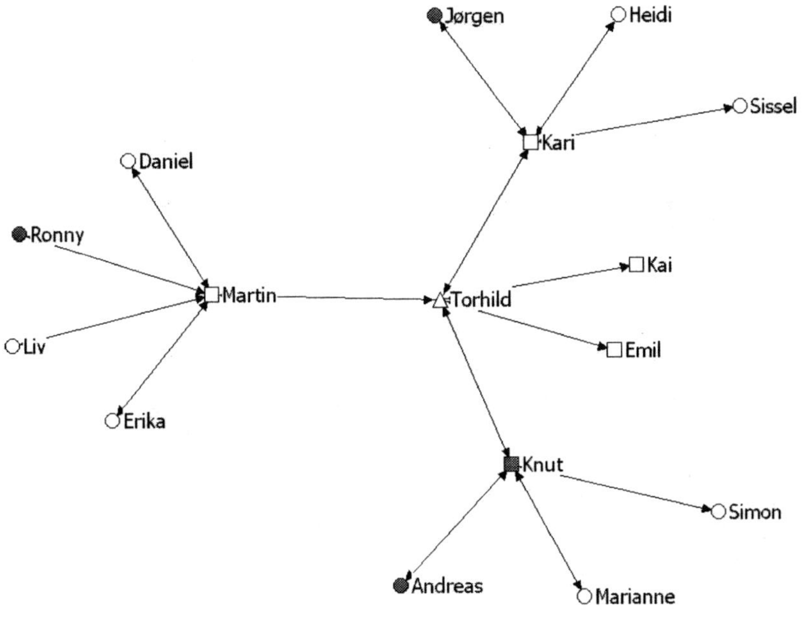

Note: Danish employees are represented in grey and Norwegian employees in white (triangles are managers, squares are sub-unit managers, and circles are employees).

Description of Relations and Networks in Omega

As it turns out, the Omega group was handling the long-distance collaboration relatively well when measured along traditional network indicators for integration and coherence. For example, when looking at interaction via email and mobile voice, none of the members were isolated from the others. All employees in the group were in contact with at least one other person during a regular week. In addition, the dialogues connected the employees through a network that crossed the geographical boundaries of the sub-units. It is easy to see, however, that email interaction followed rather closely the formal interaction lines, in particular for the group managed by Martin. It is also evident that much interaction seems to go through Martin, Kai, and Emil. The manager, Torhild, was fairly central in the information flow. The mediated relations suggested that much of the information circulated between the sub-unit managers Martin, Kari, Knut, as well as Emil (Figures 7.3 and 7.4). It is also evident that most of the Danish employees were well integrated

Figure 7.3
The email interaction network for Omega in seven days

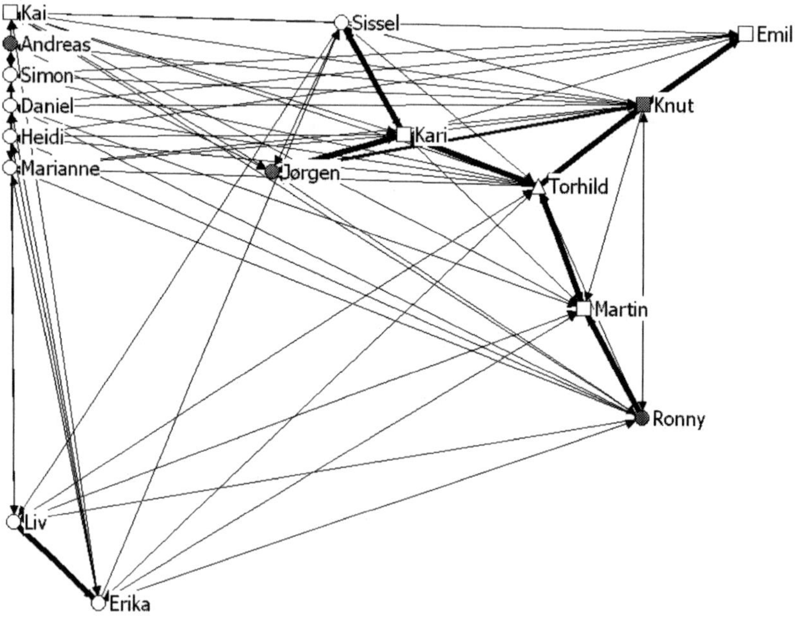

Note: Danish employees are represented in grey and Norwegian employees in white (triangles are managers, squares are sub-unit managers, and circles are employees). Tie strength indicates intensity of interaction (1 = 1-4, 2 = 5-10, and 3 = 11-20 messages).

Figure 7.4
The mobile dialogue network for Omega in seven days

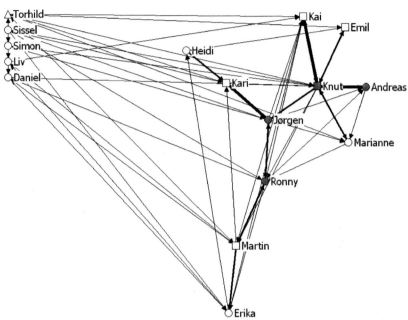

Note: Danish employees are represented in grey and Norwegian employees in white (triangles are managers, squares are sub-unit managers, and circles are employees). Tie strength indicates intensity of interaction (1 = 1-4, 2 = 5-10, or 3 = 11-20 dialogues).

in the group, despite their geographical distance from the majority of employees in Omega.

Table 7.2 gives precise details for the networks based on interactions and on the perceived relations. Among the interaction-based relations, the email network was the most active, followed by mobile phone dialogues and SMS. The email networks were denser and they also had higher reciprocity—indicating that they were not simply used to distribute information, but for two-way interaction. The lower level of reciprocity for SMS may suggest that this was a less formal channel, but also that the traffic here is less intense and task-related than in the email network. The average degree score is a ratio of the number of incoming and outgoing ties for a network of relations (Freeman, 1979). An average degree score reaching above six for email relations indicates that the average member had been in email contact with approximately six other persons in the group during the last week. The corresponding numbers for mobile and SMS were 4.1 and 2.6. The score for emails was, interestingly, also higher than the face-to-face interaction, illustrating how email connected far more people in the group than physical interaction. The core/periphery score indicates how well the registered values approximate to an ideal core/periphery structure (Borgatti and Everett, 2000). This value was relatively high for the face-to-face networks because there is a clear co-located core situated at the Norwegian headquarters, and that face-to-face follows close to this structure. This structure is softened in the mediated networks. However, while there was a relatively clear core/periphery structure reflected in the mobile network, this was less spelled out in the SMS network.

For distributed work groups it is of particular interest to see the extent to which the relations cross physical distance.[11] To compare the number of ties within and across the two involved countries, we applied the E-I Index, as developed by Krackhardt and Stern (1988). This indicator compares the external ties with the internal ties for groups within a network, ranging from -1 to 1. Given a partition of a network into a number of mutually exclusive groups, the E-I Index is the number of ties external to the groups minus the number of ties that are internal to the group divided by the total number of ties. Maximum collaboration across the boundaries is then 1 (all links are external), while equally divided links will give an index equal to zero. We categorized the employees in Denmark as "external" and the Norwegian group as "internal." None of the interaction-based relations were equally divided, but email messages were the form of interaction that was most boundary crossing (considering the national boundaries) in this group. Interestingly, SMS was more frequently used within each of the national sub-units, with mobile phone dialogues in a position in between. This shows that—at least within this

Table 7.2
Relations investigated in Omega

Interaction-based relations	Face-to-face meetings
	Mobile phone dialogues
	Email
	SMS
	Overall daily interaction
Prescribed relations	Formal work relations
Perceived relations	Trust
	Friendship
	Expertise

organization—the geography-bridging qualities of ICTs are selectively deployed; some are primarily used across larger distances, others are more commonly used within local regions. It is also interesting to observe that these technologies are important *within* co-located settings: while it is common to address the capacity of ICTs for bridging space and time, they are also used for communication with neighboring colleagues. This may be seen as an extension and generalization of norms and technical skills for communication with distant parties, or as an indication of conscious choices for media behavior, acknowledging that even in a co-located setting, face-to-face communication is not always the preferred form.

Turning to the perceived relations of trust, friendship, and expertise, these were less cohesive in Omega than the interaction-based relations: only ten friendship links (relations) and thirteen trust links were reported. The expertise network, however, was about the same density level as for mobile communication (0.28). Reciprocity is often related to trust in organizations, as trust is often seen as stronger when relations are symmetrical (Kilduff and Tsai, 2003). Interestingly, the trust relations have low levels of reciprocity, indicating that this is not a strongly interconnected network, but more open and "fluid." This indicates the "cognitive" nature of trust, since the existence of a trust tie is not always perceived equally by two individuals in a network. As displayed in Figure 7.5, the trust network actually formed a chain-like structure, with a more cohesive constellation in the Norwegian group. The trust network was also strongly embedded in the national units within the group, indicated by the high negative E/I index, while the expertise relations had a much more boundary-crossing nature.

Network Similarities

Comparing networks through general indicators gives important information regarding the general use of interaction media and the general level of trust, friendship, and expertise relations. Yet, to explore the similarities between the latent networks and the four different interaction networks further, we conducted a QAP-correlation.[12] This procedure is often used to see to what extent there are similarities between two social networks containing the same actors (Hanneman and Riddle, 2005).

As indicated in Table 7.3 the expertise network, as well as the formal network, were closely related in all the media channels.[13] In particular, the relation between expertise, email, and mobile was strong (r = 0.52 and 0.44, respectively). The mediated networks of mobile phones, SMS, and email were all highly correlated—in particular, email and mobile dialogues (r = 0.56) (all significant on a 0.01 level). This indicates that the media in Omega, to a large extent, followed the task related patterns of interaction and that the media followed highly similar patterns, in particular in the case of mobile dialogues and SMS.

The trust network, however, had no significant relation to the formal network, the face-to-face network, or the mobile communication network. It was, however, significantly but weakly related to the expertise network, the email network, and the SMS network. Trust relations were most strongly correlated to friendship relations (r = 0.28) but not at all

Table 7.3
Selected network characteristics of interaction-based and perceived relations

	Relation	Scale	Links	Density	Average degree	Reciprocity	Core-Periphery	E/I Index
Interaction-based relations	Interaction	Daily (weekly)	45	0.188 (0.546)	2.812	0.356	0.519	-0.301
	Mobile	1-4 / 5-10 / 11- 20 / >21	66	0.275	4.125	0.515	0.518	-0.208
	Email	1-4 / 5-10 / 11- 20 / >21	106	0.442	6.625	0.736	0.485	-0.083
	SMS	1-4 / 5-10 / 11- 20 / >21	43	0.179	2.688	0.512	0.370	-0.5
	Face-to face	Daily (weekly)	64	0.267 (0.733)	4	0.688	0.829	-0.375
Perceived relations	Trust	Yes/No	13	0.054	0.812	0.308	0.433	-0.818
	Friendship	Yes/No	10	0.042	0.625	0.4	0.466	-0.5
	Expertise	Yes/No	66	0.275	4.125	0.515	0.377	-0.250

with the formal relations (r = 0.07). This indicates, on the one hand, that the perceived expertise relationship was most closely related to the observable interaction that took place in Omega. This pattern also followed fairly close to the formal structure of the organization. On the other hand, the less intensive trust network diverged from the formal structure and was less similar to the mediated networks based on mobile dialogues. Yet, it had high similarity to the friendship network and also to the expertise network.

This might suggest that trust relations are more strongly supported by text-based media like SMS and email, while the more intensive work-related communication uses all media and, in particular, email and mobile dialogue. As such, it indicates that the instant problem-solving relations have other needs for communication than the more less-frequent trust and friendship ties. It is clear, however, that these relations do not operate as isolated structures, but have significant overlaps.

It should also be noted that physical closeness (i.e., face-to-face interaction) was positively correlated to the use of all media and, in particular, the SMS network; this indicates that mediated interaction is more intense among co-located workers.

Network Positions in Trust, Friendship, and Expertise Networks

As argued earlier in this chapter, relations of trust, friendship, and expertise are based on a subjective perception of others. Within an organization or a group, however, this information might be used to indicate those that more often are the object of the others' "positive expectations." The indegree centrality score is a much used indicator for measuring popularity or prestige in complete networks based on mental concepts

Table 7.4
QAP correlations for different networks (Jaccard coefficients)

	Formal	Expertise	Mobile	Email	SMS	Trust	Face-to-face
Expertise	0.316**						
Mobile	0.389**	0.435**					
Email	0.296**	0.522**	0.564**				
SMS	0.375**	0.38**	0.514**	0.393**			
Trust	0.068	0.113*	0.053	0.092*	0.12*		
Face-to-face	0.207*	0.236*	0.236*	0.295*	0.227**	0.054	
Friendship	0.1	0.086*	0.086*	0.074*	0.128**	0.278**	0.05

Note: * p < 0.05 ** p < 0.01

such as trust and friendship (Freeman, 1979; Knoke and Kuklinksi, 1982). As indicated in Table 7.4, the expertise network was strongly related to the formal structure of the group, and much of the mediated interaction followed this pattern. Trust and friendship, on the other hand, were more weakly related to the expertise network as well as to the formal structure. This suggests that the informal networks of trust and friendship were different from the formal networks although they had similarities with the advice network. An interesting question is to what extent the same people are central in the expertise network and in the trust network. As could be seen directly from the mediated interaction network above, the manager and the sub-unit managers were highly central in the interaction networks. Only some of these were, however, included in the trust network. Comparing indegree centrality, the number of incoming connections indicates that one of the "independent" sub-unit managers (Kai) is the most attractive node in the interaction network. He was the one who received most emails and mobile phone calls, and also (together with Kari) the one who had most face-to-face interaction with the others. He is also the one with the highest indegree centrality in the expertise network. Figure 7.5 illustrates the strong connection between being central in advice networks and being central in the mediated networks.

Kai is, however, not included in the trust network. In this network Martin, Marianne, Emil, and Torhild are the only ones with "indegrees" higher than two. Most central was Martin, who also had a trust-relation

Figure 7.5
Normalized indegree centrality scores for position in media network
(mean value for indegree of email, mobile phone talks, and SMS) expertise, trust, and friendship networks

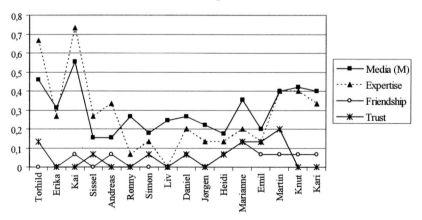

across the national boundaries. As such, he is the only person who acted like a "trust-broker" in this distributed network (Julsrud and Bakke, 2007). Thus, it seems like there are different roles and relations involved in the group, but that it is the expertise-role that most strongly generates interaction through the available media.

Supporting Relations by Email, Mobile Dialogue, and SMS

By exploring the social relations and networks embedded within a group of distributed workers in a computer company, we have seen how a set of available communication technologies was used in slightly different manners to support and sustain both work tasks and informal social relations in a group of professionals. The results from the network study suggest, first, that the trust relations in this group followed a different pattern than the work related and intensive expertise network. Individuals that were central in the expertise network were not always central in the trust network. Second, the mediated interaction networks were in general strongly related to the expertise relations, although the trust relations had a structure that related to the SMS and the email networks. Thus, this might indicate that the trust network evokes another type of "narrowband" (text-based) interaction.

In this chapter we elaborate these issues further, based on evidence from the qualitative part of the study. In particular, we will present some tentative explanations for why the trust network tended to follow other structures than the professional network, and why mobile talk and email relations seemed to be more closely related to the professional and expertise based ties.

Origins of Trust and Expertise Networks

The trust network in Omega was less dense and more locally embedded than the professional expertise network. The interviews with the members with trusting ties revealed that these relations in several instances had roots in older projects and collaborating groups. For instance, Daniel and Erika, one dyad in Omega connected by trusting ties (Figure 7.6), had both worked together in NOMO for a long time. They were both located at the same building at the Norwegian headquarters. Daniel explains that their relationship has origins from "the old NOMO company":

> At that time we were only four to five persons in this group. There were activities where family members joined, and the group was actually real close. It is not like that nowadays [with the current group]; . . . we still eat lunch together with the old group. (Daniel)

Daniel and Erika and others from the trust dyads identified in Omega, had a record of work-related collaboration that ran several years back in time. Such relationships outside their current project organization were, however, hardly visible in organizational charts or in surveys of interaction in the present organization. Another source for developing trusting ties was found in the relationship between Marianne and Heidi. These two co-located employees belonged to different sub-groups in Omega but had a strong trustful relation as well as a friendship tie. The reason appeared to be that they shared a workspace in a satellite office that was at a significant distance from the others. Their shared destiny as co-located distant workers, and their time spent together, was important for the development of solidarity and stronger ties.

A third interesting trust tie in the network was found between Martin and Ronny. In this case, the relationship actually crossed the national boundaries and the significant distance between their regular workplaces. Martin was highly trusted by Ronny, who had known him for only about 1.5 years. This was also seen as a friendship relation by one of the parties.

Figure 7.6
The trust network in Omega

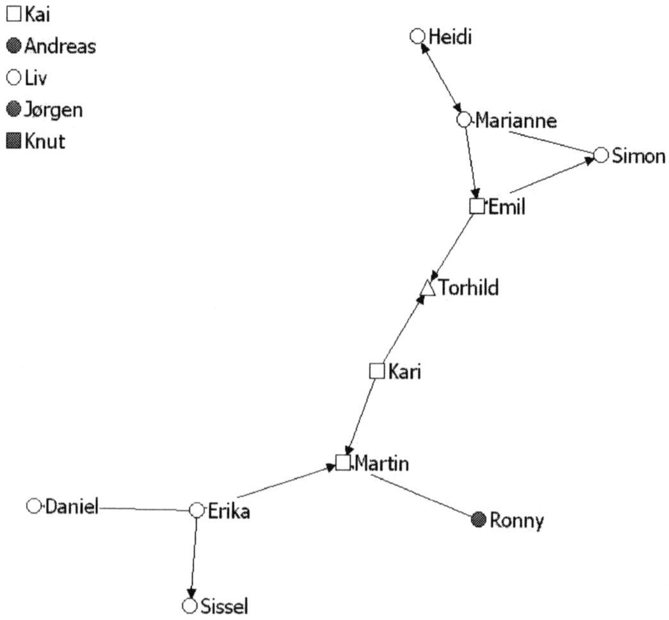

Note: Danish employees are represented in grey and Norwegian employees in white (triangles are managers, squares are sub-unit managers, and circles are employees).

In the interviews, Ronny emphasized Martin's high level of knowledge and that they shared many of the same goals and ideas for future developments. Ronny expressed that the development of a strong relation with Martin was something of a turning point for him:

> The fact that Martin now has joined the group with his high level of competence really makes me believe in this. He actually is the first Norwegian I can say that I really trust. (Ronny)

For Martin, frequent visits to Denmark together with frequent communication via electronic media appeared to be part of a deliberate effort within the group to create a better climate for collaboration. It is worth noting, however, that Ronny emphasized Martin's competence and abilities as the main reasons for trusting him. Martin's and Ronny's trusting ties are thus perhaps an example of how a relation based on rational trust and collaboration over time may transform to a stronger knowledge-based trust (Lewicki and Bunker, 1996).

These trust dyads illustrate that trust relations might have roots in collaboration and activities that took part several years previous to the study. The activities that had generated the trusting relations were in some cases participation in several former projects. Thus, they often had a longer history and duration than the patterns of the expertise network.

Media Choice, Risk, and Relations

Much of the daily interaction in the group was, as indicated above, related to formal tasks and had a professional character. For work-related tasks, email was the most obvious choice for the members of Omega in their daily routine. All formal information about meetings, change of work assignments, and relevant information about the company, was distributed by email. Written email messages also allowed for a level of precision that was essential when describing technical components, specifications, and so on. In most cases, the informants did not make sharp distinctions between email and voice mobile interaction. Both were actively used in various combinations, i.e., following up emails with mobile phone calls, but also the other way round. Kai, one of the most active users of ICT, explained that he used to combine email and mobile to get a rich understanding of how the distant colleagues were managing their tasks:

> Often I call the other colleagues in my groups just to hear how things are going. I want them to feel that there is interest for what they are doing. When you do not sit next to them and see their faces, I need to call them up and hear how things are go-

ing. You must "read between the lines" to know how they're actually doing in their work; . . . Email can be misinterpreted and read in the worst meaning. That's why I prefer telephone; it is easier to make adjustments and make sure that a meaning is correctly understood. To me, that is an important tool in a virtual organization like ours. (Kai)

This citation draws attention to the risk of misunderstanding email messages when the group members do not know each other well. Kai argued that mobile dialogues were important because they allowed for immediate correction of potential misinterpretations. In this newly merged group, there might have been a particular need for this since they were speaking different languages and were working with complex technical issues. Yet, Kai had particular advantages here since he spoke both languages fluently. He used this capability to translate and negotiate when there were misunderstandings due to language barriers—thus he can be seen as a "trust broker" between the sub-groups (for the concept of trust brokerage, see Julsrud and Bakke, 2007). The others in the group, however, found the mobile more difficult to use across the national boundaries because sometimes they found it difficult to understand the other language. This was mentioned as a problem not only for phone dialogues, but also for audio-conferences. All in all, the language differences seemed to spur the use of email rather than mobile dialogues and this was probably one reason why, in this organization, email had a more boundary-crossing usage in Omega than mobile phone dialogues (as noted previously).

The central advantage of the mobile phone dialogue was the immediacy involved. Employees in Omega stressed that they often needed to get instant feedback and clarification on issues and that mobile phones were particularly well suited for this:

When it is necessary with fast decisions I prefer to use a mobile phone. It doesn't matter if people are located in Denmark or elsewhere. (Dan)

This indicates that the combination of dialogues and email represented a powerful combination that operated in a complementary way to support the expertise based relations.

The trusting ties seemed, however, to be particularly strongly related to the use of SMS and, to a somewhat lesser degree, email. One reason for this might be, as discussed above, is that these relations often were based on former collaboration. Thus, there was not the immediate need for interacting to solve problems or immediate difficulties. The trust network was more of a "latent" network structure that was inactive in much of the daily work in the group. Another reason could be that the strong trust relations did not need the immediacy that mobile dialogues offered. It has been recognized that trusting relations may not need the same kind of immediacy as low-trust relations (McEvily, et al., 2004). Periods of silence or absence of replies could be tolerated in the case of trusting ties, but more easily perceived as hostile in relations with low trust (Licoppe and Smoreda, 2005). As such, media with high level of immediacy might be preferred where trustfulness is low—either as a deliberate choice or unconscious preference.

Thus, it might be that services like SMS were seen as little suited in relations where there are lower levels of trust. Several of the informants told us that their SMS messages were primarily used to contact friends and family, and usually not for professional acquaintances. However, this also suggested that SMS in this group of workers had another symbolic meaning for the users than email (Trevino, et al., 1987). Sending SMS messages rather than an email messages symbolized and manifested a relation that was less formal and more private.

The Technical Support of Trust, Friendship, and Expertise

In this chapter we have argued that the perceived relational structures of trust, friendship, and expertise are supported in different ways by available technologies in their communication environment. In the distributed group of product developers that was analyzed in this chapter, we found that the expertise network was mostly supported by email messages and mobile phone dialogues. The networks based on trust and friendship relations were particularly supported by SMS and email. The qualitative study suggested that, compared to the expertise network, the trust network operated on a "lower frequency" where the relations were of a longer duration, but had less frequent interaction. We also found that the email network was more boundary crossing, connecting employees from both countries, while the SMS network was more used among employees meeting face-to-face. This study adds to a growing body of research applying network analysis in investigations of media use in organizations, groups, and teams. The study also demonstrates the fruitfulness of studying technologies within a communication environment, as the study shows that technologies are important for establishing and maintaining relations within a group, and that technologies are deployed as available elements from a menu, not as singular technologies. Thereby, the chapter contributes to the rich literature on domestication of technologies—with an emphasis of the multiplicity of technologies.

The chapter also shows that the geography-bridging qualities of ICTs are selectively deployed; some are primarily used across larger distances, others are more commonly used within local regions. It is also interesting to note that these technologies are frequently used *within* co-located settings, indicating that face-to-face communication is not always the preferred form.

In accordance with some earlier studies we found that the use of mobile media, and in particular SMS, was more frequent among those who met face-to-face in their work (Ishii, 2006; Julsrud and Bakke, 2007). Thus, it seems like work tasks and social closeness are more important in spurring mediated interaction than geographical distance alone. Yet, this study also paints a slightly different picture than some earlier studies that have found that stronger relations tend to communicate more intensively and also use more numerous media (Haythornthwaite, 2002). One reason for this, we believe, is that our case involved a group of technical professionals working in permanent work groups—and although the group was newly established, the members had a history within the organization. In contrast, former studies of relations and media use in distributed environments have used empirical data from *ad hoc* teams of students collaborating in temporal, virtual teams (Haythornthwaite, 2001; Haythornthwaite, 2005) or in a community of scholars at a university (Koku and Wellman, 2004). In our group of professionals, the task-related ties were very much in focus, whereas the trust and friendship relations were less explicit. Also, this group was relatively recently established, connecting experts located in different geographical units due to a company merger. This might have made the friendship relations within the group less dense and more weakly supported by media, as compared to networks of students or university scholars. Another reason for the differences may be that we applied the term trust in addition to friendship, a term that is rarely studied in relation to mediated ties in organizations. We believe, however, that this actually unveils a relational dimension that is different from close friendship in organizations, but still important. In modern organizations it might be that it is more important—or more achievable—to have someone that you trust to discuss difficult personal matters with, than someone you consider as a close friend. Detecting these "low frequency" relations in organizational networks and how they are supported by communication media appears to be a task that is worth pursuing in future research.

Acknowledgments

The authors would like to thank the participant enterprise and the respondents—without their generous assistance and efforts, this project would not have been feasible. We would also like to thank the editors and reviewers for valuable comments and suggestions.

Notes

1. For critiques of single technology studies, see Postman, 1993; Meyrowitz, 1994; and Krotz, 2005.
2. Multiplexity is, in social network analysis, used to describe the number of relations that connects two nodes in a network. The more relations in a tie, the more multiplex it is (Garton, et al., 1997). The term "media multiplexity" is usually applied to describe the number of media that is used to support a social tie (Haythornthwaite, 2005).
3. For some notable exceptions, see the work of Erickson 1988, Ahuja and Carley 1999, Koku and Wellman 2004, Quan-Haase and Wellman 2006.
4. There are, however, also findings that suggest that denser and more interconnected groups perform better than highly centralized ones. Cummings and Cross (2003) studied 182 work groups in a large telecommunication firm and compared internal network structures with performance measures. Structures of hierarchy, degree of centrality, and managers' degree of structural holes were measured for each group and used as input in a subsequent regression analysis. In contrast to the earlier work of Ahuja and Carley (1999), this study found that hierarchal structures as well as a dominant core-periphery structures were negatively associated with performance measured by members and managers (Cummings and Cross, 2003).
5. To avoid the term "strong tie" Krackhardt has applied the term *Philos* to designate particular strong relations within organizations. Philos-relations are characterized by frequent interaction, strong affections, and a long history of interactions. (See Krackhardt, 1992).
6. This definition is much in line with later contributions where interpersonal trust is seen as a particular psychological mindset or attitude involving a deliberate willingness to be vulnerable (See Rousseau, et al., 1998).
7. Please note that the names of the organization and the groups, as well as the individuals' names, are all pseudonyms.
8. Danish and Norwegian were working languages within the groups. The languages are fairly similar, but there are certain differences that potentially can lead to misunderstandings.
9. The ego-network part of the study is documented elsewhere (See Julsrud and Bakke, forthcoming).
10. This strategy is similar to the one used by earlier network studies on trust in organizations (Krackhardt and Hanson, 1993; Krackhardt and Brass, 1994; Burt and Knez, 1996).
11. In the case of mobile work, this can of course be difficult, as these boundaries are often blurred. Yet, in this group there was one important difference between individuals situated in Denmark and those in Norway.
12. UCINETs QAP correlation procedure is based on permutation of rows and columns together of one of the input matrixes and then correlating the permuted matrix with the other matrix. This is repeated hundreds of times to build up a distribution of correlations under the null hypothesis of no relationships between the matrixes. A low p-value suggests a strong relationship unlikely to have occurred by chance.
13. Table 7.3 presents Jaccard coefficients since some relations (trust, friendship, face-to-face) are binary (Hanneman and Riddle, 2005).

Bibliography

Ahuja, Manju K. and Kathleen M. Carley. "Network Structure in Virtual Organizations." *Organization Science,* 10 (Nov-Dec 1999): 741-757.

Bernard, Russel H., Peter D. Killworth, and Lee Sailer. "Informant Accuracy in Social Network Data V: An Experimental Attempt to Predict Actual Communication from Recall Data." *Social Science Research*, 11 (March 1982): 30-66.

Borgatti, Stephen P. and M.G. Everett. "Models of Core/Periphery Structures." *Social Networks*, 21 (October 2000): 375-395.

Brehm, John and Scott Gates. "Supervisors as trust brokers in social-work bureaucracies." In *Trust and Distrust in Organizations: Dilemmas and Approaches*, edited by Roderick M. Kramer and Karen S. Cook, 41-64. New York, NY: Russell Sage, 2004.

Breiger, Ronald. "The Analysis of Social Networks." In *Handbook of Data Analysis*, edited by Melissa Hardy and Alan Bryman, 505-525. London, UK: Sage Publications, 2004.

Bryant, J. Alison, Ashley Sanders-Jackson, and Amber Smallwood. "IMing, Text Messaging, and Adolescent Social Networks." *Journal of Computer-Mediated Communication*, 11.2 (2006): 577-592.

Burt, Ronald S. *Brokerage and Closure: An Introduction to Social Capital.* Oxford, UK: Oxford University Press, 2005.

Burt, Ronald S. and Marc Knez. "Trust and Third-Party Gossip." In *Trust in Organizations: Frontiers of Theory and Research*, edited by Roderick M. Kramer and Tom R. Tyler, 68-89. Thousand Oaks, CA: Sage, 1996.

Buskens, Vincent. "The Social Structure of Trust." *Social Networks,* 20 (July 1998): 265-289.

Castells, Manuel. *The Rise of the Network Society.* Vol. 1 of *The Information Age: Economy, Society and Culture*. Malden, MA: Blackwell, 1996.

Castells, Manuel, Mireia Fernandéz-Ardévol, Jack L. Qiu, and Araba Sey. *Mobile Communication and Society: A Global Perspective.* Cambridge, MA: MIT Press, 2006.

Contractor, Noshir S. and Eric M. Eisenberg. "Communication Networks and New Media in Organizations." In *Organizations and Communication Technology*, edited by Janet Fulk and Charles W. Steinfield, 143-172. Newbury Park, CA: Sage, 1990.

Corman, Steven R. and Craig R. Scott. "Perceived Networks, Activity Coci, and Observable Communication in Social Collectives." *Communication Theory,* 4 (August 1994): 171-190.

Cross, Rob, Andrew Parker, Laurence Prusak, and Stephen P. Borgatti. "Knowing What We Know: Supporting Knowledge Creation and Sharing in Social Networks." *Organizational Dynamics,* 30 (Fall 2001): 100-120.

Cross, Rob and Laurence Prusak. "The People Who Make Organizations Go--or Stop." *Harvard Business Review,* 80 (June 2002): 104-112.

Cummings, Jonathon N. "Work Groups, Structural Diversity, and Knowledge Sharing in a Global Organization." *Management Science*, 50 (March 2004): 352-364.

Cummings, Jonathon N. and Rob Cross. "Structural Properties of Work Groups and their Consequences for Performance." *Social Networks*, 25 (July 2003): 197-210.

Duarte, Deborah L. and Nancy T. Snyder. *Mastering Virtual Teams: Strategies, Tools and Techniques that Succeed*. San Francisco, CA: Jossey-Bass, 2004.

Elsbach, Kimberly D. and Roderick M. Kramer. "Members' Responses to Organizational Identity Threats: Encountering and Countering the "Business Week" Rankings." *Administrative Science Quarterly*, 41 (September 1996): 442-476.

Erickson, Bonnie. "The Relational Basis of Attitudes." In *Social Structures: A Network Approach*, edited by Barry Wellman and Stephen D. Berkowitz, 99-121. New York, NY: Cambridge University Press, 1988.

Freeman, Linton C. "Centrality in Social Networks: Conceptual Clarification." *Social Networks*, 1 (1979) 215-239.

Garton, Linda, Caroline Haythornthwaite, and Barry Wellman. "Studying On-line Social Networks." *Journal of Computer-Mediated Communication*, 3 (June 1997).

Gersick, Connie J.G., Jean M. Bartunek, and Jane E. Dutton. "Learning From Academia: The Importance of Relationships in Professional Life." *The Academy of Management Journal*, 43 (December 2000): 1026-1044.

Giddens, Anthony. *The Constitution of Society: Outline of the Theory of Structuration*. Berkeley, CA: University of California Press, 1984.

Granovetter, Mark S. "The Strength of Weak Ties." *The American Journal of Sociology*, 78 (May 1973): 1360-1380.

Granovetter, Mark S. 1983. "The Strength of Weak Ties: A Network Theory Revisted." *Sociological Theory*, 1(1983): 201-233.

Hanneman, Robert A. and Mark Riddle. *Introduction to Social Network Methods*. Riverside, CA: University of California, Riverside, 2005. http://faculty.ucr.edu/~hanneman/nettext/.

Hartley, C., M. Brecht, P. Pagerly, G. Weeks, A. Chapanis and D. Hoecker. 1977. "Subjective Time Estimates of Work Tasks by Office Workers." *Journal of Occupational Psychology*, 50 (1): 23-36.

Haythornthwaite, Caroline. "Exploring Multiplexity: Social Network Structures in a Computer-Supported Distance Learning Class." *The Information Society*, 17 (July 2001): 211-226.

Haythornthwaite, Caroline. "Strong, Weak, and Latent Ties and the Impact of New Media." *The Information Society*, 18 (October 2002): 385-401.

Haythornthwaite, Caroline. "Social Networks and Internet Connectivity Effects." *Information Communication and Society*, 8 (June 2005): 125-147.

Haythornthwaite, Caroline and Barry Wellman. "Work, Friendship, and Media Use for Information Exchange in a Networked Organization." *Journal of the American Society for Information Science*, 49 (October 1998.): 1101-1114.

Hinds, Pamela J. and Sara Kiesler, Eds. *Distributed Work*. Cambridge, MA: MIT Press, 2002.

Hinds, Pamela J. and Cathleen McGrath. "Structures That Work: Social Structure, Work Structure and Coordination Ease in Geographically Distributed

Teams." In *Proceedings of the 2006 20th Anniversary Conference on Computer Supported Cooperative Work*, 343-352. New York, NY: Association for Computing Machinery, 2006.

Hollingshead, Andrea B., Janet Fulk, and Peter Monge. "Fostering Intranet Knowledge Sharing: An Integration of Transactive Memory and Public Goods Approaches." In *Distributed Work*, edited by Pamela J. Hinds and Sara Kiesler, 335-355. Cambridge, MA: MIT Press, 2002.

Ishii, Kenichi. "Implications of Mobility: The Uses of Personal Communication Media in Everyday Life." *Journal of Communication* 56 (June 2006): 346-365.

Julsrud, Tom E. "Behavioral Changes at the Mobile Workplace: A Symbolic Interactionistic Approach." In *Mobile Communications: Re-negotiation of the Social Sphere*, edited by Richard S. Ling and Per E. Pedersen, 93-112. Secaucus, NJ: Springer-Verlag, 2005.

Julsrud, Tom E. and John W. Bakke. "Boundary Spanners, Close Collaborators and Old Friends: An Exploratory Analysis of Distributed Knowledge Workers' Personal Networks." Forthcoming.

Julsrud, Tom E. and John W. Bakke. "Building Trust in Networked Environments: Understanding the Importance of Trust Brokers." In *Computer-Mediated Relationships and Trust: Organizational and Managerial Effects*, edited by Linda L. Brennan and Victoria E. Johnson. Hershey, PA: Igi Global, 2007.

Kadushin, Charles. "Networks and Small Groups." *Structure and Dynamics: eJournal of Anthropology and Related Science*, 1.1 (September 2005): Article 5.

Kilduff, Martin and Wenpin Tsai. *Social Networks and Organizations*. London, UK: Sage, 2003.

Knoke, David and James H. Kuklinksi. *Network Analysis*. London, UK: Sage, 1982.

Koku, Emmanuel F. and Barry Wellman. "Scholarly Networks as Learning Communities: The Case of TechNet." In *Designing Virtual Communities in the Service of Learning*, edited by Sasha A. Barab, Rob Kling, and James H. Gray. Cambridge, UK: Cambridge University Press, 2004.

Krackhardt, David. "Cognitive Social Structures." *Social Networks*, 9 (June 1987): 109-134.

Krackhardt, David. "The Strength of Strong Ties: The Importance of Philos in Organizations." In *Network and Organizations: Structure, Form and Action*, edited by Nitin Nohria and Robert G. Eccles, 216-239. Boston, MA: Harvard University Press, 1992.

Krackhardt, David. "The Ties That Torture: Simmelian Tie Analysis in Organizations." *Research in the Sociology of Organizations,* 16 (1999): 183-210.

Krackhardt, David and Daniel Brass. "Intraorganizational Networks: The Micro Side." *Advances in Social Network Analysis: Research in the Social and Behavioral Sciences*, edited by Stanley Wasserman and Joseph Galaskiewicz, 207-229. Thousand Oaks, CA: Sage, 1994.

Krackhardt, David and Jeffrey R. Hanson. "Informal Networks: The Company Behind the Chart." *Harvard Business Review,* 71 (July-August 1993): 104-111.

Krackhardt, David and Robert N. Stern. "Informal Networks and Organizational Crises: An Experimental Simulation." *Social Psychology Quarterly,* 51(June 1988): 123-140.

Kramer, Roderick M. and Karen S. Cook, Eds. *Trust and Distrust in Organizations: Dilemmas and Approaches.* New York, Russell Sage Foundation, 2004.

Tyler, Tom R. and Roderick M. Kramer. "Whither Trust?" In *Trust in Organizations: Frontiers of Theory and Research,* edited by Roderick M. Kramer and Tom R. Tyler, 1-15. Thousand Oaks, CA: Sage Publications, 1996.

Kristoffersen, S. and F. Ljungberg. "Mobility: From Stationary to Mobile Work." In*Planet Internet,* edited by Kristin Braa, Carsten Sorensen, and Bo Dahlbom, 137-156. Lund, Sweden: Studentlitteratur, 2000.

Krotz, Friedrich. "Mobile Communication, the Internet and the Net of Social Relations." In *A Sense of Place: The Global and the Local in Mobile Communication,* edited by Kristóf Nyíri, 447-458. Vienna, Austria: Passagen Verlag, 2005.

Lewicki, Roy L. and Barbara B. Bunker. "Developing and Maintaining Trust in Work Relationships." In *Trust in Organizations: Frontiers of Theory and Research,* edited by Roderick M. Kramer and Tom R. Tyler, 1-15. Thousand Oaks, CA: Sage Publications, 1996.

Lewis, J. David and Andrew Weigert. "Trust as a Social Reality." *Social Forces,* 63 (June 1985): 967-985.

Licoppe, Christian and Zbigniew Smoreda. "Are Social Networks Technologically Embedded? How Networks are Changing Today with Changes in Communication Technology." *Social Networks,* 27 (October 2005): 317-335.

Lipnack, Jessica and Jeffrey Stamps. *Virtual Teams: People Working Across Boundaries with Technology.* New York, NY: John Wiley & Sons, 2000.

Massey, Doreen. *Space, Place and Gender.* Minneapolis, MN: University of Minnesota Press, 1994.

Mayer, Roger C., James H. Davis, and F. David Schoorman. "An Integration Model of Organizational Trust." *Academy of Management Review,* 20 (July 1995): 709-734.

McEvily, Bill, Vincenzo Perrone, and Akbar Zaheer. "Trust as an Organizing Principle." *Organization Science,* 14 (January 2003): 91-103.

McKnight, D. Harrison, Larry L. Cummings, and Norman L. Chervany. "Trust Formations in New Organizational Relationships." *The Academy of Management Review,* 23 (July 1998): 473-490.

McPherson, Miller, Lynn Smith-Lovin, and James M. Cook."Birds of a Feather: Homophily in Social Networks." *Annual Review of Sociology,* 27 (2001): 415-444.

Meyrowitz, Joshua. "Medium Theory." In *Communication Theory Today,* edited by David Crowley and David Mitchell, 50-77. London, UK: Polity Press, 1994.

Nardi, Bonnie A., Steve Whittaker, and Heinrich Schwarz. "It's Not What You Know, It's Who You Know: Work in the Information Age." *First Monday,* 5.5 (May 2000): http://firstmonday.org/issues/issue5_5/nardi/index.html.

Postman, Neil. *Technopoly: The Surrender of Culture to Technology.* New York, NY: Vintage Books, 1993.

Quan-Haase, Anabel and Barry Wellman. "Hyperconnected Net Work: Computer-Mediated Community in a High-Tech Organization." *The firm as a collaborative community: reconstructing trust in the knowledge economy,* edited by Charles C. Heckscher and Paul S. Adler, 281-333. New York, NY: Oxford University Press, 2006.

Rousseau, Denise M., Sim B. Sitkin, Ronald S. Burt, and Colin Camerer. "Not So Different After All: A Cross-Discipline View of Trust." *Academy of Management Review,* 23 (July 1998): 393-404.

Scott, John P. *Social Network Analysis: A Handbook.* 2nd ed. Thousand Oaks, CA: Sage, 2000.

Shapiro, Debra L., Blair H. Sheppard, and Lisa Cheraskin. "Business on a Handshake." *Negotiation Journal,* 8 (October 1992): 365-377.

Silverstone, Roger and Leslie Haddon. "Design and the Domestication of Information and Communication Technologies: Technical Change and Everyday Life." In *Communication by Design: The Politics of Information and Communication Technologies,* edited by Robin Mansell and Roger Silverstone, 44-74. Oxford, UK: Oxford University Press, 1996.

Trevino, Linda K., Robert H. Lengel, and Richard L. Daft. "Media Symbolism, Media Richness, and Media Choice in Organizations." *Communication Research,* 14 (October 1987): 553-574.

Urry, John. "Mobile Sociology." *British Journal of Sociology,* 51 (January-March 2000): 185-203.

Wasserman, Stanley and Katherine Faust. *Social Network Analysis: Methods and Applications.* Cambridge, UK: Cambridge University Press, 1994.

Wellman, Barry. "Computer Networks as Social Networks." *Science,* 293 (September 2001): 2031-2034.

Wellman, Barry and Stephanie Potter. "The Elements of Personal Communities." In *Networks in the Global Village: Life in Contemporary Communities,* edited by Barry Wellman, 49-82. Oxford, UK: Westview Press, 1999.

Wellman, Barry, Janet Salaff, Dimitrina Dimitrova, Laura Garton, Milena Gulia, and Caroline Haythornthwaite. "Computer Networks as Social Networks: Collaborative Work, Telework, and Virtual Community." *Annual Review of Sociology,* 22 (1996): 213-238.

Wellman, Barry and Scot Wortley. "Different Strokes from Different Folks: Community Ties and Social Support." *American Journal of Sociology,* 96 (November 1990): 558-588.

Wenger, G. Clare. "A Network Typology: From Theory to Practice." *Journal of Aging Studies,* 5 (Summer 1991): 147-162.

Yuan, Y. Connie and Geri Gay. "Homophily of Network Ties and Bonding and Bridging Social Capital in Computer-Mediated Distributed Teams." *Journal of Computer-Mediated Communication,* 11 (July 2006): Article 9, http://jcmc.indiana.edu/vol11/issue4/yuan.html.

8

Negotiations in Space: The Impact of Receiving Phone Calls on the Move

Ann Light
Sheffield Hallam University

It could be said that telephony has only come of age with the cellular phone, in that wireless technology allows a move from location-centered to person-centered phoning. Stripped of the cables that tied phones to a particular point, the full sense of tele-phoning (from the Greek *tele* = far away and *phone* = voice) can be enacted[1]. Phones are now associated with discrete voices. This reflects a change in use as well as in technology: whereas households and businesses primarily had landline phones, cell phones quickly attached themselves to individuals. Person-centered phoning embodies new relationships. The defining quality might be summed up as mobility through possession. These different aspects of the new relationship are captured by the names that the new phones have come to be known by, e.g., "mobile" in Britain, "handy" in Germany, "keitai" in Japan.

It has been a fast transition to a new version of the possibilities for communication. Ferraris (2005) wittily observes that the caller's opening question has gone from "Who are you?" to "Where are you?" as we no longer ring a location and attempt to reach a person, but ring a person and attempt to locate them. But, with increased take-up, location has already become less of a focus. The first mobile phones were expensive and novel, and mostly used alongside landlines—they were there to do mobile things (see Laurier, 2001). Over the last few years in Europe, traditional and mobile phoning practices have amalgamated as homes without landlines and mobile phones with inclusive tariffs replace the old systems (Haddon, 2005). A further element blurring the distinction between landline and cellular is the appearance of short-range wireless (roaming) landline phones.

Thus, the mobility of the cell phone is becoming a truism—an obvious feature of phoning to be used when we ourselves are not stationary. Our phone follows us on our daily rounds, and we, augmented by extensive wireless operator networks and further promise in the form of the mobile internet, carry with us a halo of extended connections. Undeniably, our social shape has changed with the possibility of instant union with friends, work associates, and emergency services across remote spaces. What this chapter concentrates on is the way that personal shape has changed too.

This chapter looks closely at the experience of phoning and assesses how this quality of person-centeredness—that allows us to situate calls almost anywhere and then move while still talking, and that allows us to put all this capability on our person—alters our understanding of the physical relationships we hold. To do this, sections of several accounts of phone use will be scrutinized and used as a basis for discussion.

Phones: The Social and the Physical

Many studies on the use of mobile phones concern social dynamics and how these relate to the physical and geographical context in which calls are made and received. Within this field, the impact of mobile communications has been discussed at different scales. For instance, Castells, et al. (2006) have identified a change in the concepts of space and time at a societal level across the world, in a cross-cultural study that relates this to changing communicative practices. Specifically, they argue we have entered a period when "timeless time" and "the space of flows" structure our everyday lives, as networks compress and reorder our experience of time and prioritize connections and the movement between places rather than locations themselves. Rheingold (2002) considers the collective behavior of groups as phones allow for spontaneous gatherings of friends and relative strangers, focusing in particular on their role as activists and how phones help to organize their use of space. Hulme and Truch (2005), on the other hand, explore the construction of individual identity, discussing how phone contact in the "interspace" between key zones like places of home, work, and leisure can be challenging for call participants as they feel required to adopt extra social roles. Looking at other individual practices with phones, Taylor and Harper (2003) focus on rituals and the "gifting" between friends made possible with SMS, recommending that devices could relate stored messages to location.

Of particular relevance here is research that concentrates on individuals, talk, and specific contexts and places of use. Early qualitative work was often concerned with the acceptability of behavior with phones in public. Palen, et al. (2000) interview new phone users over time to reflect on the changing nature of their perceptions of where and how phones should be used. Palen, et al. (2001) develop this to look at the tensions that arise in using a phone in a public space, conceptualizing it, after Ling's work on Goffman (1996, cited in Palen, et al., 2001) as, in part, a matter of a conflict between social spaces in which people assume different faces. If mobile phone users are simultaneously in two spaces, "the space they physically occupy, and the virtual space of the conversation" (2001: 121), then which face takes precedence, they ask. More recently, Love and Kewley (2005) have looked at the impact of making calls on other people in the vicinity, interviewing disinterested bystanders. Ito's (2005) ethnography presents young Japanese people's mobile phone use as highly nuanced and place-sensitive, especially when used in transit. Specifically, this chapter records one woman, whom the author observed using a phone on public transport. It describes how her exchanges embedded "subtle clues that indicate her status and availability for communication keyed to her physical location," and how, "as she prepares to get off the train, she initiates a change of topic . . . as an indicator that the conversation has come to an end" (2005: 144).

Another related branch of work is conducted on mobile phone conversations to look at formulations of space and location. Weilenmann considers the impact of location on availability to others, captured in the title of her 2003 piece, "I Can't Talk Now, I'm in a Fitting Room." Laurier (2001) considers the much observed tendency for people to ask each other where they are, and Arminen (2003) answers him with a suggestion that, while the location of the participants is commonly mentioned, it is not discussed in geographical terms but rather is made relevant as part of the joint activities engaging call participants. There also exists a tangential literature on how people talk together about place, such as the experiments of Zhou, et al. (2005) that are not technology-specific, but show how context-dependent descriptions are likely to be.

All these studies relate to the work presented here in that they consider the relationship between place and phone call. What distinguishes this research is its interest in how individuals regard their personal space while using phones and how this relates to both social spaces and the environment around them.

One other pertinent area where the impact of the local environment on phoning has been studied is within cognitive psychology—in the context of driving. Quantitative analysis of behavior during laboratory simulations has suggested that the use of phones (handheld or hands-free) disrupts performance by diverting attention; an effect attributed "in large part to the distracting effects of the phone conversations" that direct attention "away from the external environment and toward an internal cognitive context associated with the phone conversation" (Strayer, et al., 2003: 31). Of note here are the following findings from Strayer and Johnston (2001) and Strayer, et al. 2003:

- Even when participants' eyes are directed at objects in the driving environment, they are less likely to remember them if conversing on a phone.
- Neither attending to auditory input nor producing vocal outputs by themselves are sufficient to produce impairments in driving performance.
- Conversation with a passenger in the vehicle is qualitatively different in these respects from conversations on a phone.
- Participants commented that they found it no more difficult to drive while using a phone than to drive without. There appears to be a disconnect between the self-perception of one's driving performance and objective measures.

Strayer and his team suggest these findings indicate that the competition for attention takes place at a central attentional level in the brain and cannot be due to structural interference or overload of a perceptual or response channel. By contrast, analysis of brain activity has been used to support a model of divided attention (Shomstein and Yantis, 2004). They argue that attention is finite and, when deployed to one modality such as talking on a phone, it necessarily extracts a cost on another modality, such as the visual task of driving.

A phenomenological approach is taken here in contrast to quantitative or cognitivist readings of how attention works during phone calls, which will be further explained in the next section.

Concepts of Space

This section defines two contrasting perspectives on space used in analyzing the accounts collected. The first is a familiar characterization of physical space: the world of geographical coordinates and map readings. We encounter it in this chapter in the shape of distances walked, as well as turnstiles, staircases, and car interiors moved through. These entities remain measurable and constant, regardless of the practices involving them.

In the following discussion, physical space will be juxtaposed with phenomenological space, or *spatiality*, as depicted by Heidegger. Spatiality might be crudely characterized as our experience of space as we act within it. Heidegger argues that one can only come to know any more abstract conception of space—such as that described as "physical space" above—through innate spatiality. In moving, finding things, seeing other people, or choosing direction, we experience space very differently from the measurable and constant abstraction that we talk about. Heidegger contrasts the remoteness of the street—in contact with our shoes, but uninteresting to us—with the acquaintance we meet upon it. The latter is phenomenologically closer because it is to them that our attention goes as we notice them: interestedness or "concern" at the time "brings something close by" (1962, 141-2). For Heidegger, something is near if it is "*both* something I am coping with and something absorbing my attention" (Dreyfus, 1991: 134). Coyne (2001) notes that the commuter on her mobile phone is measurably close to her fellow travelers in the railway carriage but nearer ontologically to the person on the end of the phone.

In physical closeness, concern precedes our bodies. It is already with the acquaintance on the street when we are still twenty paces away. How anticipation and the projection of concern to the other speaker in a call affects people's willingness to converse on the phone has already been discussed (see Light, 2008). It was found that expected calls, known callers, and predicted topics all contributed to a seamless transition into a call from other tasks. In other words, expectation had a major effect on the call. In addition, it was found that anticipation had a part to play in people's spatial response to what was going on during a call. This aspect is the focus of this chapter, using the concepts of concern, projection towards, and anticipation in the following analysis.

Two Changing Contexts of Personal Space

The changes made possible by adoption of personal wireless phones can be broadly divided into two categories: our experience of space as the phone (a) becomes one with our body and (b) follows us about.

First, there is the transition to the individual, as the phone becomes a personal possession. This shift sees phones following the contours of the body, developing close links to ears, eyes, and mouths and, in some cases, ceasing to be a single gadget. Phones have shrunk. Many are now used attached to the body as hands-free earpieces or through headphones and a microphone suspended at the neck. The phone has moved from *beyond* the person to *with* or *on* the person. If we are to believe certain commentators, the next move may be integral—to *in* the person. Clark (2003) calls the increasing association of telephony with the individual and the gadgets that enable this to take place "prime, if entry-level, cyborg technology" (27). He goes on to discuss the impact of a phone apparatus "lightly implanted in the skull" (171).

Actual moves toward integration with the body, so far, seem largely driven by a desire to integrate phoning activities with other mobile practices and, indeed, other technologically mediated activities such as driving or listening to recorded music on the go. A typically iterative process of changes in form and function can be mapped as person-centeredness alters the meaning of the device.

If we continue to take a Heideggerian view of our relation to the world, then the integration of the device does not depend on design or embedding, so much as how far the kit manages to operate so that we don't think about it. After all, in using the phone we may wish to show off our purchasing power or our appreciation of style or technology. Primarily, however, we wish to engage through it, so our concern can remain with the person at the other end.

If we return to Heidegger's example of meeting an acquaintance, the medium equivalent to the phone is the street: something to be stood upon, not considered. The act of using something effortlessly sends the medium into inconspicuousness. It takes a breakdown in immersion in the activities in which we are engaged for us to notice peripheral features; in other words, something has to go wrong. Heidegger discusses the mediating technologies of the body: "equipment for . . . hearing, such as the telephone receiver, has what we have designated the inconspicuousness of the proximally ready-to-hand" (1962: 141). Thus, another phenomenological concept of value in this chapter is the idea of "ready-to-hand" inconspicuousness and its opposite, "breakdown," when tools are not inconspicuous. We will relate this phenomenological idea of integration to the actual integration of phone with body.

Thus, the value of using Heidegger's approach to phenomenology is that it involves a notion of transparency through use—also well illustrated, for instance, by Merleau-Ponty's (1962) discussion of a blind man and his cane—and a developed consideration of how concern travels beyond us, often as a precursor to action.[2]

Research Approach

The study described below relies on an analysis of accounts of receiving phone calls, gained by interviewing people who use both landline and mobile phones. Interviewing was chosen as the method of data gathering because mental activities were under review.[3] The particular form of interviewing employed (described below) precludes observation and is related to critical incident interviewing (see Urquhart, et al., 2003). This approach was used because it has proved effective for working at the level of subtle changes in attention (see Light and Wakeman, 2001; Light, 2006; and Light, 2008).

The focus was placed on received calls, for two reasons. First, there is a tendency in phenomenological literature to regard the phone as an enabling device, extending the body out of its biological sphere. But the phone might also be considered *penetrative* in that framing. The study reported chose to focus on this less acknowledged aspect, exploring the phone as a two-way instrument, as a medium as well as a tool. Second, although the presence of local environmental factors may be felt by both caller and recipient, recipients have not chosen the moment of the call, and therefore have not chosen the context in which it arrives; they have less time to prepare for any change in context that answering the phone might introduce.

A sample of British professionals was interviewed in great depth about phone calls they had received. All were aged between thirty and fifty and were regular users of landlines before adopting mobiles as part of their social and work life. This profile was chosen to place attention upon what mobile phoning has introduced to those for whom it was a transition from landlines, as opposed to a younger group for whom mobiles would have always been part of life. For this study, ten people (five males and five females) were chosen who (1) regularly use both kinds of phone and (2) regularly explain their ideas. Seamon (2002) argues that when using what he calls an existential-phenomenological approach, some people will be more appropriate than others to invite as participants. Chosen participants met his two conditions: that they (1) must have had the experience under investigation; and (2) be able to express themselves clearly and coherently in a form relevant to the investigation.

Participants agreed to describe in great detail the last time they had received a call on a mobile phone and the last time they had received a call on a landline phone and to accept interruptions of clarification and probing. After giving both accounts, they were invited to make a comparison by reviewing what they had recalled and, in comparing the two moments of remembering, commenting on what they had learned. In this way, comparison was invited from the individuals concerned, but the process was prevented from affecting initial recall.

No other direction was given and no formal structure was imposed, other than to keep the interview directed towards the specific instances of practice chosen to discuss. Interviews were non-directive in order to gather accounts in the participants' own words about the things that they felt were relevant to mention. People were encouraged to describe the phenomena they mentioned in considerable detail and to evoke the events and thoughts that had accompanied receiving the calls, using a Rogerian non-directive interviewing technique adapted to delve deeply into people's descriptions of encountering technology (described in Light and Wakeman, 2001; see also Light, 2006). By using evocation, the method gets as close to an immersive form of recollection as is possible in the essentially reflective space of an interview. Vermersch (1994), who developed the underlying *explicitation* technique for remedial tuition in French schools, shows how it can elicit accounts of process in sufficient detail to support interviewees in learning about and refining their practice (see also Vermersch and Maurel, 1997).

A retrospective interviewing method acknowledges the importance of discussing naturally occurring phenomena so that motivation, expectation, and other contextual factors are not distorted before the event. This precluded recording the calls involved (for a fuller discussion of this aspect, see Light, 2006). One feature of this technique is an absence of control over the context of what is described. In all, interviewees talked about twenty-four calls, including the unanswered, a message centre call-back, a long and involved discussion with an old friend, a series of calls to find someone, sales calls, and the swift query of an unknown journalist. Equally, the equipment used varied widely. In each case, an outline was gathered so that this could be considered in relation to accounts of experience, since equipment is obviously a significant contextual factor, especially when considering the increasing integration of kit into personal space.

As stated, the content of the interviews was largely determined by the interviewees. Interviewers, using echoing techniques, engaged in neutral questioning and checking back (as in a therapeutic form of interview) to go into further and further depth as a way of focusing the attention on the activity of recall. Using this method, emphasis is placed on remembering to keep interviewees in a particular relationship with what they are describing. It is argued (Light, 2006) that this encourages an explanation where the purpose is held constant, rather than attempting to maintain inter-subject consistency or consistency of language. By this means, the method acknowledges the way that people's accounts are designed for particular interactions, as highlighted by Antaki (1994), Atkinson and Silverman (1997), and others. Indeed, Potter and Wetherell's (1987) guidance on discourse analysis, with its emphasis on context of delivery and what it is meaningful to analyze, informed the design (for greater details of the interviewing technique, see Light and Wakeman, 2001 and Light, 2006).

The accounts were transcribed and analyzed as examples of discourse. They were not regarded as representative of the calls in more than a general way. As noted, there was no accompanying transcription of phone calls. In this respect, the work differs from much discourse analysis relating to phone calls (from Schegloff, 1972 to Weilenmann and Leuchovius, 2004). It also differs in the level of transcription seen as useful. The focus of the analysis was based on choice of language, syntax, and juxtaposition. Thus, the notation ignores tone and the finer temporal aspects of the talk, though repetitions, false starts, and other textual aspects are included. Participant responses are quoted extensively below so as not to privilege the researcher's view.

The accounts were scrutinized for the kind of discovery that might be useful in considering what happens when people receive calls and where their concern takes them. The structure of the accounts was of interest for what it might reveal about the shifts in attention of the individual (see Light and Wakeman, 2001).

Participants were not asked for an account of their experience, as such. Practically, this would have taken questioning to a higher conceptual level than was useful. Philosophically, it would have posed the problem of whether it is meaningful to talk in the terms of researching experience, per se. Instead, the term "experience" is used here to provide shorthand for people's encounters with phones and of the thoughts and feelings that accompanied the process of encountering to facilitate comparing accounts. Within the phenomenological framework, it is assumed that people do have thoughts and feelings during the process of encountering technology. Specifically, the approach suggests that engagement in activity is primary, and reflection is one form of activity, limited to occurring at moments of "breakdown" when concern moves from doing to thinking about doing. So, *how* participants talked about *what* they talked about is important for the light it sheds on their experience. The accounts are not intended to represent what people did, but to bear some relation to what they noticed they did and what they saw as significant about this to mention (assuming that this reflects both on the experience they had and the context in which they are discussing it). With a phenomenological approach, this notice of significance by the interviewee allows the interviewer, in turn, to form insights.

Discoveries: Four Accounts of Mobility

Analysis of the accounts showed that space and location were important to participants in different ways. For instance, if we examine an interviewee's account of being at home using a mobile phone, a number of interesting introductory observations can be made in what is essentially a static situation.

In AB's account, he describes how he uses his Bluetooth earpiece:

AB: You don't wear it all the time, so you have to really be expecting a call for it to be valuable. Because if you are not expecting a call you will actually reach and automatically answer it with the phone; you won't take the Bluetooth device out, put it round your ear and then answer the call. . . .

. . . I will often use [the call] as a pause to go and get some coffee. Because I'm not watching or listening to anything or reading anything. You get off the sofa, walk into the kitchen, put the kettle on, make up a cup of coffee or whatever . . . still talking, because you can do both things simultaneously.
Interviewer: Can you tell me more about doing "both things simultaneously?"

AB: Well, the advantage is that your hands are both free, so you are not holding a phone to your ear, you are not distracted in any way; you've actually got a device deliberately designed to allow you to do other things at the same time, so that's what you do. So if I had to answer a phone without a headset, then I have to hold it to my ear constantly which means I'm tied up and I don't know if you've ever tried making coffee one-handed but it's not easy, so I wouldn't do it. . . . Can't think of anything else I would do.

Interviewer: Just coffee? . . .

AB: I'm trying to think back. Just coffee. I find I talk for longer.

In the first paragraph, we learn that, far from being integrated, AB regards use of the earpiece as less natural than his use of the phone. He has to concentrate to interrupt his usual pattern. In this respect, the technology intrudes to cause breakdown. It is not invisibly "ready-to-hand," either physically (he has to reach for it and attach it, as he has chosen to ignore its designed quality to sit on his ear in readiness) and phenomenologically (he temporarily switches concern from preparing to engage with his caller to considering the earpiece and its location).

Later, he notes that he is not holding a phone to his ear, and thus "not distracted in any way." At this point, one could argue that the seamless potential of the earpiece has kicked in. Wireless technology allows him to stroll around his flat and engage his hands. He does something that he might do if the caller were in the room with him. Prepared for the call and in control of environment, he talks of conducting an additional task that has an impact on the activity of phoning. This second aspect of the account shows both the potential to be engaged with one's local environment while on the phone and, further, a way that the integration of the phone with the body affects the potential to operate in surrounding physical spaces.

Here, as with other accounts, though some aspects of the phone's opportunities for mobility were exploited, mobility was not a primary condition of the interviewee. By contrast, the following three examples are provided to interrogate the particular phenomenon of being on the move with a phone. All three concentrate on being a mobile recipient and each shows a different condition: being moved about, driving oneself, and walking.

Being Moved About

CS is upstairs on a bus, reading, when the phone rings. Thus, she is stationary, but moving relative to the world; she is being taken to work by someone with whom she has little influence and no contact. She takes the phone out of her pocket, notes the caller, M, and answers it:

CS: So, the phone rang and the thing that was in my mind was that I was in an insecure situation because I was on the bus. I had a laptop, a bag with my lunch in it and I was on the top deck and there aren't any buttons to press to stop the bus and it was a 28, so it wasn't going to go into [my workplace]; it was going to whip up the A27 and I was going to have to stop it, so when the phone rang my first thought was, "Oh god, I've got to juggle with the phone and cope with getting off the bus."

Interviewer: Were you nearly about to get off the bus?

CS: I was kind of getting that way.

Interviewer: How did that feel?

CS: It probably made me talk faster.

Interviewer: Were there other moments when the world about you affected the call?

CS: Really my kind of awareness of the outside world was limited to clocking the point at which I was going to have to terminate that part of the conversation and trying to remain empathetic and pleasant to her, though feeling a bit stressed. . . . [She] wanted to talk some stuff through and she asked me if it was a good time and I said it was absolutely fine, but that I would probably . . . the thing that I was really scared of was trying to hold the phone and talk whilst also walking down the stairs, 'cos of my shoulder being bad. And I was a bit panicked about that, so I said that I was going to have to stop the phone conversation and phone you back so we talked a bit and then I said, "I'm gonna have to stop now," and so I stopped the call, went downstairs, got off the bus and then phoned her again and carried on the conversation.

In CS's account, we see the relative vulnerability of the recipient compared to the caller. This was not a welcome moment for a call. The language ("insecure," "urgent," "panicked," "stressed") and the emphasis of constraints that make the call inconvenient both point to discomfort. CS immediately turns these constraints into hurdles to overcome—concerning jumping ahead towards the moment when she has to leave the bus. We hear a swing between solicitude for the caller and anxiety about her physical location and the approaching need to "juggle" the phone. Some of this tension is arguably relived as she slips grammatically, from the use of reported speech to direct speech, during her description: "I was a bit panicked about that, so I said that I was going to have to stop the phone conversation and phone you back."

CS prioritizes getting to work over talking to M—at no point is there any consideration that she might remain on the bus, miss her stop, and continue the conversation. It appears that, unquestioningly, the conversation must be interrupted at a moment dictated by her location, which is outside her direct control, so that the pressing circumstances of negotiating her exit can take precedence. We can observe the management strategy that CS adopts: acquainting her caller with her anticipated circumstances. As the call begins, she has already predicted the need to end the call abruptly, perhaps when the caller is in mid-sentence, and so she leads the opening exchange to focus upon the behavior that she will take because of her location (but not specifically upon location itself). In this way, she juggles her needs: getting off the bus, averting apparent rudeness, and devoting attention to the caller. This management strategy works, as she describes listening to M to the exclusion of other matters: "awareness of the outside world was limited to clocking the point at which I was going to have to terminate that part of the conversation." When pushed by the interviewer to remember at what point this was, or how she made the transition, she has no clear recollection. She has been able to absorb herself in the shared space of the call, at least partially.

Elsewhere, she describes the kind of engagement she experiences in talking to M when they can talk without the breakdowns introduced by CS's anticipatory anxiety. She gives a description of ringing M back. CS is now absolutely stationary and in charge of her environment. However, she is still on the same phone, a demonstration that it is not the mobility of the technology, but the circumstances of the user, that make the difference to the potential quality of the experience:

> I realized, at the end of the call, that all the way through the call I'd been really focused on her, and my presence in the place where I was was really rather bodily—it was like the shape of me but actually I was somewhere else in this kind of non-space which was the space of my phone call. It's not like I'm with the other person, it's like I'm in an abstracted place. . . . We're used to it on the fixed phone that this will happen to us and we've got special rooms for it to happen in—but with mobile phones it can happen to you anywhere: you are anywhere and then you're not actually there at all because you're in this place which is the place of your encounter.

In this description, we hear CS use the language of phenomenological space as she struggles to express a feeling of being on the phone and absorbed. It is in marked contrast to how she speaks about talking to the same person, on the same phone, on a bus.

CS's account of her bus journey suggests how the immediate environment can affect the experience of phoning, even when nothing is directly disturbing the traveler. She reports no loud noises or competing conversations, as other interviewees reported. She was sitting still at the time of the call. Her distractions are a consequence of location and of relative mobility, and they take the form of a projection ahead to the approaching bus stop. Her strategy is to limit the duration of engagement she is prepared to offer and return in time from the phenomenological space of engagement to leave herself free to negotiate the bags and staircase wholly in the space of the bus.

In the next account, we look further at the effects of being mobile by considering an account of driving.

Driving

SL is driving towards a junction when the phone rings. Thus, she is in control of her own motion, though it is mediated by a vehicle that is about to demand both a decision about direction and some maneuvering. She does not answer the phone, but devotes considerable thought to her decision:

> I remember feeling quite harassed. It was my work phone and my work phone rings quite a lot. So quite often I don't want to answer it 'cos I'm not necessarily in the right space to deal with whatever the person wants to know from me. I find mobile phones to be quite intrusive . . . I felt it was demanding my attention and I wanted to put my attention into finding out which road I needed to get on to get to [a major road in the south of England].
>
> I think it was a mixture of emotions, because part of me wanted to find it to answer it and part of me thought, "That's not a good idea, because you are driving and if you

> lean forward to find out which bag it's in, you're likely to take your eye off the road and that's probably not a good idea at the moment." . . . And then I remember thinking about those people that go around with those hands-free headsets and thinking, "Would I want one of those or not?" Probably not, 'cos then you'd have to answer the phone and the phone calls I get are members of the public who want something from me. So you might get someone ringing you up when you are on [the London ring road] saying, "Can you tell me how you can help me with my scriptwriting project?" And I kind of like things to be in compartments. So I like to be in a scriptwriting space when someone rings me up about that.

In SL's account, we can again see emotional language ("harassed," "mixture of emotions," "intrusive," "demanding"). Again, conflicting feelings cause tension. However, this time it is not only the anticipated demands of the environment that are cited as causing conflict, although they clearly play a part.

There is a further concern: SL talks about not being "in the right space" for the activities that she anticipates needing to engage in if she answers the phone: "I like to be in a scriptwriting space when someone rings me up about that." This introduces a different dimension to her decision not to receive the call. There is an ambiguity as to which type of space the right/scriptwriting space is. Here, it could be an appropriate office, or a shared phenomenological space in which SL can follow the concerns of her caller, as her utterance, "I kind of like things to be in compartments," might indicate. There is evidence for both interpretations later in her account. Contrast the two passages that form part of her subsequent discussion of the call. The former is clearly about a physical space of activity; the latter about what happens to where her concern is:

> . . . Because quite often the sorts of requests people have involve looking at diaries . . . I much prefer to be able to help someone when I am sitting somewhere where I can deal with it . . .
>
> I would always like to be able to give people as much attention as I can when they phone me up. . . . So it really is about feeling I've got space at that time to accommodate them and when I think of phones I do often think of them as . . . breaking into something I'm already doing and demanding that what that person wants takes precedence.

This is more than concern with immediate difficulties. SL is navigating as the phone rings—about to move from one main road to another and not sure of her route. Furthermore, she doesn't know where her phone is, and looking for it would be dangerous, as would answering it would be if she could find it. However, her more global problem with the phone ringing in the car is that the car is the wrong place for dealing with the substance of the call. She has jumped to the locations necessary to handle the activities of a call ("a scriptwriting space," "sitting somewhere where

I can deal with it") and, without learning the nature of the call, she has already prejudged that to do it justice she needs to be otherwise engaged. In the old days, the work phone would ring in the office and the chances of the caller finding SL in the right space, in both senses, would have been higher. By taking her work phone out with her and keeping it switched on,[4] SL appears to prioritize contact but this sits at odds with her desire to match task with setting.

SL's projection toward a space of joint activity is a step beyond the projection that concern for the caller generates in that it involves anticipatory concern for the caller's concern. And this other person's concern could take her anywhere. SL's preoccupation with this aspect of being phoned reflects interestingly on the business of driving. Not only would she be trying to be in two places, but they are both conceived of as activity spaces with their own demands. SL potentially has the option to stop the car, find, and answer the phone (though other drivers and environmental conditions might make this too dangerous). Again, this degree of disruption isn't even entertained. Her management strategy is not to negotiate between spaces; she doesn't pick up.

The final example looks further at competing activities, this time accompanying the activity of walking.

Walking

CG is walking to the train station and listening to music through a headset when the phone rings. Thus, like SL above, he is in control of his own motion. He answers the phone by pushing a button on his MP3 player.

> CG: The reason I remember quite clearly is that it has quite an abrupt ring and it's quite loud. . . . And it's a really nice part of the canal walk, and I'm listening to music, walking along and suddenly this really loud ring. . . . Generally I wouldn't think of it as intrusive, but on this occasion very loud, very obnoxious, jarring.

> I do the walk every day so I have a routine, I know exactly where I am going, counting the steps while listening to the music. If I listen to the same album for periods at a time, I'd know when certain things would be happening in the song.

> . . . That stretch of river is where I would be thinking about my day, what happened the day before and if there was anything I was supposed to do. Once I turn the corner from the river, the whole pace changes. . . .
> Intrviewer: So how was it doing the walk and taking the call?

> CG: A lot quicker. Not really conscious of everything going on around me, I mean conscious of it but not taking it in or aware of things. And I would have tried to end the call just before I got through the turnstile at the station. . . .

> I had a predetermined need to end the call. Unless the call was really important and then I would have stopped but I don't think I've had one of those calls in a really long

time. And I would know I had to end the call before I had lots of other people moving around me. Because a) it's a bit rude, and b) it's a different speed in [hometown, as opposed to London] so I need to be conscious of other things around me moving around. And I wouldn't be able to focus on the call and people moving around me slowly while I am trying to walk very fast. . . . As I'm entering the station, if anything else is to be discussed, I don't mind picking the call up again once I'm on the train.

CG's account raises new aspects of the relationship between environment, phone, and concern. CG, too, is disconcerted by the call, but he is more disturbed by the nature of the interruption, rather than the circumstances of his location. The call is "abrupt," "very loud, very obnoxious, jarring." This sounds unlike anticipation. It is the visceral discomfort of having a familiar piece of music cut into by a loud noise.

The ringing phone is graceless, a breakdown. With the commencement of the ringing, CG is neither absorbed in his daily walk nor in the caller's world; he is shocked. By contrast, the start of the call (once the technology has resumed its inconspicuousness) marks a more interesting transition, as his description of his activity spaces shows.

Much of what he describes relates to the activity spaces he was occupying before the call. There are two notable features. First, it seems that the music has integrated into the walk and become part of being by the canal: "I'd know when certain things would be happening in the song." The music is not distracting him from the physical space he occupies; it enhances the routine. It is treated very differently from the call. Second, it seems he is projecting toward the day before and the day to come as he moves, so that he is not fully engaged in taking the canal walk even before the phone rings. Arguably, he is already in multiple phenomenological spaces. So, when the call starts, it interrupts the activity spaces of his planning, as well as distracting him from what he is walking past.

Once on the phone, he initially allows his projection toward the caller to dominate his description, and he devotes himself to absorption in the call. His music has turned itself off and the landscape has never even competed with his counting activities. CG's account briefly shares features with CS's account above, in that he struggles with the language to describe this state: "Not really conscious . . . I mean conscious of it but not taking it in or aware of things." But, as he continues his description, we hear about another balancing act between phone and environment.

CG feels that it is inappropriate to be on the phone as he arrives at the station. Here, it is other people who provide the thing to be coped with, and more subtly, he includes the local culture in this: "people moving around me slowly while I am trying to walk very fast," which he elsewhere notes is an undesirable quality of the town in which he lives. Even as he distances himself from his environment in terms of behavior, he recognizes social concern for the people with whom he has physical proximity: "it's a bit rude." Like CS and SL, he employs a management strategy. He uses the stretch between entering the station and reaching the turnstile to wind the call up, he explains elsewhere. Like CS, he anticipates resuming the call, if necessary, once the most difficult section to negotiate is over. Unlike CS and SL, he contemplates the possibility that the call might take precedence over his progress and cause him to stop.

Summary

The three accounts explored above have significant qualities in common. They suggest that the recipients have a reaction to being called where they find themselves. This relates to being interrupted in what they are doing. The passages quoted show a diversity of ways that interruptions manifest: by coming at the wrong time (approaching a critical bus stop), in the wrong place (away from the office), by being different in quality from what went before (loud ringing), by competing with complex motion (negotiating moving bodies, descending an unstable staircase, or taking a corner), and intentions (getting to a destination). The list may look little different from those constructed before the advent of mobile phones in that variants on most of these types of interruption have always been possible. For instance, cooking can involve complex, time-sensitive physical maneuvering of a kind that might lead someone to ignore a call. Also, phones have a long history of disturbing people by waking them. However, getting a call while mobile is a particular challenge because it often introduces environmental elements outside the recipient's control—elements that have nothing to do with the call. This is another factor that all three accounts share; not only is the call imposed on them, but it has nuisance value. In different ways, mobility increases day-to-day uncertainty and risk.

In each account, the response to this is the same. All the interviewees' talk of location and mobility segues seamlessly into a discussion of how they managed to deal with it. Taking charge of the immediate situation would seem to be a necessary precursor to enjoying any other phenomenological closeness. They are only able to allow the tools they are using (the bus, the car, the phone) to become inconspicuous once they have coped with the interesting aspects of their mobility (anticipated competition between activity spaces and technologies) by devising a strategy (anticipating a resolution to this competition). This inconspicuousness can then last until the interviewee has to actually cope with the conflict set up in using the technology (getting off the bus, moving through the confined space of the station). SL, who cannot anticipate a resolution, never starts the competition.

Two accounts do show successful negotiation of spaces. Despite the timing of the interruption, two interviewees choose to take their call and commit to it. The recipients then engage with the caller enough to lose sight of where they are, even though they know they must use a sense of their location to end the call in a short time to come. How they monitor their progress would not appear to be information available to them.[5]

From a phenomenological perspective, however, even without information on the mechanism of these shifts, the flow of attention between spaces forms an elegant dance, creating new personal shapes as a result of these negotiations. It is compelling to return here to the literature on driving and phoning. Despite coming from a very different research tradition, the findings of Strayer, et al. (2003) seem borne out of the analysis of these accounts. We don't always see what is in front of us when we are on the phone. As we become mobile, this matters. Strayer, et al. attribute this distraction to "an internal cognitive context associated with the phone conversation" (31). This chapter argues that phoning is a complex activity because the phenomenologically close spaces of phoning do not necessarily reflect the demands of the person's physical location, but rather compete by offering new activities to share outside it. As soon as the environment gets lively, as it does when we leave rooms designed to hold the telephone and step outside, the dance begins. So, we could argue here that Strayer, et al. (2003) and Palen, et al. (2001), in conceptualizing the multiple demands upon a person on the phone, underestimate the number of spaces that are useful to consider. What might be learned if Palen, et al.'s (2001) discussion of the management of face was not only based upon "the space [participants] physically occupy, and the virtual space of the conversation," but also upon the further activity spaces possible to identify by taking a phenomenological approach?

If we look at the literature more generally, we see other stories of management, as in Ito's (2005) work, cited earlier, on a Japanese woman's strategy for managing her phone in the context of the social disapproval of speaking on public transport. Though Ito bases this interview on previous observation, the similarity is encouraging and suggests some value in the discoveries described here—looking more directly at managing spatial factors.

We can look critically at the methodology used in the study and argue that the interviewees gave a dramatic account of the risks and emotions that they encountered as part of using their phone, and that this dramatization occurred as a response to the interest and close questioning of the interviewer. Perhaps more worthy of note, then, is the valence of the feeling and the way that each interviewee moved from giving these colorful descriptions of their spatial problems and frustrations with their equipment straight into describing their management strategy, linking it with subtler discussions of spatiality. This juxtaposition of ideas in the accounts is revealing and exists independently of the more self-conscious act of choosing the language in which to portray the activities under review. In all the accounts, people could be seen attempting to manage spatial transitions gracefully in response to the activities of being on the phone. Because this observation can be based on account structure and participant orientation rather than solely content, it has greater validity as a discovery (Potter and Wetherell, 1987). In conclusion, it suggests a way that the advent of person-centered phoning has added considerable complexity to the spatial management needed to be on the phone, but complexity that people are taking in their stride.

Before finishing, let us consider the other strand introduced by person-centered phoning—that of integration. Two of the examples under discussion involve a handheld phone and a phone with a plugged-in wearable headset (hands-free). Is this significant?

In the accounts, both CS and SL are made aware of the demands of using their phone by the physicality of it. Breakdown here has some value. Without a hands-free device, part of managing their call involves a need to locate and then hold their phone while wanting to do other things (go down a staircase, drive onto a major road). The physical act of making contact with the phone can represent the phenomenological "bringing close" of a remote connection. A seamless shift would have felt different. Might it have led to more daring—possibly foolhardy—behavior, such as navigating the staircase or the motorway while trying to stay engaged? Questions of this kind raise subtle design challenges.

CG is hands-free but chooses to end his call at the point where the environment becomes more complicated. His wearable headset is interesting in another respect. As well as sitting closer to the user, the technology integrates multiple media in one device. CG only has to contend with one set of headphones to listen to his music and use his phone, and can switch between the two by pressing a button. However, the experience of using both is far from integrated. First, his account gives a brutal picture of what is involved in the transition from music to phone; the call is disruptive to the point of "jarring." Second, the spaces the two activities occupy are different in quality. The music is part of the physical space he walks through; it has become attached to moments and sights in the walk. Whereas, in using the phone, he takes himself out of this space and into another where he is unaware of what is around him. The device cannot follow these subtle shifts of attention. It is not yet person-centered; it treats activities as separate functions not part of the stream of life. Telephony may have come of age, but telephones have not.

Conclusion

This chapter has set out to show that it is not so much mobility per se, but absorption into the person and what they are doing—a quality of person-centeredness—that characterizes what is new as phones lose their wires. In doing so, it has begun to show the impact on people's management of space. In focusing on the personal, rather than shared, concerns of call recipients, the chapter seeks to complement existing research into mobile communication while challenging some interpretations of how attention is distributed.

Taking a phenomenological perspective with a particular focus upon the impact of mobility, this study has looked at the nature of a sudden connection to another place while negotiating an existing one and explored the factors that influence the opportunity for engaging with the caller. Adopting a Heideggerian account of people's relationship to space, the activities of receiving and responding to a call on the move have been viewed as involving a series of breakdowns and the ensuing behavior regarded in terms of anticipation and shifts in concern between competing spaces of activity. This approach has allowed us to consider the interaction between physical location, the complexity of the demands made upon the person, and the individual's activity.

The data are indicative of profound shifts of awareness in people's negotiation of communication on the move. Analysis suggests that the new contexts of communication introduced by mobility affect our experience of space in subtle and complex ways.

In addition, by taking a phenomenological approach, it has been possible to consider movement in terms of shifts in attention and projection into spaces ahead of actual activity and show that this can be fruitful as an adjunct to considering movement as a physical phenomenon. Findings suggest that it is these transitions between spaces of concern and activity that are made interesting by the mobility of the people involved. In managing their phones across a new range of physical environments and in a new relationship to their bodies, people are weaving patterns of attention into a rich spatial fabric.

Notes

1.   Oxford English Dictionary, Oxford University Press, 2005.
2.   For an analysis of phone calls which describe both the transparency of the equipment in use and how a person can feel projected into the same space as their caller, see Light, 2008.
3.   Mental activities cannot be observed or directly investigated, making the empirical processes we can use open even wider to debate and criticism than those used for interpreting physical activities. Although individuals' assertions about what they are thinking may be regarded as a useful source of insight, they raise many issues, both in respect to what can be observed by the interviewee and to how their observations can be meaningfully interpreted by the interviewer. Atkinson and Silverman (1997) argue that social scientists with research based exclusively on personal interview data are in danger of recapitulating one of the key features of contemporary society, rather than examining it. They express concern that personal interviewing may produce a version of social inquiry that is devoid of social organization and in which categories such as "experience" are treated without question. This danger is acknowledged. At no point in this study is any discourse treated as an unmediated account of mental activities, rather than one prepared for a particular audience in a particular context. Last, the method described here cannot be held up to direct comparison with others for validation and so can only be viewed as providing suggestions and provocations to supplement existing literature that considers what goes on in people's heads.
4.   The interview was conducted before it became illegal to keep a handheld set switched on by the driver of a car in the country of interview.
5.   This is consistent with literature on introspection, with Strayer, et al.'s (2003) findings and with the intuition that if they were able to give a good account of their own shifting patterns of absorption, then much of the alleged absorption must have given way to self-reflection in addition to looking out for significant signals in the landscape.

Bibliography

Antaki, Charles. *Explaining and Arguing: The Social Organization of Accounts.* London, UK: Sage, 1994.

Arminen, Ilkka. "Location: A Socially Dynamic Property: A Study of Location Telling in Mobile Phone Calls." Paper delivered at The Good, the Bad, and the Irrelevant Conference. 3 September 2003, Helsinki, Finland.

Atkinson, Paul and David Silverman. "Kundera's *Immortality*: The Interview Society and the Invention of Self." *Qualitative Inquiry*, 3 (September 1997): 304-325.

Castells, Manuel, Mireia Fernandéz-Ardévol, Jack L. Qiu, and Araba Sey. *Mobile Communication and Society: A Global Perspective.* Cambridge, MA: MIT Press, 2006.

Clark, Andy. *Natural-Born Cyborgs: Minds, Technologies, and the Future of Human Intelligence.* Oxford, UK: Oxford University Press, 2003.

Coyne, Richard D. *Technoromanticism: Digital Narrative, Holism, and the Romance of the Real.* Cambridge, MA: MIT Press, 2001.

Dreyfus, Hubert L. *Being-in-the-World: A Commentary on Heidegger's "Being and Time," Division 1.* Cambridge, MA: MIT Press, 1991.

Ferraris, Maurizio. "Where Are You? Mobile Ontology." Paper delivered at the Seeing, Understanding, Learning in the Mobile Age conference. 29 April 2005, Budapest, Hungary: http://www.fil.hu/mobil/2005/Ferraris.pdf.

Haddon, Leslie. "Communication Problems." In *Thumb Culture: The Meaning of Mobile Phones for Society,* edited by Peter Glotz, Stefan Bertschi, and Chris Locke, 89- 100. New Brunswick, NJ: Transaction Publishers, 2005.

Heidegger, Martin. *Being and time.* Translated by John Macquarrie and Edward Robinson. New York: Harper and Row, 1927/1962.

Hulme, Michael and Anna Truch. "The Role of Interspace in Sustaining Identity." In *Thumb Culture: The Meaning of Mobile Phones for Society,* edited by Peter Glotz, Stefan Bertschi, and Chris Locke, 137-148. New Brunswick, NJ: Transaction Publishers, 2005.

Ito, Mizuko. "Mobile Phones, Japanese Youth, and the Re-placement of Social Contact." In *Mobile Communications: Re-negotiation of the Social Sphere,* edited by Richard S. Ling and Per E. Pederson, 131-148. London, UK: Springer-Verlag, 2005.

Laurier, Eric. "Why People Say Where They Are During Mobile Phone Calls." *Environment and Planning D,* 19.4 (2001): 485-504.

Light, Ann. "Adding Method to Meaning: A Technique for Exploring Peoples' Experience with Technology." *Behaviour & Information Technology,* 25.2 (2006): 175-187.

Light, Ann. "Transports of Delight? What the Experience of Receiving (Mobile) Phone Calls Can Tell Us About Design." *Personal and Ubiquitous Computing,* 2008.

Light, Ann and Ian Wakeman. "Beyond the Interface: Users' Perceptions of Interaction and Audience on Websites." *Interacting with Computers,* 13 (February 2001): 325-351.

Love, Steve and Joanne Kewley. "Does Personality Affect Peoples' Attitude Towards Mobile Phone Use in Public Places?" In *Mobile Communications: Re-negotiation of the Social Sphere,* edited by Richard S. Ling and Per E. Pederson, 273-284. London, UK: Springer-Verlag, 2005.

Merleau-Ponty, Maurice. *Phenomenology of Perception.* Translated by Colin Smith. London, UK: Routledge & Kegan Paul, 1945/1962.

Palen, Leysia, Marilyn Salzman, and Ed Youngs. "Going Wireless: Behavior and Practice of New Mobile Phone Users." In *Proceedings of the 2000 ACM conference on Computer Supported Cooperative Work,* 201-210. Philadelphia, PA: ACM, 2000.

Palen, Leysia, Marilyn Salzman, and Ed Youngs. "Discovery and Integration of Mobile Communications in Everyday Life." *Personal and Ubiquitous Computing,* 5 (July 2001): 109-122.

Potter, Jonathan and Margaret Wetherell. *Discourse and Social Psychology: Beyond Attitudes and Behaviour*. London, UK: Sage, 1987.

Rheingold, Howard. *Smart Mobs: The Next Social Revolution*. Cambridge, MA: Perseus Publishing Group, 2002.

Schegloff Emanuel A. "Sequencing in Conversational Opening." In *Directions in Sociolinguistics: The Ethnography of Communication*, edited by John J. Gumperz and Dell Hymes. 346-380. New York, NY: Basil Blackwell Inc., 1972.

Seamon, David. *Phenomenology, Place, Environment, and Architecture: A Review of the Literature*. 2002. http://www.phenomenologyonline.com/articles/seamon1.html.

Shomstein, Sarah and Steven Yantis. "Control of Attention Shifts Between Vision and Audition in Human Cortex." *The Journal of Neuroscience*, 24 (November 2004): 10702-10706.

Strayer, David L., Frank A. Drews, and William A. Johnston. "Cell Phone-induced Failures of Visual Attention During Simulated Driving." *Journal of Experimental Psychology: Applied*, 9 (March 2003): 23-32.

Strayer, David L. and William A. Johnston. "Driven to Distraction: Dual-task Studies of Simulated Driving and Conversing on a Cellular Telephone." *Psychological Science*, 12 (November 2001): 462-466.

Taylor, Alexander and Richard Harper. "The Gift of the *Gab*?: A Design Oriented Sociology of Young People's Use of 'MobilZe!'" *Computer Supported Cooperative Work*, 12 (September 2003): 267-296.

Urquhart, Christine, Ann Light, Rhian Thomas, Anne Barker, Alison Yeoman, Jan Cooper, Chris Armstrong, Roger Fenton, Ray Lonsdale, and Siân Spink. "Critical Incident Technique and Explicitation Interviewing in Studies of Information Behavior." *Library & Information Science Research*, 25 (Spring 2003): 63-88.

Vermersch, Pierre. *L'Entretien D'Explicitation*. Paris, France: ESF, 1994.

Vermersch, Pierre and Maryse Maurel, Eds. 1997. *Pratiques de L'Entretien D'Explicitation*. Paris, France: ESF, 1997.

Weilenmann, Alexandra. "'I Can't Talk Now, I'm in a Fitting Room': Formulating Availability and Location in Mobile Phone Conversations." *Environment and Planning A*, 35.9 (2003): 1589-1605.

Weilenman, Alexandra H. and Peter Leuchovius. "'I'm Waiting Where We Met Last Time': Exploring Everyday Positioning Practices to Inform Design." Paper delivered at the 3rd Nordic Conference on Human-Computer Interaction. 23-27 October 2004, Tampere, Finland.

Zhou, Changqing, Pamela Ludford, Dan Frankowski, and Loreen Terveen. "Talking About Place: An Experiment in How People Describe Places." Presented at the 3rd International Conference of Pervasive Computing (PERVASIVE). May 10 2005, Munich, Germany.

9

Mobile Phone "Work": Disengaging and Engaging Mobile Phone Activities with Concurrent Activities

Marc Relieu
Ecole Nationale Supérieure des Télécommunications

Given the growing ubiquity of interactional communication devices, it is not surprising that several studies have been devoted to analyzing, through more or less systematic observations, how various kinds of "remote" communications are juxtaposed or intertwined with the proximal settings in which speakers are located (Ito and Okabe, 2005; Koskinen, 2005; Ling, 1997, 2002; Weilenmann, 2003). Because mobility expands the variety of occasions and places for remote talking or writing, there is a growing interest in how we solve the various organizational issues linked to remote activity—turn taking, sequential ordering, etc.—while simultaneously walking, driving, or talking with a co-present partner. Mobile phone exchanges affect how users manage their relationship with co-present others and their engagements in other current activities. Users either actively disengage from current activities in order to be involved in mobile phone activity, or actively involve others in their mobile phone activities.

The aim of this chapter is twofold. First, I introduce some methodological issues raised by the study of the situated use of mobile technologies. In this context, I discuss a specific video recording kit best suited for observing these situations. Second, in order to focus as clearly as possible on boundary issues during mobile phone use, I examine how an intermittent, text-based chat interacts with proximal activities such as eating, drinking, and looking at one's physical surroundings.[1] My focus will be on the detailed analysis of the practices through which users combine various features of a remote exchange (e.g., reading and writing short text messages) while simultaneously involved in the interactions and activities embedded in their proximal contexts (e.g., talking to nearby others).

Studying Mobile Phone Situated Activities

Studies of mobility have stressed the mobility of portable phone users. However, mobile phones are themselves mobile objects: they are portable, relatively light, and are held and manipulated by hand. Mobile phones can be grasped, turned over, oriented in various perspectives, and can be shown or lent to others. This micro-mobility[2] of portable devices allows us to configure their role in the unfolding organization of activities and participation frameworks[3] around them (Goffman, 1981; Goodwin and Goodwin, 1992). In effect, mobile phone use creates new opportunities for overhearing a conversation or for seeing others' text messages. As such, understanding the relationship between remote telephone exchanges and activities in the nearby environment require us to look more closely to the mobility of the mobile phones themselves.

For instance, text-based activities require the user to focus on the mobile phone screen and the manipulation of the handset. At first glance, this focus appears to increase the so-called individualization of mobile phone users, especially in public places. In particular, the screen encourages a front-to-front relationship, brought about by the need for hand-eye coordination. This mobile interface disengages the individual, to an extent, from their physical environment; however, these affordances do not determine what users actually do. In accordance with other ethnographic studies (see Weilenmann and Larsson, 2001), my observations show that people orient themselves to the handset in various embodied and dynamically managed ways. Nearby friends glance at the screen and comment on the content of text messages that have been written or read. In addition, people speaking on the phone covertly communicate disaffiliating displays to other co-located individuals about what they are telling to their remote partner.

Several artful practices are used in order to make sense of mobile phone use. Observations of mobile phone users in public spaces help to distinguish two aspects of this work (Ling, 1997, 2002; Relieu and Morel, 2004). On the one hand, people have to deal with different contingencies. For example, new incoming calls, text messages, or funny pictures of friends are unpredictable events. In public places, the mobile phone owner has limited possibilities to disguise who will hear or see what has been received. On the other hand, for those communication events where the individual initiates the call or writes the text, he or she can be more or less carefully prepared. In this case, the person initiating the contact can negotiate who is co-present and who will have the right to overhear or read the communication. Therefore, boundaries between what constitutes a "private" interaction isolated from parallel proximal activities and a shared, co-produced interaction are not necessarily marked in advance; rather, they can be systematically achieved. In any case, the onset and the conclusion of those boundaries have to be made explicit by those participating in the mobile communication.

Although the micro-mobility of mobile phones is a pervasive feature of contemporary society, several methodological constraints arise for those who wish to carry out systematic video-based observation of mobile-based activities. Audio-video records present several advantages for the analysis of practical action in context (Pomerantz and Fehr, 1997: 70; Sacks, 1984). In particular, they give access to the interactive features that are not accessible in any other way, they preserve the relevant details of activities, and they make it possible to examine, "again and again," the ongoing process of interaction (Sacks, 1984: 26).

Two main problems in capturing mobile telephony in this context center on the visibility of the mobile phone screen and the mobility of the mobile phone user. The former requires a solution for capturing screen events and the latter requires a solution that is able to follow mobile users. For instance, it is impossible to capture the process of writing or keying text with a wide-angle camera. Conversely, a higher-resolution camera that would capture writing makes it difficult to capture wider, contextual features of the social interaction. As pointed out before (Mark, et al., 2001; Zouinar, et al., 2004) a fixed camera is inadequate for tracking unpredictable and often unplanned situations of use. For instance, Short Message Service (SMS) writing and reading can be done anywhere and at anytime. Unlike large computer screen-based activities, non-vocal mobile phone uses (SMS, WAP) are difficult to capture using classical recording approaches. In order to find a solution for recording the situated use of mobile devices, I use a micro-camera, with a build-in microphone mounted on glasses, in addition to an external recorder.

This observational tool—called the GlassCam—is wearable and delivers low-quality images that are sufficient for research purposes. The angle preserves the main features of the interaction with the handset[4] while capturing the main interactions with co-present others.[5] Because this video equipment is a specific, uncommon, wearable device, informants were provided with detailed explanations of its use. In addition, there were two interviews before the informants started to use the system. The first explored their general background with information and communications technology (ICT) use, with a specific interest in the duration and location for each type of use (SMS, vocal, etc.). In the second interview, the informant was presented with the observational kit and was taught how to use it. Moreover, the decision as to when and for how long the respondent would be recorded was a joint agreement between the researcher and the participants.[6]

SMS Chat in Context

SMS Chat is an application that enables two-way chatting via SMS text messaging, during which users type a text message into the phone. To subscribe to this service, mobile phone owners dial a special number and receive a list of instructions and rules. Users create a Chat ID (Nickname) and select a "room" devoted to a specific thematic interest. A profile can also be written and sent to other participants. Messages can be sent to all channel members or just to a single user.[7]

Because they are not confined to the same temporal expectations as synchronous vocal conversations, most SMS chats are intermittent exchanges,[8] providing more extended opportunities to be interlaced with other proximal activities. The reception, reading, and response cycle is likely to become a local event that is a feature of the local environment.

Establishing a Joint Attention to the Remote Exchange

In this first segment, two male high school students, Kim (age eighteen) and Denis (age nineteen), are sitting outside a fast food restaurant in Paris. A preliminary interview has revealed that Kim used to chat on his mobile phone during lunchtime. Kim has agreed to use the GlassCam during two lunchtime breaks. The following abstract shows how Kim and Denis orient themselves to an incoming message by coordinating several pending activities.

Having bought lunch, Kim and Denis both sat at a table. As they begin to eat, Kim becomes involved in an SMS Chat session. At that very moment, the participation framework in which the chat takes place had not been discussed. Kim could either engage in the chat alone or collaborate with Denis. The following exchange reveals how this issue became relevant to the participants' lunch experience:

Figure 9.1
Kim and Denis's lunch, taken from the GlassCam

1.   Denis: >you have sent a message already?<
2.   *-------→
3.   ((incoming new message ring tone starts)
4.   ((K takes the straw to his lips))
5.   Kim: >yeah!<
6.   -------→

Kim had just sent the "READ" instruction to the SMS Chat operator before the beginning of this exchange, which allowed him to receive the profiles of other participants in the chat. Then he put his phone on the table, unpacked his hamburger, and was about to drink from his cup with his extended finger and hand (Figure 9.1). As Kim re-engaged himself in the meal, Denis introduced a verification question, trying to evaluate the degree to which Kim was already involved in the chat (line 1). The ringing, which began at the end of this question, was potentially disrupting both for the trajectory of the pending hand gesture and for the production of the expected answer. Kim found an embodied way to solve this multi-activity puzzle: first, he took his cup, produced a minimal answer for Denis, took a sip from his straw and, finally, picked up his phone as it was still ringing.

Kim, therefore, took several pending actions and was able to accomplish a temporal distribution that set up a participation framework. Kim was still involved in drinking from his cup. Later, Denis glanced at the phone screen on the table and asked a new confirmation question (line 7), which indicated that he had read the message displayed on the handset:

7.   D: Three received messages?
8.   K: Yeah, three received messages, yes.
9.   K: It doesn't stop ringing.
10.   ((ring tone still playing; display of a new message))
11.   K: Three, four received messages!

This question (line 7) indicated that Denis was not only attending to the chat (already the case in line 1), but also that he was able to observe the rest of the remote exchange. That is, incoming messages were liable to be questioned.

While Denis treated the ringing phone as an occasion to look at the screen, thereby giving him participation status in the chat activity, he never actually handled the mobile by himself. Thus, the position he claimed indicated limited access to the phone, and displayed a certain orientation toward its ownership. Through his answer and further comment about the ongoing ringing and displayed messages (lines 8-11), Kim ratified this position and made what was still happening on his phone publicly available to Denis. At the end of this sequence, it became possible to characterize a participation framework in which: (1) Denis could glance at the mobile phone screen, (2) comment on visible or audio items, (3) question Kim about the chat course, and (4) Kim could read what was coming in on the screen aloud.

Moreover, this participation framework nicely articulated the two main activity streams (the proximal talk and the remote exchange) into a joint, locally embedded coordination. Remote contributions would be either read and discussed between co-present partners or written collaboratively. In brief, the "remote" exchange, far from keeping the mobile phone's owner apart from his co-present mate, became a constitutive part of their common activity.

Keeping Writing Isolated from Interaction

Further dialogue showed that sharing the activity on the mobile phone was never officially, or formally, established. On the contrary, the co-participants reorganized their conduct in relation to the ongoing order of events. Contingencies linked to the temporal organization of the meal, visually relevant happenstances, or the incipient state of talk was suit-

Figure 9.2
A GlassCam view of the visual puzzle: the van's sliding door,
partly open, turns the logo of "Croix Rouge Francaise," or "French Red Cross,"
into "Croix Rose," or "Pink Cross"

able to generate a local contextual work by which the involvement in the chat was reorganized.

In the following fragment, for example, the content on the handset and a feature of the proximal context turned out to be a potentially conflicting issue for the participants' divided attention. In this case, Denis invited Kim to look at a Red Cross van that had stopped just behind them and happened to present an interesting visual puzzle.[9]

[K (Chat message to "angela25"): *hi you look interesting*]

1. D: Look, that makes a reddish cross
2. ((K follows D's eyes and turns head towards a van))
3. K: ((Coming back to the handset)) yeah?
4. D: Look, that makes a reddish cross instead of a red cross
5. ((K resumes SMS writing))
6. D: Look at the van!
7. ((K turns head toward the van))
8. D: As there are the two doors, that makes the reddish cross
9. ((K comes back to the screen then looks at the van again))
10. K: Pink!
11. ((back to screen))
12. D: ((Still watching the van)) Yes, the pink cross or the reddish cross.
13. ((K resumes writing))

While Kim was writing a new message (line 1), Denis directed Kim's attention to a feature of the proximal environment (line 2). This invitation had two interrelated components. First, it included a combination of communication resources with which Kim was encouraged to find what, in his surroundings, was signified by Denis's use of "that." The command "look" was used in order to launch the next relevant action. During this conversation, the images from the GlassCam indicated that Denis turned his gaze to the van. This head movement was a visible gesture indicating where Kim should look to find the target. Because Kim was visibly involved in typing a message, this directive implied that he should break off the writing process to focus on a proximal visual resource. Second, this deictic pointed not to a simple object, but to the identification of a phenomenal, contingent configuration. The van's sliding side door had been partly opened, which produced a truncation of the label normally displayed on the van. The text was transposed into another color label, "croix rose," or "reddish cross," resulting in a visual and linguistic riddle.

Thus, the situation presented the two with a visual puzzle where Denis requested Kim's assistance in resolving the riddle. However, Denis had to first redirect Kim's attention towards the van. The visual search was then woven into the talk. Not only was the accomplishment of the look conditionally relevant to the previous directive, but it was also the first part of a two-part utterance. This second part consisted of a verbal assessment of the visual riddle. It solicited Kim's engagement not only in talk, but also in collocated activity. This sequence nicely combined an invitation for Kim to become involved in a mutual interaction with Denis, via an examination of a visual target in their physical surroundings.

Following Denis's eyes, Kim briefly looked at the van but then refocused on the mobile handset, producing an utterance which can be seen as a minimal acknowledgment of the puzzle. This one-word turn ("yeah," line 3) is similar to a "so what" component, and was uttered with a rising pitch. In essence, it indicates that Kim invited Denis to produce a further explanation. The material from the GlassCam indicated that Kim then immediately returned his visual attention to the mobile phone screen. Thus, while Kim was not looking at the van, he had not entirely closed his participation to the incipient talk. Afterwards, Denis repeated the initial invitation to look, adding an explicit explanation of the visual in order to help Kim understand the point (line 4). This repeated utterance shows that Denis was not only dissatisfied with Kim's assessment of the puzzle, but also that his previous turn failed to elicit Kim's attention.

Thus, Denis directed Kim's attention to the Red Cross van one more time. By this time, Kim had already re-engaged his attention towards the mobile phone activity and did not produce any further proximally relevant actions (line 5).

At this point Denis produced yet a third version of the directive, turning it into an overt command to look at the van (line 6). Once Kim looked at the van, Denis produced a more detailed characterization of the "reddish cross." He explained how the object configuration had produced a surprising, unintended outcome. This explanation was provided the solution of the riddle. However, instead of accepting this interpretation, Kim offered an alternative reading (a "pink cross," line 10). By doing this, he displayed an overt recognition of the puzzle while also disagreeing with Denis's interpretation. Kim then looked back to the mobile handset while Denis took this new reading into account (yet questioned it to some degree).

We can see from the exchange that the initial interaction disturbed Kim's production of SMS Chat text. Looking at the van meant that Kim had to turn away from the screen and therefore had to pause in his writing. Kim underscored the disturbance by affording only a minimal level of participation in the dialogue with Denis. Eventually, Kim artfully engaged in the interaction with his nearby friend, and then again resumed writing his message without making it public.

This weak participation establishes an order of priority, albeit a local one that was open to changes as different exigencies arose. The writing of the text message gained status as the main activity, the exchange with Denis becoming secondary. It was something to which Kim returned after a brief (re)involvement with the secondary activity stream. The analysis of this fragment allows us to see that the stability of a participation framework is a potential issue for those who are engaged in a proximal setting. This is particularly the case when one member is involved in both a remote and a proximate interaction.

Making Sense of Categories: A Situated Reception of a Message

New SMS Chat messages are signaled by ring tones. In social situations, they often contain news that can be introduced into the co-present conversation. Reading incoming messages also introduces pauses and hesitations that open up new occasions for talk. In the following fragment, Kim reads a message he has just received aloud. His tripping over a word initiates a clarification sequence:

1.   K: Then "Makliz" ((reading the message)) *Young girl from Morocco would like to talk (.) to a be/*
2.   *berkani?* What's that. (0.8) *Or an oudji? or from the neighborhood a cool person from Paris or*
3.   *beside.*
4.   (----)
5.   K: What is a berkani?
6.   D: I guess it is a, uhm ::[::
7.   K: [Bertrand?
8.   D: No, I guess it is like berbers, kabyls and so on.
9.   K: Or idji? or from °the same area°. no no no no no this is not for me.
10.   ((K comes back to the message list and opens a new SMS))
11.   D: I guess it's the different, uh (-) regions from (-) Arabic countries.
12.   D: >I guess uhm!<
13.   (-)
14.   : eh I thought I had four messages where ( ) the others?

The message Kim read was sent to all SMS chat participants, and had adopted a classical self-presentation format: the sender (Makliz) described herself and proposed a very precise identification of the kind of person with whom she wanted to chat. It included the use of nicknames and the availability for more focused interaction (de Fornel, 1989; see also Ten Have, 2000). The woman's public form of self-presentation was a potential preface to beginning of an exchange.

In lines 1-2, Kim read the message aloud and discovered that the sender was looking for rather specific types of individuals. Kim trips over the category label as he reads it (line 1) and requests a clarification ("what's that," line 2). The orientation of this question was not clear; it could have been either a self-interrogation embedded in the reading or a question directed to Denis. Denis's response heads the potential to define the term as a new conversational item, or as a comment set apart from the reading of the message. In this case, Denis did not produce any answer. He was busy eating his hamburger and was absorbed in that activity. Kim, after a short pause, resumed the reading and came across another term that he did not understand (as indicated by the pitch in tone). Once he reached the end of the message, and after a long pause, he repeated the question about the first unknown item. This question was only then explicitly divorced from the reading.

In contrast to the first question about "berkani" people, which was not answered by Denis, Kim specifically solicited a response the second time. After a short collaborative search, Denis proposed an answer. To make sense of the categories proposed, he compared them with other ethnic categories. The outcome is a list that exhibits a possible, not uttered, but understandable, collection of "similar" categories: Moroccan ethnic groups. At the end of Denis's turn, which opened a new opportunity for him to talk, Kim went back to reading aloud. This reading was both a conversational expansion of the last turn as well as a new transition to the mobile phone screen. After reading aloud the other two categories, Kim went back to the message reception. At that point, the reading was still deeply intertwined in the talk. Through this artful hybrid turn, which belonged both to the talk and to the reading, Kim managed to complete the clarification sequence while resuming the chat. Finally, he added one last turn in which he concluded that he was not a convenient addressee of the SMS message (line 9). As such, when Denis expands his previous point by proposing a definition of the relevant ethnic group (lines 11-12), no answer is given. The final comment produced by Kim confirmed that he had already closed both the vocal sequence and the reading of Makliz's message.

During this sequence, the potential of the proximal conversation was linked to the reading of the message and was closely embedded in the search for a possible answer to the remote exchange. Because the message proposed a list of potential partners, the reading turns into an inspection of a possible correspondence between the proposed characterizations and a possible self-selection of Kim as a suitable chat partner. The reading of the message brings Denis into the interaction, but Kim keeps ultimate control over how to end this sequence.[10]

Conclusion

In the analysis presented here, we see how the remote and the local are woven into a unified sequence. However, special skills are needed if we are to embed remotely produced messages into proximal interactions. These messages have the ability to affect the trajectory of the local interaction.

In this chapter, I have presented a new methodological approach (the GlassCam) and examined its relevance in the analysis of how one organizes remote mobile phone communication in a local space. Video-based studies of concrete, tangible activities done with mobile phones shed light on how we interlace the local and the remote. Far from being divorced from their surroundings, these remote contributions are being "made at home" with mundane practices (Sacks, 1992). The diffusion of the mobile phone underscores the importance of this articulation work. We have to learn how to tailor and time our involvement in various simultaneous streams of activity.

Remote conversations have been examined as situated phenomena, embedded in the organization of multi-activity settings and their particular ongoing participation frameworks. In order to analyze the local constitution of "remote" exchanges, we need to understand the various ways in which vocal or textual contributions gain a precise role in the situated, socially and materially, embedded situation. As it has been shown, some contributions gain a hybrid nature, belonging to both the remote and the local realms. Other contributions to the remote exchange are kept in isolation from the local circumstances.

While favoring the constitution of a common communication space, modern technologies generate a split between the remote and the local. Thus, by focusing on how mobile technology—and the remote communication that it supports—fits into specific places and interactions, we can begin to meet the challenge of understanding how the far and the near constitute a coherent course of action. From this perspective, activities linked to media use (e.g., surfing the web, taking pictures, sending an MMS, viewing TV on a phone) are deeply embedded in the social organization of ordinary courses of action. However, to understand how media uses merge with other observable activities, we need to explore the details of how participants constitute an understanding of these articulations. Once we will be able to compare, in a more systematic way, how various media features contribute to this articulation, we will gain a better understanding of our increasingly technological but still common world.

Appendix: Transcription Conventions

Italics	Used exclusively for representing the written text, as readable on the mobile phone screen.
°word°	Indicates that the speech is produced at an attenuated sound level compared to what follows and precedes
word::::	Underlines the notable lengthening of the preceding syllable. The number of points indicates the relative length of the lengthening.
(.)	Marks a micro-pause of less than two tenths of a second

(-)   Indicates a more extended silence

(.5)   Silence of 0.5 seconds

(word)   Indicates uncertainty about the transcription of an
                item

((sentence/text)) Introduces a description

[ ]   Indicates overlapping of speech between two or
                several speakers

>a little time< Frame a segment that is accelerated compared to the
                rest of the speech.

*------→   Indicates an interruption of the preceding segment

Notes

1. Numerous issues discussed in this paper have been discussed in various presenta-
    tions at L'Ecole des Hautes Etudes en Sciences Sociales, France Telecom Research
    and Development, and the International Conference on Conversation Analysis at
    Copenhagen (Relieu, 2002).
2. As defined by C. Heath and P. Luff, "micro-mobility" refers to "the way in which an
    artifact can by mobilized and manipulated for various purposes around a relatively
    circumscribed, or 'at hand'" (1996: 306).
3. Goffman (1981) defines participation frameworks in a structural way: "When a
    word is spoken, all those who happen to be in perceptual range of the event will
    have some sort of participation status relative to it. The codification of these vari-
    ous positions and the normative specification of appropriate conduct within each
    provide an essential background for interaction analysis—whether (I presume)
    in our own society or any other" (3). For an example of how this notion has been
    built upon, see Goodwin and Goodwin, 1992.
4. The quality of recordings depends on ambient light, screen quality, and numerous
    other partially uncontrollable local conditions. In the work reported on here, less
    than 20 percent of the data could be used for research purposes. It is also important
    to note that the ego-centered view does not reflect the sight of the user. In other
    words, it is impossible to distinguish head movements from eye orientations.
5. It would be more rigorous to capture multiple perspectives in a single location, for
    example, combining a close-up camera on the handset/screen with a wide-angle
    camera to record the interaction with others (see Goodwin, 1996). However, it is
    difficult to set up multiple recording devices in public areas and it is not easy to
    track mobile phone use in successive natural settings.
6. In some cases, I was present during the actual recording. In these cases, I acted
    as an observer and noted down the progress of the interaction. In other cases, the
    informants took the equipment with them and used it over several days.
7. Compared to current Internet chat systems, SMS Chat on the mobile phone is a
    very primitive service. For instance, it is not possible to open several frames and
    chat simultaneously with different people or groups.
8. When participants sustain a shared involvement in the rhythm of the reading and
    writing of their textual productions, SMS exchanges display a quasi-conversational
    structure. Each new SMS is produced with the expectation that it will be read as
    soon as received and "immediately" replied to. The timing of the delivery and
    the reading and writing process of each participant defines a "normal" delay for

the other and displays her interest for the other. The temporal order of the textual exchange constitutes a normative basis for the detection of "lapses" and the attribution of motives.

9. Several studies have investigated the act of seeing as embedded within complex webs of activities (Lynch, 1988; Goodwin, 1996, 2000).

10. Note that the message is not a private message addressed to Kim but a public proposal sent to everyone in the chat. It is, therefore, "safe" to read it aloud since there is no risk of unveiling private content.

Bibliography

de Fornel, Michel. "Une Situation Interactionnelle Négligée: La Messagerie Télématique." *Réseaux*, 38 (1989): 31-48.

Goffman, Erving. *Forms of Talk*. Philadelphia, PA: University of Pennsylvania Press, 1981.

Goodwin, Charles. "Transparent Vision." In *Interaction and Grammar*, edited by Elinor Ochs, Emanuel A. Schegloff and Sandra A. Thompson, 370-404. Cambridge, UK: Cambridge University Press, 1996.

Goodwin, Charles. "Practices of Seeing: Visual Analysis; An Ethnomethodological Approach." In *The Handbook of Visual Analysis*, edited by Theo Van Leeuwen and Carey Jewitt, 157-182. London, UK: Sage Publications, 2000.

Goodwin, Charles and Marjorie H. Goodwin. "Context, Activity and Participation." In *The Contextualization of Language*, edited by Peter Auer and Aldo Di Luzio, 77-99. Amsterdam, Netherlands: John Benjamins Publishing, 1992.

ten Have, Paul. "Computer-mediated Chat: Ways of Finding Chat Partners." *M/C: A Journal of Media and Culture,* 3 (August 2000): http://www.api-network.com/mc/0008/partners.php (accessed 31 August 31, 2007).

Heath, Christian C. and Paul Luff. "Convergent Activities: Line Control and Passenger Information on the London Underground." In *Cognition and Communication at Work*, edited by Yrjo Engeström and David Middleton, 96-129. Cambridge, UK: Cambridge University Press, 1996.

Ito, Mizuko, and Daisuke Okabe. "Technosocial Situations: Emergent Structurings of Mobile Email Use." In *Personal, Portable, Pedestrian: Mobile Phones in Japanese Life,* edited by Mizuko Ito, Daisuke Okabe, and Misa Matsuda, 257-273. Cambridge, MA: MIT Press, 2005.

Koskinen, Ilpo. "Seeing with Mobile Images: Towards Perpetual Visual Contact." In *A Sense of Place: the Global and the Local in Mobile Communication,* edited by Kristóf Nyíri, 339-348. Vienna, Austria: Passagen Verlag, 2005.

Ling, Richard S. "The Social Juxtaposition of Mobile Telephone Conversations and Public Spaces." Paper delivered at the Conference on the Social Consequences of Mobile Telephones. July 2002, Chunchon, Korea.

Ling, Richard S. "'One Can Talk About Common Manners!' The Use of Mobile Telephones in Inappropriate Situations." In *Themes in Mobile Telephony:*

Final Report of the COST 248 Home and Work group, edited by Leslie Haddon. Farsta, Sweden: Telia, 1997.

Lynch, Michael. "The Externalized Retina: Selection and Mathematization in the Visual Documentation of Objects in the Life Sciences." *Human Studies*, 11 (April 1998): 201-234.

Mark, Gloria, Urik Christensen, and Michael Shafae. "A Methodology Using a Microcamera for Studying Mobile IT Usage and Person Mobility." Paper delivered at the Annual Conference on Human Factors in Computing Systems (CHI), 1-2 April 2001. Seattle, Washington.

Pomerantz, Anita and B.J. Fehr. "Conversation Analysis: An Approach to the Study of Social Action as Sense Making Practices." In *Discourse as Social Interaction*, ed. Teun A. van Dijk, 64-91. London, UK: Sage Publications, 1997.

Relieu, Marc. "The 'Glasscam' as an Observational Tool for Studying Screen-based Mobile Phone Uses and Management of Parallel Activities." Paper delivered at the International Conference on Conversation Analysis (ICCA), 20 May 2002. Copenhagen, Denmark.

Relieu, Marc., and Julien Morel. "L'hybridation contrôlée des usages du mobile en public: une approche située (Mobile phone uses in public: a situated approach of how to manage hybridization)". In *Mobilités.net: Villes, Transports et Technologies Face aux Nouvelles Mobilités*, edited by Daniel Kaplan and Hubert Lafont, 175-181. Paris, France: FING, 2004.

Sacks, Harvey. "Notes on Methodology." In *Structures of Social Action: Studies in Conversation Analysis*, eds. by John M. Atkinson and John Heritage, 21-27. Cambridge, UK: Cambridge University Press, 1984.

Sacks, Harvey. *Lectures on Conversation*, edited by Gail Jefferson. Oxford, UK: Blackwell Publishing, 1995.

Weilenmann, Alexandra. "Doing Mobility." Ph.D. dissertation, Göteborg University, Swede, 2003.

Weilenmann, Alexandra and Catrine Larsson. "Local Use and Sharing of Mobile Phones." In *Wireless World: Social and Interactional Aspects of the Mobile Age*, edited by Barry Brown, Nicola Green, and Richard Harper, 92-107. London: Springer Verlag, 2002.

Zouinar, Moustafa, Marc Relieu, Pascal Salembier, and Guillaume Calvet. "Observation and Capture of Multimodal Interaction in Mobile Situations." In *The Proceedings of the 1st French-speaking Conference on Mobility and Ubiquity computing (UbiMob)*, 5-8. Nice, France: ACM Press, 2004.

10

Beyond the Personal and Private: Modes of Mobile Phone Sharing in Urban India

Molly Wright Steenson
Princeton University School of Architecture

Jonathan Donner
Microsoft Research India

Arundathi is a college student in Bangalore. As she sits in one of the city's many new popular coffee shops, her mobile rings. Although the young woman on the other end of the line is not looking for Arundathi, she has not misdialed, either. The caller asks if Arundathi's friend Neema is there. Indeed, she is, and Arundathi happily passes over the handset. The caller was trying to locate Neema but did so by contacting *someone* else, not *someplace* else. This incident is both an example of mobile sharing, and how the use of mobile phones complicates and restructures physical and social space. As sharing mobiles is relatively common but not well represented in the research literature, this chapter explores the connection between mobile sharing and social space.

Of course, the mobile phone is designed to be moved from place to place and allows users to connect with others no matter where they might be. It is a simple proposition, but one with significant impacts on daily life. Inquiry around these impacts is advancing, led by the development of mobile theories with a specific focus on spatial issues, such as the real-time city (Townsend, 2000), absent (Gergen, 2002) or connected (Licoppe, 2004) presence, and hyper- and micro-coordination (Ling and Yttri, 2002). Yet, as the theme of this volume makes clear, decades into the mobile communications age we are still making sense of how mobile communications both reflect and reconstruct spaces.

This chapter contributes to the overall dialogue on the significance of mobile communication for human, social space by expanding the inquiry into one of the world's largest communities of mobile users, India. In this context, we draw on ethnographic research to identify various modes of mobile phone sharing that cannot be entirely explained by economic necessity and instead reflect deeper processes of human organization. In the process, this chapter further illustrates how mobile communication helps people create and alter the social spaces around them.

Background

To begin, we briefly review existing literature on three distinct conceptual threads: the relationship of mobiles and other information communication technologies to space, the sharing of mobile communication devices, and the growing importance of mobile communication in the developing world. We then synthesize these threads to present our ideas about how mobile phone sharing in India relates to the reconstitution of space.

Social Space and Mobile Space

Lefebvre, Appadurai, and Castells remind us that space is structured by the humans who occupy it. For Lefebvre (1991, 26), "(Social) space is a (social) product," marked by "spatial practice." Appadurai defines "locality" and "neighborhood" in this regard: locality is "primarily relational and contextual" rather than "scalar or spatial" (Appadurai, 1996, 178); neighborhoods are "situated communities characterized by their actuality, whether spatial or virtual, and their potential for social reproduction" (179).

The use of communication technologies challenge and reconstruct these social spaces. Castells (2000) suggests that space is "not a reflection of society, it is its expression . . . space is not a photocopy of society, it is society." To Castells, "the space of flows," brought about by the widespread use of communication technologies, is the material form of the informational society (441). Like other communication technologies, mobile use pressures older concepts of space (Nyíri, 2005), divides attention between proximate and distant subjects (Gergen, 2002; Licoppe, 2004), creates tension between private conversations and public venues (Höflich, 2006), and enables coordination and simultaneity over distances (Ling and Yttri, 2002; Townsend, 2000). Overall, the research suggests that like its antecedent, the landline (Gottmann, 1977), the mobile telephone is a powerful mediator and disruptor of these human social spaces and is a new addition to the growing tensions "between the space of flows and the space of places" (Castells et al., 2007; Castells and Susser, 2002, 397).

Sharing Mobiles

Sharing is among the core subjects of social inquiry (Huntsman and Hooper, 1996; Mauss, 1990). However, research on the sharing of mobile phones is relatively rare. Weilenmann and Larsson (2001) argue that sharing behaviors challenge the dominant, default view of mobile phones as personal, individual devices (e.g., Katz and Aakhus, 2002). They describe how Swedish teens shared mobiles in a "minimal" way by exchanging messages across handsets, and in a "hands on" manner by sharing time on a single call, through borrowing and lending phones both among friends, and, occasionally, to proximate strangers. Taylor and Harper (2003) identify sharing as a critical component of mobile use by teens, describing the "gifting" of SMS messages between proximate users as they leaning over each other's handsets. Bell (2005) notes that while mobile use in Asia may be mostly individualistic, sharing behaviors are common in families.

Different Contexts, Different Uses—Mobiles in the Developing World

The third conceptual thread involves distinct patterns of mobile use in the developing world, where connectivity is now possible for millions who previously could not afford a landline. In India, for example, between March 2003 and September 2006, mobile subscriptions increased tenfold, from 13 million to 129 million. By contrast, fixed line growth has been relatively stagnant, with 40 million lines currently in operation (Telecom Regulatory Authority of India, 2007).

Reviews of the social and economic implications of this sudden availability (Castells et al., 2007; Donner, 2008), suggest that for much of the world, mobile use is substantially and symbolically distinct from use in the prosperous global North. On the one hand, mobile use in the developing world is defined and structured by persistent conditions of economic scarcity and low tele-density, particularly in rural areas (Cartier et al., 2005; Zainudeen et al., 2006). These conditions encourage reliance on pre-pay cards (Minges, 1999), public pay-per-use mobile phones (Sey, 2006), and the use of beeping, flashing, and missed calls as strategies to keep mobile expenditures low (Donner, 2007; Zainudeen et al., 2006). Even in urban contexts, among emerging middle-class families, telecommunications expenditures can be a significant proportion of household income, leading to careful assessments of if, when, and how to place a call (Donner et al., 2008). Looking beyond economic scarcity, other researchers are exploring how socio-cultural differences structure mobile use (Campbell, 2007; Horst and Miller, 2006; Leonardi et al., 2006). Still others argue that the mobile is a global device with strong and problematic symbolic value as a consumerist, individualistic tool (Kavoori and Chadha, 2006).

Synthesis and Research Problem

Both central concepts of this paper (mobiles and space, mobiles and sharing) have been studied in developing-world settings, both rural and urban. Mobile use sets norms and helps individuals carve "personal" spaces out of crowded urban environments. Maroon explores mobile use in the changing urban spaces of Morocco, emphasizing how it is as "culturally-situated bodies that people utilize inventions with the power to reorganize normative modes of sociality" (201). Writing about the Philippines, Paragas (2005) explores norms of mobile use on Manila's crowded public busses, while Pertierra (2005) explains how Filipinos, "without a room of their own," use the mobile to create private spaces. Conversely, in rural areas, mobiles help conquer distance and isolation by linking villages and individuals to the rest of the nation and beyond (Tall, 2004).

Recent research has also begun to explore mobile sharing behaviors in developing-world settings. Perhaps most salient is the mobile kiosk, made famous by Grameen's formal, franchised Village Phones in Bangladesh (Aminuzzaman et al., 2003). The transactional model of mobile phone as public payphone is actually quite varied, encompassing both formal ventures, such as Village Phone or Vodacom's community phone shops in South Africa (see Reck and Wood, 2004), to grey-market "umbrella ladies" who offer little more than a lawn chair and a handset (Sey, 2006). These shared-access models extend telecommunications services to rural and urban poor alike (Donner, 2005; Reck and Wood, 2004).

Sharing is not limited to these formal, transactional venues, however. For example, Chiphcase and Tulusan (2007) detail a variety of ways in which sharing occurs over and around handsets. Their field notes from Uganda describe pooling minutes, coordinating electric charges (Samuel et al., 2005), beeping/intentional missed calls (Donner, 2007), and electronic banking and remittances (Ivatury, 2006). In rural villages, many handsets may be gifts from family members who have moved to the city or overseas (Tall, 2004).

Looking at urban areas, Konkka (2003) stresses the importance of sharing and collectivist approaches to the handset to Indian consumers. Other research from urban India suggests that within families, children often share handsets with parents (Donner et al., 2008; Horst and Miller, 2005), and wives share handsets with husbands (David, 2005); in both cases, the negotiations around mobile use reflect and restructure family dynamics.

Nevertheless, these sharing studies are at the periphery of a research literature that mostly assumes that the mobile is owned and operated by a single user. It is against this backdrop—a relative lack of research on mobile sharing, a growing interest in distinct forms of mobile use in the developing world, and continued interest in the complex relationship between mobiles and space that we embarked on our Bangalore study. Our study involved a set of interviews and observational visits centered on relationships between location, space and sharing behavior. We focus on non-transactional sharing behaviors that involve the handset itself. We distinguish this physical, visible sharing from the "minimal" forms identified by Weilenmann and Larsson (2001), from the village phone or commercial phone kiosk, and from the broader array of sharing behaviors identified by Chipchase and Tulusan (2007).

At the outset, we had no *a priori* categorization of mobile phone sharing behaviors. Though we set out to interview people at a variety of socio-economic levels in urban Bangalore, we expected to see more instances of sharing among relatively poorer individuals and households, since these groups would be less likely to afford (own) mobiles of their own. We also expected to see relatively formalized sharing arrangements, such as explicit device sharing and people sharing one handset with multiple SIM cards, something we had heard of anecdotally. Instead, we found little evidence of a strong economic demarcation of sharing and observed plenty of mobile sharing, even among middle-class Bangalorians.

Mobile Phone Sharing in Bangalore: An Ethnographic Study

Our study consisted of interviews with thirty-nine residents of Bangalore, conducted in July and August of 2006; eighteen were male, twenty-one were female. Interview subjects fit into three groups: students or recent college graduates and their family members (fifteen students, eight parents or elder relatives), service workers (five men and six women, who fill a number of small service jobs), and micro-entrepreneurs (three from a large street market, two with businesses in a Bangalore apartment complex). We used three overlapping methods to recruit interview participants. Working with research assistants from Bangalore fluent in Hindi and the local language, Kannada, we identified an initial small set of middle-class interview subjects and moved from there, via referrals, to their friends and neighbors. Next, we visited seven homes in Bangalore's largest slum thanks to Geeta Menon of Stree Jagruti Samiti, an organization that aids domestic workers. Finally, we re-contacted a vendor with whom we were acquainted from a previous study on low-income micro-entrepreneurs (Donner, 2006), as a point of departure for observing sharing activity in Bangalore's Gandhi Market. From his post, we sat back from the street, watched activity and approached people when we noticed sharing behaviors, interviewing those who consented to speak with us. We conducted our interviews in homes, workplaces, and cafés, where the people sharing phones were likeliest to be most comfortable. In some situations, we conducted interviews in group settings of friends or family members; this sometimes offered a different perspective than we realized from individuals.

Through observations and interviews, we identified various forms of sharing. Table 10.1 illustrates two spatial dimensions to these behaviors, which in turn became the basis for our categorization of sharing behaviors. First, some behaviors were *proximate*, meaning the sharing was initiated between two or more people co-present in a location. Often, but not always, this resulted in one person borrowing a handset from another to place a call. Other forms were *distributed*, meaning that the sharing behavior was prompted by an incoming call from somewhere else.

Second, spatial factors restricted distinct sharing behaviors to certain social-spatial domains: different spatial contexts (domestic, out and about, marketplace, and village-to-urban) fostered different forms of sharing. Both dimensions illustrate how mobile use complicates what was once more straightforward: when all telephones were landlines, people called *places*; now, people call *people* (Wellman, 2001). The various forms of sharing we identified (conspicuous, stealthy, person-seeking, and place-seeking) are discussed below.

Conspicuous Sharing

Although the mobile may be a personal device, it is not necessarily a *private* device—people borrow handsets. This most obvious and natural form of mobile sharing is the "hands on" approach described by Weilenmann and Larsson (2001: 104). Such conspicuous, informal sharing is born out of social and spatial proximity. We saw this form of sharing in every spatial context we visited: within the home, out and about, in

Table 10.1
Kinds of sharing across various settings

Co-Presence	Sharing Behavior	Spatial Context			
		Domestic	Out & about	Marketplace	Village-to-urban
Yes - Proximate	Conspicuous	Yes	Yes	Yes	Yes
	Stealthy	Yes			
No - Distributed	Person-seeking	Yes	Yes		Yes
	Place-seeking	Yes		Yes	Yes

the marketplace, and between urban workers and their families in rural villages.

In domestic settings, mobiles come out of pockets and purses, and are placed on tables and countertops, both for recharging and for easy accessibility. These visible resting places may prompt mobiles to temporarily take on "landline" characteristics and enable and encourage conspicuous sharing. We saw this pattern in the family of Sushma, a forty-eight-year-old middle-class housewife with a home-based life insurance business. Sushma's husband, sister, mother, twenty-five-year-old daughter visiting from the United States, and twenty-year-old son all make use of her phone even though many of them have mobile phones of their own. The situation is similar in twenty-year-old Girish's family. He, his mother, and his father all charge their mobiles on a table in the front hallway. Though Girish and his father both own the same, relatively fancy handset model, he freely uses his father's phone. As he wryly puts it, "What's mine is mine, what's theirs is mine too." While Girish acknowledges he uses his father's phone when he has his own, economically, it all comes from the same place—Girish's father pays for his son's calls, which amount to Rs. 300 a month (about $7 USD). Yet Girish does not like using his mother's phone. This is not for an economic reason but rather because his mother receives too many business calls on it.

Siblings, too, use each other's mobile phones, particularly when a younger sibling does not yet own a mobile. When Ajay, twenty, shares with his eighteen-year-old brother Abhishek, Abhishek uses it to text or call his friends while the two of them are watching TV. The case is similar with Raghu, twenty, who comes home from school and places his shiny 3G handset on top of the television set ("It's India's place to leave things," he explains). Inevitably, his sixteen-year-old brother will grab it, but not to make calls or send text messages: his friends don't have their own mobiles either, so he uses the phone to play games or listen to the radio.

The rationale for such sharing is not purely economic, and instead reflects deeper family dynamics. In particular, the patterns of sharing between husbands and wives reflected differences in gender roles. These gender differences are not unique to India—for example, Ling (2001) observed a gendered component to mobile phone non-ownership (rejection) in Norway, but they were particularly evident among the homes we visited in Bangalore. Dickey (2000) writes about the predominance of traditional gender roles: men are viewed as primary earners who make household decisions; women maintain the home and kinship network and raise children, regardless of employment outside the home. Tying into this is the cultural ideal of modesty for Indian women, crossing caste, class, and religion. Some of the more prosperous women we interviewed expressed little interest in owning their own mobile phones. Lata, forty-four, said she never wanted to own a mobile phone; her two landlines were sufficient. When she goes out, she says she can use the family driver's phone, a phone booth, or the phone of a vendor to call home. Only when we asked explicitly did Lata reveal that she shares her husband's mobile: she shares it when they are in the same place, but would not consider taking it with her, away from him. Like other women we interviewed who do not carry mobiles, sharing with a spouse is so commonplace it isn't even mentioned. Jyotisana, forty-three, also a traditionally dressed housewife, uses her husband's new mobile phone. "I'll never get my own mobile," she says; she insists that her twenty-year-old daughter, Soumya, will not get one unless she moves away for a job. Clearly, the mobiles are shared between husband and wife, but not on equal terms (David, 2005).

When a family goes out, the assumptions around mobile sharing become particularly evident. Anasuya, twenty-three, a recent master's graduate, has carried a mobile phone since early 2004; her sister, Aparna, twenty-seven, has carried one since 2001. But when the two sisters go out with their mother, only the mother carries a mobile. Similarly, everybody has the mobile number of Sushma, the housewife and insurance agent mentioned above; they reach the family through her. When we shared these stories within our research lab, one researcher said her family did the same thing: only her mother carried a mobile when the family went out. When asked how we would reach her, she said, "If you were meant to reach me at dinner with my family, you would already have the number!"

This behavior illustrates the blurry boundaries between the handsets, the numbers, and the individuals who supposedly are reachable by those numbers; when the family is in one place, it may require only one handset, which in turn reinforces the cohesiveness of the family unit.

We also saw this lack of correspondence between handsets and individuals among the groups of friends we visited. While "out and about," Raghu prolifically shares his mobile phone not only with his brother, but also with his friend, Rajesh, twenty-one. Without asking first, Rajesh picks up the phone and freely texts friends in the group. He also answers the phone for Raghu when he is Raghu's moped passenger. In the same group of friends, Rajesh also uses the phones of friends Gautam and Minthu, who each claim not to mind at all. Text messages are essentially free within the prepaid mobile phone plans they have, but the freedom of sharing seems to extend beyond economic argument. The frequent sharing of handsets, messages, and message credits among the group reinforces the close relationships between its members. Moreover, Rajesh carries on the communication with and for the group, which serves the collective good. But these interactions are bounded; Rajesh does not use his friends' mobile phones outside of the group situation; he does not borrow it to take home at night, for example. This out-and-about behavior resembles the sharing behavior of wives who reject mobile ownership in favor of sharing with their husbands. Ironically, Rajesh could have owned a mobile phone if he had wanted one, but perhaps he knew he could count on his friends' handsets. His parents gave him the money for a mobile, but he chose to spend it on clothes and a DVD burner.

In addition, conspicuous cell phone sharing happens outside of close relationships. Within other mutually beneficial exchanges, mobile phone sharing is a courtesy. In Bangalore's Gandhi Bazaar, a thriving market street, we approached fruit vendor, Mahadev, thirty-two, after observing him lend his phone to another vendor. The other vendor used it to place an outbound call because he was out of credit on his own phone. Though not close friends, the two were familiar to each other; Mahadev has worked at Gandhi Bazaar since he was twelve and in his current location for fifteen years. It was no matter to extend the courtesy to the other vendor.

The forms of mobile sharing described in this section are conspicuous and common, which is why we start with this category in our observations. Certainly, economic constraints shape the form mobile sharing takes (Haddon and Vincent, 2005). Among the young middle-class users we spoke to, it was more common to share lower-cost text messages and free features on the phone like games, radio, or MP3, rather than outbound voice calls. The more economically-constrained users in our discussions reported using mobiles only for incoming calls, going to one-rupee (about $0.02 USD) phone booths to make return calls; they also used the phone to place "missed calls" (Donner, 2007). However, as these observations show, non-economic factors structure the ways people overtly share mobile phones. In the home, territoriality and positioning shape proximity—while rules and mores determine appropriateness of use; as occurs elsewhere in the world, the handsets are "domesticated" according to deeper patterns and expectations of family dynamics (Haddon, 2003). In the middle-class homes in urban India we visited, those expectations include the sharing of handsets according to a blend of communal and hierarchical family roles. Among students, friends who share minutes and message credits or tease each other by nabbing and hiding mobiles, demonstrate in-groups and outsider status by their target choices.

Stealthy Sharing

A second form of sharing happens among people proximate in space without agreement or explicit consent. Simply put, our interviews with family members illustrated that occasionally, young people in the household borrow phones from their parents without their parents' knowledge.

Stealthy mobile phone sharing circumvents rules parents or other authority figures put in place. Ashita, a twenty-four-year-old architecture student, has owned a mobile since 2002 but says she always runs out of currency on her prepaid plan. Her parents know she has a boyfriend, but the family does not discuss him. When Ashita runs out of credit on her phone, she sometimes uses the mobile of her father, Avani, fifty-three, to text the boyfriend, carefully erasing the sent message in the call register. Yet, she also openly uses her father's mobile to text her friends. "It's this mobile freakiness," Avani says. "She can't do without it." Ashita also reaches out to her neighbor friends when she needs to use a mobile phone. When she ran out of currency in the middle of a fight with her boyfriend, she bolted to the apartment of Nishita, twenty, to finish the argument on Nishita's mobile. But if Ashita lent her phone to her friends, she would likely erase her personal information before doing so—as her twenty-year-old neighbor, Vicky, told us, anybody his age erases personal messages and call registers before sharing their mobiles.

If this stealthy use were a clear-cut case of theft or stealing, we would not count it as sharing.[1] But as we discussed previously, the personal-not-private nature of the mobile blurs lines of behavior. The difference arises in the level of transparency of phone use in terms of who the phone is used to contact and how frequently. If the conspicuous forms help reinforce and restructure family and friendship ties, then these surreptitious forms may undermine or subvert them.

Person-Seeking: "Approxi-Calling"

So far, we have described two modes of sharing that are relatively straightforward, since they occur among co-present actors—people use another's handset to make out-calls with permission (conspicuously) or without it (stealthily). Other modes are more complex, as in-calls involve actors distributed in geographic and social space.

At the beginning of this chapter, we described Arundathi and Neema's "out-and-about" sharing at a café, when Arundathi's personal mobile phone rang with a call for Neema. The interaction seems simple, but it requires a tacit understanding among the participants that one person can call a second person and expect that second person to (a) be near the actual call target and (b) be willing to pass the phone over to the target. It is a similar story to the one reported by Weilenmann and Larsson in Sweden:

> A girl sitting at a table at the far end of the café has a phone that is ringing loudly. The girl, A, stands up and begins running across the café, while holding the ringing phone in her hand. She runs to the other end of the room, ten tables away. Four ring signals have now been heard. She gives the phone to a girl, B, sitting at a table. B answers the phone. A walks back to her table. B talks for a while, then puts on her coat and leaves the café together with her friend, and the phone: A remains seated in the café. (100)

Parents know how to contact their non-mobile-owning children via their friends' mobile phones. If Nimisha, twenty-three, is not at home or school, she is likely with her best friends Supriya, Anu, or Anasuya. Her mother, Lata, knows how to reach her, even though Nimisha does not carry a mobile phone. Lata simply calls one of the three young women's mobile phones, knowing she will eventually find her daughter. This is not very different from recent landline-only circumstances where she might have called the homes of each of the young women to touch base with her daughter. However, even though the young women may be at someone's apartment where she could call a landline, Lata still calls their mobiles. This reflects a hybrid of person-to-person and person-to-place calling as described by Wellman (2001). Nimisha's friends do not mind fielding the calls and sharing the handset, even though the purpose of the call may be just to keep in touch or exchange a trivial piece of information.

Approxi-calling is not restricted to family members and cliques of friends. Anand, thirty-three, a personal driver, and Santosh, twenty-seven, a caretaker, both accept calls for other workers at the apartment complex where they work. The workers call their families back from one-rupee phone booths. Anand and Santosh both come from villages far from Bangalore. When they each moved to the city, they relied on others to share phone messages from their families. Ultimately, this proved unreliable and, in Santosh's case, tragic when he did not receive the news that a family member was critically ill. He made it back to his family's village in Kerala too late. The crisis sparked each man to get his own mobile phone. Now, both Anand and Santosh serve as connection points for numerous people; they field approxi-calls from the families of other workers at the apartment complex, passing on messages to the workers, who in turn call their families from one-rupee phone booths. Anand and Santosh try to be more trustworthy than the people they originally relied upon before they had mobile phones. In turn, these sharing transactions create and reinforce not only the social bonds between the phone owner and the call target, but also in an overall ecosystem connecting rural villages to the urban apartment complex.

Place Seeking and Fixing: Landline Substitutes

In areas where landlines are scarce, the mobile is often used as a substitute for a landline, rather than as a complement to it (Hamilton, 2003). As we described above, the mobile on the kitchen counter might be used similarly to a domestic landline, but we found other manifestations of this substitution effect in sharing behaviors outside the home, as, in some instances, callers sought to speak to someone (anyone) at a location, rather than to a specific person (Wellman, 2001).

In Gandhi Bazaar, we spoke to locksmith Venkatesh, forty-four, who has worked in the same location at the market for thirty years. His workplace consists of a bench with a vice, bags of different keys, a small cabinet, and a trunk that also serves as a place to sit. At night, he puts away these items in a nearby building. He has owned two mobile phones in three years (he gave his first to a vendor around the corner). Though his workplace is in the open air, uncovered, and portable, his mobile phone affords his business a degree of predictable reachability previously available only to more formal enterprises with permanent structures to support a landline. At work, Venkatesh places the mobile phone on top of or inside of his cabinet. It is answered by whoever is around, most likely him, his son, or the vendor next to him. If he leaves town, as he does for his annual holiday, the locksmith who works in his location uses his mobile. Thus, Venkatesh's locksmith business shares the mobile in the same way it would share a landline. People who call Venkatesh's mobile aren't necessarily calling Venkatesh, the individual; they are calling the locksmith in Gandhi Market.

Sharing as a Contextual Lens

We have discussed four forms of mobile sharing, as observed across different physical and social spaces. Not all forms of sharing happen in all social-spatial contexts. Mobile phones are shared freely in the home, by necessity when out-and-about, as an approxi-calling method to reach someone in a social network, and as a substitute for landlines in small business settings. Mobile sharing in urban India exemplifies the themes outlined by Castells and Appadurai, demonstrating the tensions at play between the global and the local, as well as the "local interaction" of mobile phones, used and shared in a local situation, as outlined by Weilenmann and Larsson (2001: 92). Most importantly, the notion of mobile phone sharing provides a contextual lens, through which we can better understand the interactions between people, their mobile phones, and human space. Sharing marks the production of social space, to follow Lefebvre's (1991) concept. Mobile sharing not only highlights the configuration of communities but also the ways these practices reproduce themselves in different social settings. Following this thread, one way to understand the concept of home is as a set of interactions between its occupants: every time family members share a mobile phone, they reaffirm roles of who and what belongs inside and outside the home, as well as the purposes of the home itself. At the neighborhood and inter-neighborhood level, the sharing helps reinforce community ties—and binds villages and the immigrant communities in urban areas.

This is not to say that everyone shares. Girish, mentioned above, uses his father's mobile regularly but will not share his phone with others. Ashita did not share her mobile phone with her mother, twenty-three-year-old sister (who do not own mobiles), or father. Although Girish and Ashita are middle-class students, we also found this non-sharing behavior in a family we interviewed in Bangalore's largest slum. We assumed that a mobile phone in a lower-class family would be a *de facto* shared resource, used as the main telephone. But this was not always the case. Rafiq, a twenty-six-year-old steel fabricator, lives with his mother, brother, father, sister, uncle, and two cousins in a very small slum dwelling. He owns a mobile phone and will not let anyone else use it. Rafiq aspires to a business context use for his mobile, in which the phone is a consistently private device and not for sharing.

This established mode of use is the case with Vipim, forty-two, a businessman working in electronics and manufacturing, who largely uses his phone for business purposes. He calls his handset an "office asset"—his employees provide their own handsets and the company pays for the mobile phone plan. Avani, fifty-three, a government official mentioned earlier in this article, has a similar perspective: "You never do that [share mobiles] at a particular level—nobody shares that way." Thus, Rafiq's decision to not share the mobile is consistent with our observations of all people we spoke to who used a mobile for business purposes—only when family members run a business together do they share mobile phones (as was the case with a family of vitamin distributors and a couple who owned several small bakeries). The comments of these businessmen suggest that there is a both a functional and symbolic component to the role of the mobile in a business, and that, perhaps, by electing not to share their handsets with people, they are reaffirming their status as autonomous economic actors.

This study raises many priorities for future research and deeper explanation. Our own research interests will likely draw us toward further study of the spatial indications of these various modes of sharing within both marketplaces and the domestic setting. For others interested in exploring sharing behavior, we suggest that each behavior type we identified could be delved into more deeply, with a closer look at conspicuous, stealthy, people-seeking, and place-seeking sharing. In each case, the "tensions" between when to share and when to withhold might be explained by additional inquiry into the socioeconomic factors at work—class, income, and vocation may influence sharing behaviors in ways this brief review only begins to address.

Conclusion

Within our study, we saw at least four kinds of sharing, across multiple physical contexts (domestic, public, commercial, and long-distance). In every case, the sharing that occurred was structured by, and helped to restructure, social space. We found a rich set of interactions at play within the sharing behaviors in their spatial environments, with the mobile phone acting as a fulcrum on the axis of communalism and individuation. Even when mobile phone users strive toward greater individuation, many remain open to sharing the mobile phone in a variety of social spheres:

at home, moving between places, in the marketplace, and as a conduit to disparate, dislocated social networks.

The observations from the Bangalore phone sharing study outlined four key sets of ideas. First, regardless of mobile ownership, informal sharing occurs extensively. Certainly, in many cases this is marked by proximity, friendship, and kinship, but other informal sharing happens at the neighborhood level without close bonds. Second, sharing is structured by constraints (e.g., economic, family mores, literacy) that permit and restrict certain behaviors. Third, though the mobile is a flexible device, it fixes and reaffirms space, whether domestic or commercial. Finally, mobile sharing bridges social networks in a set of ecologies between neighborhoods and rural villages.

It is worth considering non-sharing behaviors to illuminate issues of socioeconomic mobility and domestic dynamism. Mobile phone users exercise power dynamics regarding who may or may not share a mobile and under which conditions. In most interviews, we observed a tension between the imperative to share (with family, with friends, with customers) and the imperative to control, as illustrated by the comments of Vipim and Rafiq—and by the rules of mobile use negotiated between parents and their children. In terms of socioeconomic mobility, Rafiq's non-sharing behavior reflected that of personal business use, as opposed to the more communal sharing we observed between vendors in the market. His family prioritized this personal business use over the collective household use of a phone. They did not indicate they were put out by this behavior, much the same as middle-class families agreed that mobile use for business made the phone unsuitable for sharing unless all parties conducted business together. At the same time, rejecting the mobile helps to reinforce and control appropriateness of behavior within the domestic boundary, as interviews with non-sharing housewives indicates. But where it intrudes upon this boundary, it is also a point of play, such as between Avani and his daughter Ashita. The father knows his daughter surreptitiously uses his phone; the family knows she has a boyfriend, but charade and the stealthy sharing it requires are part of a larger family dynamic.

Mobile penetration in India (and elsewhere in the developing world) is in the midst of a virtuous cycle. As the middle class grows and prosperity increases, more people are able to purchase handsets of their own. At the same time, coverage is reaching small towns and villages, and the price of handsets continues to fall, allowing people of extremely modest economic means to also become handset owners. As penetration rises, the proportion of people who must share mobiles for purely economic reasons will fall further. However, this chapter has illustrated a variety of situations in which sharing seems not to be purely derived from economic constraint. Thus, we do not expect it to disappear entirely. In domestic settings, among teens, and between the rural villages and prosperous urban areas, the micro-contexts of domestic and intra-group social spaces will persist—and so will the sharing that these spaces enable. Understanding what happens when there are fewer mobiles than people in the room (or the restaurant, or the marketplace) will remain a fruitful and important line of inquiry.

Note

1.   Stealth behavior can spur identity management through Subscriber Identity Module (SIM) card swapping with oneself. In the case of Sushma's twenty-year-old son, Vicky, a mechanical engineering student, this practice allowed him to hide from his parents a girlfriend he met on the Orkut social networking website. Vicky's parents pay for his calls and receive a paper bill each month. Though Vicky carefully erased messages and his call register on his phone, he did not calculate that this paper bill would list all of his calls. His father showed him the bill and asked about a frequently occurring number. "Just a friend!" Vicky said. When his father saw the number again, he asked, "Her again?" Now Vicky uses an old SIM card solely to contact the girlfriend and puts all of his pocket money toward its credit. He swaps a SIM in to call his girlfriend and quickly swaps it back afterwards. He laughs and says that in order to avoid further embarrassing questions from his family, he has avoided being alone with his father for the last two weeks.

Bibliography

Aminuzzaman, Salahuddin, Harald Baldersheim, and Ishtiaq Jamil. "Talking Back! Empowerment and Mobile Phones in Rural Bangladesh: A Study of the Village Phone Scheme of Grameen Bank." *Contemporary South Asia,* 12 (3, 2003): 327-348.

Appadurai, Arjun. *Modernity at Large: Cultural Dimensions of Globalization.* Minneapolis, MN: University of Minnesota Press, 1996.

Bell, Genevieve. "The Age of the Thumb: A Cultural Reading of Mobile Technologies from Asia." In *Thumb Culture: The Meaning of Mobile Phones for Society,* edited by Peter Glotz, Stefan Bertschi, and Chris Locke, 67-88. New Brunswick, NJ: Transaction Publishers, 2005.

Campbell, Scott W. "A Cross-cultural Comparison of Perceptions and Uses of Mobile Telephony." *New Media & Society,* 9 (April 2007): 343-363.

Cartier, Carolyn, Manuel Castells, and Jack Linchuan Qiu. "The Information Have-Less: Inequality, Mobility, and Translocal Networks in Chinese Cities." *Studies in Comparative International Development,* 40 (June 2005): 9-34.

Castells, Manuel. *The Rise of the Network Society.* Vol. 1 of *The Information Age: Economy, Society and Culture.* Malden, MA: Blackwell, 1997.

Castells, Manuel, Mireia Fernandéz-Ardévol, Jack L. Qiu, and Araba Sey. *Mobile Communication and Society: A Global Perspective.* Cambridge, MA: MIT Press, 2006.

Chipchase, Jan and Indri Tulusan. "Shared Phone Practices: Exploratory Field Research from Uganda and Beyond." 2007. *Future Perfect.* http://www.janchipchase.com/sharedphoneuse (accessed 6 March, 2007).

David, Kalpana. "Mobiles in India: tool of tradition or change?" Paper delivered at the Pre-Conference on Mobile Communication of the International Communication Association. 26 May, 2005, New York, NY.

Dickey, Sara. "Permeable Homes: Domestic Service, Household Space, and the Vulnerability of Class Boundaries in Urban India." *American Ethnologist,* 27 (May 2000.): 462-489.

Donner, Jonathan, Nimmi Rangaswamy, Molly W. Steenson, and Carolyn Wei. "'Express Yourself'/ 'Stay together': The Middle-class Family." In *Handbook of Mobile Communication Studies,* edited by James E. Katz. Cambridge, MA: MIT Press, 2008.

Donner, Jonathan. "Internet Use (and Non-Use) Among Urban Microenterprises in the Developing World: An update from India." Paper delivered at the Conference of the Association of Internet Researchers (AoIR). 28-30 September 2006, Brisbane, Australia.

Donner, Jonathan. 2008. "Research approaches to mobile use in the developing world: A review of the literature." *The Information Society,* 24 (3): 140-159.

Donner, Jonathan. 2007. "The rules of beeping: Exchanging messages using missed calls on mobile phones." Paper delivered at the 55th Annual Conference of the International Communication Association. 27 May 2005, New York, NY.

Donner, Jonathan. "The Social and Economic Implications of Mobile Telephony in Rwanda: An Ownership/Access Typology." In *Thumb Culture: The Meaning of Mobile Phones for Society,* edited by Peter Glotz, Stefan Bertschi, and Chris Locke, 37-52. New Brunswick, NJ: Transaction Publishers, 2005.

Gergen, Kenneth J. "The Challenge of Absent Presence." In *Perpetual Contact: Mobile Communication, Private Talk, Public Performance,* edited by James E. Katz and Mark Aakhus, 227-241. Cambridge, UK: Cambridge University Press, 2002.

Gottmann, J. "Megalopolis and Antipolis: The Telephone and the Structure of the City." In *The Social Impact of the Telephone,* edited by Ithiel de Sola Pool, 303-317. Cambridge, MA: MIT Press, 1977.

Haddon, Leslie. "Domestication and Mobile Telephony." In *Machines That Become Us: The Social Context of Personal Communication Technology,* edited by James E. Katz, 43-55. New Brunswick, NJ: Transaction Publishers, 2003.

Haddon, Leslie and Jane Vincent. "Making the Most of the Communications Repertoire: Choosing Between the Mobile and Fixed-line." In *A Sense of Place: the Global and the Local in Mobile Communication,* edited by Kristóf Nyíri, 231-240. Vienna, Austria: Passagen Verlag, 2005.

Hamilton, Jacqueline. "Are Main Lines and Mobile Phones Substitutes or Complements? Evidence from Africa." *Telecommunications Policy*, 27 (February-March 2003): 109-133.

Höflich, Joachim. "Places of Life—Places of Communication: Observations of Mobile Phone Usage in Public Spaces." In *Mobile Communication in Everyday Life: Ethnographic Views, Observations and Reflections*, edited by Joachim R. Höflich and Maren Hartmann, 19-51. Berlin, Germany: Franks and Timme, 2006.

Horst, Heather and Daniel Miller. "From Kinship to Link-up: Cell Phones and Social Networking in Jamaica." *Current Anthropology* 46 (December 2005): 755-778.

Horst, Heather and Daniel Miler. *The Cell Phone: An Anthropology of Communication*. Oxford, UK: Berg, 2006.

Huntsman, Judith and Antony Hooper. *Tokelau: A Historical Ethnography*. Honolulu, HI: University of Hawaii Press, 1996.

Ivatury, Gautam. "Using Technology to Build Inclusive Financial Systems." Consultative Group to Assist the Poor, Focus Note, no. 32. Washington, DC, 2006.

Katz, James E. and Mark A. Aakhus. "Making Meaning of Mobiles: A Theory of *Apparatgeist*." In *Perpetual Contact: Mobile Communication, Private Talk, Public Performance*, edited by James E. Katz and Mark Aakhus, 301-318. Cambridge, UK: Cambridge University Press, 2002.

Kavoori, Anandam and Kalyani Chadha. "The Cell Phone as a Cultural Technology: Lessons from the Indian Case." In *The Cell Phone Reader: Essays in Social Transformation*, edited by Anandam P. Kavoori and Noah Arceneaux, 227-240. New York, NY: Peter Lang, 2006.

Konkka, Katja. "Indian Needs: Cultural End-User Research in Mombai." In *Mobile Usability: How Nokia Changed the Face of the Mobile Phone*, edited by Christian Lindholm, Turkka Keinonen, and Harri Kiljander, 97-112. New York, NY: McGraw-Hill, 2003.

Lefebvre, Henri. *The Production of Space*. Malden, MA.: Blackwell, 1991.

Leonardi, Paul, Marianene E. Leonardi, and Elizabeth Hudson. "Culture, Organization, and Contradiction in the Social Construction of Technology: Adoption and Use of the Cell Phone Across Three Cultures." In *The Cell Phone Reader: Essays in Social Transformation*, edited by Anandam P. Kavoori and Noah Arceneaux, 205-226. New York, NY: Peter Lang, 2006.

Licoppe, Christian. "'Connected' Presence: The Emergence of a New Repertoire for Managing Social Relationships in a Changing Communication Technoscape." *Environment and Planning D: Society and Space*, 22.1 (2004): 135-156.

Ling, Rich S. "'We Release Them Little by Little': Maturation and Gender Identity as Seen in the Use of Mobile Telephony." *Personal and Ubiquitous Computing*, 5 (July 2001): 123-136.

Ling, Rich S. and Birgitte Yttri. "Hyper-Coordination via Mobile Phones in Norway." In *Perpetual Contact: Mobile Communication, Private Talk, Public Performance*, edited by James E. Katz and Mark Aakhus, 139-169. Cambridge, UK: Cambridge University Press, 2002.

Maroon, Bahíyyih. "Mobile Sociality in Urban Morocco." In *The Cell Phone Reader: Essays in Social Transformation*, edited by Anandam P. Kavoori and Noah Arceneaux, 189-204. New York, NY: Peter Lang, 2006.

Mauss, Marcel. *The Gift: The Form and Reason for Exchange in Archaic Societies*. London, UK: Routledge, 1990.

Minges, Michael. "Mobile Cellular Communications in the Southern African Region." *Telecommunications Policy*, 23 (August 1999): 585-593.

Nyíri, Kristóf. ed. *A Sense of Place: the Global and the Local in Mobile Communication*. Vienna, Austria: Passagen Verlag, 2005.

Paragas, Fernando. 2005. "Being Mobile with the Mobile: Cellular Telephony and Renegotiations of Public Transport as Public Sphere." In *Mobile Communications: Re-negotiation of the Social Sphere*, edited by Richard S. Ling and Per E. Pederson, 113-129. London, UK: Springer-Verlag, 2005.

Pertierra, Raul. "If You Can't Afford a Room of Your Own, Buy a Mobile Phone." Paper delivered at the Conference on Mobile Communication and Asian Modernities. 8 June 2005, Hong Kong, SAR.

Reck, Jennifer. and Brad Wood. "Vodacom's Community Services Phone Shops." *Small Enterprise Development*, 15 (December 2004.): 31-37.

Samuel, Jonathan, Niraj Shah, and Wenona Hadingham. "Mobile Communications in South Africa, Tanzania, and Egypt: Results from Community and Business Surveys." Moving the Debate Forward: The Vodafone Policy Paper Series #2, 2005 http://www.vodafone.com/assets/files/en/AIMP_09032005.pdf. (Accessed 17 September 17 2006).

Sey, Araba. "Mobile Payphone Systems in Africa: The Social Shaping of a Communication Technology." Paper delivered at the 56th annual Conference of the International Communication Association. 23 June 2006, Dresden, Germany.

Susser, Ida, ed. *The Castells Reader on Cities and Social Theory*. Malden, MA: Blackwell, 2002.

Tall, Serigne Mansour. "Senegalese Emigrés: New Information & Communication Technologies." *Review of African Political Economy,* 31 (March 2004): 31-48.

Taylor, Alexander and Richard Harper. "The Gift of the *Gab?*: A Design Oriented Sociology of Young People's Use of Mobiles." *Computer Supported Cooperative Work*, 12 (September 2003): 267-296.

Telecom Regulatory Authority of India. The Telecom Services Performance Indicators: July-December 2006. New Delhi, 2007.

Townsend, Anthony M. "Life in the Real-time City: Mobile Telephones and Urban Metabolism." *Journal of Urban Technology,* 7 (August 2000): 85-104.

Weilenmann, Alexandra and Catrine Larsson. "Local Use and Sharing of Mobile Phones." In *Wireless World*: *Social and International Aspects of the Mobile Age*, edited by Barry Brown, Nicola Green, and Richard Harper, 99-115. London, UK: Springer-Verlag, 2002.

Wellman, Barry. "Physical Place and Cyberplace: The Rise of Personalized Networking." *International Journal of Urban and Regional Research,* 25 (2, 2006): 227-252.

Zainudeen, Ayesha, Rohan Samarajiva, and Ayoma Abeysuriya. "Telecom Use on a Shoestring: Strategic Use of Telecom Services by the Financially Constrained in South Asia." Learning Initiatives on Reforms for Network Economies (LIRNE), 2006.

Conclusion

Mobile Communication in Space and Time— Furthering the Theoretical Dialogue

Scott W. Campbell
University of Michigan

Rich Ling
Telenor Research/University of Michigan

Revisiting the Space of Flows

The contributions to this volume illuminate the ways in which mobile communication alters how people experience space and time, with important consequences for coordination, social cohesion, and the management of daily life activities. In this concluding chapter, we draw from the contributions to further the theoretical dialogue on the space-time implications of mobile communication. As demonstrated in several of these chapters, this is not the first attempt at theory building in this area. Most notably, Castells, et al. (2007) address the spatio-temporal changes that come out of the adoption and use of wireless technologies in their discussion of "the space of flows" and "timeless time." The space of flows refers to "the material organization of simultaneous social interaction at a distance by networking communication, with the technological support of telecommunications, interactive communication systems, and fast transportation technologies" (171). This is not to suggest that places are no longer relevant during mobile communication and other forms of electronic communication. Rather, places take on new meaning as they are conceptualized and utilized for their ability to support networked flows through information and communication technologies (ICTs). For example, today's coffee shop with WiFi access is regarded and used quite differently as a mediated environment than the typical coffee shop a generation ago. Like places, time also takes on new meaning in the network age, as it becomes desequenced or compressed through networked interactions (hence, the phrase "timeless time").

The concepts of the space of flows and timeless time are not exclusively tied to mobile communication. In fact, they come out of Castells' earlier research and theory building on the evolution of the Information Age and the resulting transformations at the cultural, economic, and political levels (see for example Castells, 1989, 2000). Castells' thesis is that in recent decades ICTs have nourished (but not caused) a shift in social order characterized by decentralized, flexible, network nodes based on shared interests and need for information rather than shared geographic space. Castells' theory building on the Information Age and the rise of a Network Society has largely been fueled by the diffusion of computing and Internet innovations—although he is careful to acknowledge the importance of other electronic and transportation technologies that support this new networked order. As such, the body of work addressing the space of flows and timeless time so far emphasizes ICTs other than on mobile telephony, with the very notable exception of a chapter in Castells, et al.'s (2007) cross-cultural analysis of wireless and mobile communication in a global context. Although the chapter in that book helps develop the concepts of space of flows and timeless time in a wireless context, its principal contribution is the overall conclusion that mobile communication extends the logic and practice of this new spatio-temporal order. Here, we see an opportunity to deepen the dialogue by drawing from the detailed accounts provided in this volume.

Furthermore, much of Castells' (2000) previous explication of the space of flows and timeless time emphasizes the impacts on cities, which are increasingly becoming globally connected hubs of networked activity. We see this as another opportunity for theoretical development, as the contributions to this volume highlight the implications of mobile communication for interpersonal relations and how daily life is carried out at the individual level.

Finally, we see an opportunity to bring attention to non-material aspects of social life that play a role in the transformation of places into spaces of networked flow. As explained above, the space of flows is defined as the "material organization of simultaneous social interaction at a distance." What is important to note here is the attention paid to "material" forms of support for networked communication and information flow. That is, in order for a place to become a space of flow in the network society, it must have the material features that allow for the exchange of information and networked communications. These "material" features include technology, such as electronic circuits, as well as physical places that can serve as network nodes and hubs. Castells does not suggest the space of flows is entirely material in nature. Indeed, he recognizes that "this material support is embedded in communication systems, and in the social geography and cultural context of these communication systems" (Castells, et al., 2007: 178). As such, we do not consider our discussion here as a departure from the thinking of Castells and his colleagues, but rather as an extension of it—an opportunity to shed new light on the social context surrounding the formation of the space of flows through the emerging practice of mobile communication.

Marc Relieu's chapter on mobile phone work highlights competence at negotiating social context as a non-material factor that can play a key role in the transformation of a place into a space of flow. His study illustrates this point by exploring the intricate nuances involved in fitting mobile communication into the circumstances of the local setting. Relieu shows how individuals must carefully strike a balance between attending to local activity and the flow of mobile-mediated interaction. As he demonstrates, sometimes the "artful practice" of this type of mobile phone work involves building connections between two disparate social spheres. His observational account of two friends having lunch shows how one of the parties, Kim, incorporates an SMS chat session into the local situation without alienating Denis by incorporating him into the flow of networked interaction. As the author points out, Kim must solve a "multi-activity puzzle" if he is to competently use the seating area outside of the restaurant as a space of flow.

Steenson and Donner's chapter also highlights how the non-material social dimension can play a key role in the formation of the space of flows. Through their accounts of mobile sharing in India, the authors reveal that the flow of networked interaction can be just as beholden to the nature of one's local relationships as it is to the material elements in the surrounding environment. In other words, "social proximity" to friends, family, and co-workers can be just as important as physical proximity to circuits and other such resources that support the space of flows. As the authors point out, the nature of this "social space" shapes the form of mobile sharing that takes place, whether it is conspicuous, stealthy, or otherwise. But generally, the different forms of mobile sharing tend to have the effect of tightening social space. By situating their research in India, Steenson and Donner manage to not only provide a glimpse into the social influences on the space of flows and timeless time, but to also bring much needed visibility to emerging mobile communication practices in the developing world where wireless diffusion rates are among the highest.

Beyond these social dimensions that influence whether and how the space of flows takes shape, the chapters in this volume also reveal that local time can serve as an important non-material element. As Castells (2000, Castells, et al., 2007) explains, time is rendered "timeless" by becoming de-sequenced or compressed when a space of place is utilized as a space of flow. Castells (2000) asserts that certain structural elements must be in place for the construction of timeless time, which leads him to the hypothesis that "space organizes time in the network society" (408). While this is certainly true, several studies in this collection bring attention to how time plays a multi-faceted role in networked sociability by also playing a formative role in the space of flows.

Returning to Relieu's study, we see how the "work" performed to fit mobile communication in a local context can entail waiting for the right moment to engage in mediated interaction so as not to disrupt the activity stream in the proximal environment. Ann Light's research on the phenomenology of mobile communication also illustrates how timing can be a critical element in many mobile-mediated situations. For example, Light notes, "cooking can involve complex, time-sensitive physical maneuvering of a kind that might lead someone to ignore a call" (207). Light's study reveals that the temporal context surrounding networked interaction not only shapes *whether* a place becomes a space of flow, but the experience and nature of that flow as well. In her account of the episode on a bus, an incoming call at the wrong time (i.e., when the user is about to exit the bus) forces changes in communication. The person exiting the bus not only talks faster, but also experiences feelings of stress, anxiety, and even panic; this reveals how timing can affect one's phenomenological experience of networked interaction. Doring and Poschl's chapter on nonverbal cues also demonstrates how the local context of time can shape how one experiences the space of flows. In their study, text messages that were sent at night were perceived as more intimate than messages sent during the day, while daytime messages were perceived to be significantly more dominant. Thulin and Vilhelmson's study also illustrates how time can change attitudes toward mobile communication. As participants in their study became older, more experienced users, they felt more burdened by the intrusions of mobile communication and developed new strategies for managing immediate and permanent access, while at the same time reporting increased levels of dependence on the technology.

Collectively, these findings highlight that non-material, as well as material, aspects of local context can play a formative role in supporting the transformation of place into a space of flow and how individuals, as network nodes, experience the flow of networked interaction. Beyond highlighting non-material dimensions that support the space of flows, we consider these findings valuable in the way they bring focus to the micro-level circumstances surrounding the space of flows constructed through mobile communication.

The Personalization of Mobile Media

In addition to distinctive social, spatial, and temporal qualities, personalization—which cuts across various dimensions—is a distinguishing feature of mobile communication and how it plays out in everyday life. Without doubt, the adoption, use, and ramifications of mobile telephony can be placed in a broader technosocial context. The article by Arminen, as well as that by Diminescu, Licoppe, Smoreda and Ziemlicki, help us to understand how the rise of mobile communication is part of the larger shift in social order from placed-based sociability to decentralized, flexible, network nodes supported by numerous transportation and communication technologies. Julsrud and Bakke show how this larger movement is taking place not only in personal community networks, but in the working world as well. While it is part of this sweeping movement, we believe mobile communication embodies unique qualities that manifest in particular ways throughout social life. Certainly one of those qualities is the mobility that the technology affords. Mobility lowers the threshold for communication by loosening the traditional constraints of space and time (Ling, 2004). However, chapters in this volume draw attention to another important aspect of the technology that seems to be just as important, if not more so, than mobility—the personalization of mobile communication technology.

The personalization of mobile telephony is apparent in many facets of how the technology is perceived and used. Perhaps the most obvious form of it is in the way the technology is tied to an individual user (Ling, 2008). Of course, one notable exception is in the case of mobile sharing. But even when the technology is shared, it is still characteristically personal. As Steenson and Donner point out, "when all telephones were landlines, people called *places*; now, people call *people*" (236).

In her chapter, Ann Light discusses how the personalization of mobile telephony alters how people ordinarily relate to communication technology. She explains that the embodiment of mobile telephony engenders a "transition to the individual, as the phone becomes a personal possession. This shift sees phones following the contours of the body, developing close links to ears, eyes and mouths, and, in some cases, ceasing to be a single gadget" (195). In many cases, the technology has become such a personal artifact that the lines distinguishing object from subject become blurred (Hashimoto and Campbell, 2007).

We agree with Light's argument that "Person-centered phoning embodies new relationships" (191). The chapters in this volume show how the personalization of mobile communication technology alters how people relate not only to the technology, but to space, time, and each other, often resulting in increased social cohesion among friends, family members, and loved ones. Fernando Paragas' chapter serves as an excellent case in point. In his study, migrant workers embraced the mobile phone much more rapidly than traditional mass media and the landline telephone. Paragas attributes the explosive growth of mobile communication to the personalization the technology affords in private interaction, noting the "use of landline phones in the host country had not risen because access to the units was often shared with other people, precluding their viability for personal conversations" (59). In this case, the mobile phone served as an umbilical cord to family members back home, which reduced feelings of homesickness. As Paragas explains, "the mobile phone, as a deeply personal medium, imbued [overseas Filipino workers] with an intimate sense of connection to their otherwise geographically distant relations" (58).

The contribution from Ito, Okabe, and Anderson also highlights consequences of the shift from location-based networking to person-based communications. Like others, the authors remark on the cohesive effects that come out of person-centered telecommunication by acknowledging emerging themes in the research such as "full-time intimate communities" (Yoshii, et al., 2002), "virtual walled communities" (Ling, 2004), and "telecocoons" (Habuchi, 2005). These observations hint at a potential downside of the technology—that social network ties may actually become *overly* configured through mobile communication. While it is true that "the cell phone now serves as an instrument par excellence for endogenous strengthening" (Gergen, 2002: 237), there is the concern that this may be happening at the expense of weak ties, which play an important role in our social lives.

Beyond direct person-to-person connection, Ito, et al. draw attention to another aspect of personalization afforded by mobile technologies in the way they are used to carve out individual territories in public and semi-public settings. Their study shifts focus from the interpersonal uses of mobile phones and other portable media devices as they are used individually to establish embodied presence in urban spaces. While these uses of the technology differ from the interpersonal connections reported in other chapters, they share similarities in the way they engender personalization. In this case, mobile media are used to personalize public space, and this can lead to its own version of a cocooning effect. Ito, et al. note how individuals "appropriate public and semi-public spaces by pulling out a laptop in a café, or donning headphones in a crowded train to create a private cocoon" (71). The mobile phone too is appropriated in this way as people increasingly use the technology to play games, listen to music, access the Web, capture and review photos, etc. As in the case of social networking, the personalization of public space through mobile technologies offers both promise and peril. On the one hand, individuals have increased opportunities to work, play, and resurrect "dead time." On the other hand, these uses of mobile technologies can cut individuals off from co-present others in their proximal environment. Goffman (1963) discussed the importance of "civil inattention" in populated urban areas. Civil inattention refers to demonstrated awareness of co-present strangers without directly engaging in a threatening or overly friendly manner. According to Goffman, civil inattention allows for the sharing of communal space without imposition. In addition, it makes individuals available to one another in times of need, such as asking for directions. The use of mobile media in public settings is altering the extent to which civil inattention is practiced in modern society.

Another area in which mobile technology contributes to personalization is message content. Just as it is used as a resource for logistical coordination, so too has the mobile phone become an important means for socio-emotional exchanges among friends, family, and romantic partners. Even text messaging, which is characteristically low in media richness (Daft and Lengel, 1984, 1986), is commonly used for the exchange of highly intimate messages. In fact, some even prefer SMS to face-to-face communication for delivering sensitive messages (Ishii, 2006). Paragas' study of migrant workers shows how the personalization of mobile-mediated content extends beyond the individual and network levels to the national level as well. Using mobile telephony in concert with channels of mass communication, such as television, radio, and video, migrant workers operate in a multi-sourced media environment in which information flows in both downward and upward directions. As Paragas explains, "National and global events gleaned from traditional media were discussed at the personal level through mobile communications. Conversely, personal stories exchanged over the phone are contextualized in public events" (45). For example, the kidnapping of a Filipino bus driver in Iraq became one of the personal discourses of migrant workers that made it to the national, even global, stage.

The personalization of mass media content offers increased potential for ordinary citizens to bring about social and political change. Castells (2007) agues that the media constitute the space where political power is decided, which has traditionally been located in mass communication channels such as radio, television, and newspapers. The rise of mobile telephony and other personal communication technologies has engendered new spaces in which power, as well as counter-power, is played out. According to Castells (2007), "the rise of insurgent politics cannot be separated from the emergence of a new kind of media space. . . . Appropriating the new forms of communication, people have built their own system of mass communication, via SMS, blogs, vlogs, podcasts, wikis, and the like" (246-247). Personalized mass media content certainly offers benefits by appealing to specialized interests and aiding in political mobilization, however this may also come at a social cost. In particular, some are concerned that the personalization of the media can have a fragmentary effect on society by creating echo chambers of like-minded interests (see for example, Sunstein, 2002).

A Look to the Future

With subscriptions well into the billions worldwide and growing, the social implications of mobile telephony are both profound and far-reaching. Use of the technology gives rise to new forms of sociability, new meanings for space and time, and new levels of personalization in how people orient to the media and each other. As the burgeoning field of mobile communication studies grows, the power of the technology to bring about social change becomes increasingly evident. Researchers are making huge strides in identifying key areas of social change. However, important questions remain about whether these changes ultimately help or hinder society.

As we see in this volume and elsewhere, one of the effects of mobile communication is in bringing people together. But it also seems the solidarity that comes out of it is bounded and potentially fragmented, evidenced by the discussion of "tele-cocoons" and "virtual walled communities." Furthermore, mobile telephony is such a personal technology that it cultivates individuation, as seen in its use for music, gaming, and other individual practices. This tension between social connection, overly configured networks, and individuation raises important questions about social capital in the emergent "mobile network society."

In order to address these concerns, the next volume in the Mobile Communication Research Series explores the theme of "Mobile Communication: Bringing Us Together or Tearing Us Apart?" Like this one, Volume II will include investigations from various perspectives and across various levels of social order. As we look to the future with Volume II, our aim is better to understand ways that mobile communication can bring people together and/or create social division, and the social consequences that come out of these processes, whether they are relational, psychological, political, or otherwise.

Bibliography

Castells, Manuel. *The Informational City: Information Technology, Economic Restructuring and the Urban-Regional Process*. Oxford, UK: Blackwell, 1989.

Castells, Manuel. *The Rise of the Network Society*. Vol. 1 of *The Information Age: Economy, Society and Culture*. Malden, MA: Blackwell, 1996.

Castells, Manuel. "Communication, Power and Counter-power in the Network Society." *International Journal of Communication, 1* (2007): 238-266, http://ijoc.org/ojs/index.php/ijoc/article/view/46 (accessed 7 April 2007).

Castells, Manuel, Mireia Fernandez-Ardevol, Jack Linchuan Qiu, and Araba Sey. *Mobile Communication and Society: A Global Perspective*. Cambridge, MA: MIT Press, 2007.

Daft, Richard L. and Robert H. Lengel. "Information Richness: A New Approach to Managerial Behavior and Organization Design." In Vol. 6 of *Research in Organizational Behavior*, edited by Barry M. Staw and L.L. Cummings, 191-233. Greenwich, CT: JAI Publishing, 1984.

Daft, Richard L. and Robert H. Lengel. "Organizational Information Requirements, Media Richness and Structural Design." *Management Science, 32* (May 1996): 554-571.

Gergen, Kenneth J. "The Challenge of Absent Presence." In *Perpetual Contact: Mobile Communication, Private Talk, Public Performance*, edited by James E. Katz and Mark Aakhus, 227-241. Cambridge, UK: Cambridge University Press, 2002.

Goffman, Erving. *Behavior in Public Places: Notes on the Social Organization of Gatherings*. New York, NY: Free Press, 1963.

Habuchi, Ichiyo. "Accelerating Reflexivity." In *Personal, Portable, Pedestrian: Mobile Phones in Japanese Life*, edited by Mizuko Ito, Daisuke Okabe, and Misa Matsuda, 165-182. Cambridge, MA: MIT Press, 2005.

Hashimoto, S.D. and Scott W. Campbell. "The Life of Mobile Data: Traces of Self and Other." Paper delivered at the 20th Simposio Internacional Comunicacion Social. January 2007, Santiago, Chile.

Ishii, Kenichi. "Implications of Mobility: The Uses of Personal Communication Media in Everyday Life." *Journal of Communication, 56* (June 2006): 346-365.

Ling, Richard S. *The Mobile Connection: The Cell Phone's Impact on Society.* San Francisco, CA: Morgan Kaufmann, 2004.

Ling, Richard S. *New Tech, New Ties: How Mobile Communication Reshapes Social Cohesion.* Cambridge, MA: MIT Press, 2008.

Sunstein, Cass R. *Republic.com.* Princeton, NJ: Princeton University Press, 2002.

Wellman, Barry. "Physical Place and Cyberplace: The Rise of Personalized Networking." *International Journal of Urban and Regional Research, 25* (February 2001), 227-252.

Yoshii, H., M. Matsuda, C. Habuchi, S. Dobashi, K. Iwata, and N. Kin. *Keitai Denwa Riyou no Shinka to sono Eikyou.* Tokyo, Japan: Mobile Communications Kenkyuukai, 2002.

About the Contributors

Ken Anderson is in Intel Research where he conducts ethnographic research of human cultures and social practices to inform corporate strategy and technology development. His current foci are on social relationships, identity, and time. Ken is a symbolic anthropologist by training; his dissertation topic was on intertextuality and Azorean identity, which explored the space of media, identity, and culture. Prior to coming to Intel, Ken was at AT&T, MediaOne, US West, and Apple where he worked to bring a better understanding of people's everyday lives into corporate product and strategy development. He has also played the role of itinerate academic teaching at University of Colorado Health Sciences Center, Bethel College and Seminary, University of Minnesota, and Brown University.

Ilkka Arminen, Ph.D. is professor of Sociology and Social Psychology at the University of Tampere, Finland. His research has focused on communication and social interaction. His special interest is on the uses of mobile media and communication technologies, both at everyday contexts and workspaces. His current work concerns mobile telephony and social changes in social networking. He is the leader of the media, technology, and interaction team that addresses interaction design in various contexts. His work has been done in collaboration with number of industrial partners, such as Elisa, Finnair, the Finnish Aviation Ministry, Nokia MP, and Radiolinja. He has published in numerous journals, including *Acta Sociologica*, *Discourse & Society*, *Discourse Studies*, *Personal and Ubiquitous Computing*, *Journal of Pragmatics*, and *The Sociological Quarterly*. His books include *Institutional Interaction—Studies of Talk at Work* (2005, Ashgate).

John Willy Bakke works as a research scientist at Telenor Research and Innovation, where his primary areas of research are flexible work arrangements and user interpretations and user acceptance of technologies. Recent projects include studies of teleworking, the role of ICTs and workplace design for work task execution and collaboration, and trust and social capital in distributed groups. He has published a number of articles and papers in these areas, and is also the editor and co-editor of books on telework, distributed work, and workplace design.

Scott Campbell, Ph.D. is assistant professor and Pohs Fellow of Telecommunications in the Department of Communication Studies at the University of Michigan. His research explores the social implications of new media, with an emphasis on mobile communication and social engagement. Professor Campbell's research appears in *Communication Education, Communication Monographs, Communication Research Reports, International Journal of Communication, Journal of Applied Communication Research, New Media & Society, Qualitative Research Reports in Communication, Sociology Compass*, and other scholarly venues. Prior to joining the University of Michigan in 2005, Professor Campbell worked in the wireless industry and was on faculty at Hawaii Pacific University on the Hawaiian island of Oahu.

Dana Diminescu is associate professor in the Department of Social and Economic Sciences at the Ecole d'Ingénieurs Télécom ParisTech and director of the "IT/Migrations" scientific program in the Maison des Sciences de l'Homme—Paris. Her research field is sociology of mobility and migration.

Jonathan Donner is a researcher in the Technology for Emerging Markets Group at Microsoft Research India, where he studies the social and economic impacts of mobile communication technologies in developing countries. Some of his recent research appears in *Information Technologies and International Development, The Journal of Computer-Mediated Communication*, and the *Handbook of Mobile Communication Studies*. Between 2003 and 2005, he was a postdoctoral research fellow at the Earth Institute at Columbia University. He earned a doctorate in Communication Research from Stanford University in 1999 and has worked for Monitor Company and the OTF Group, both consultancies in Boston, MA.

Nicola Döring, Ph.D. is professor of Media Design and Media Psychology in the Department of Media and Communication Studies at Ilmenau University of Technology. Her current research interests include social and psychological dimensions of online and mobile communication, learning and teaching with new media, gender and sexuality studies, and evaluation research.

Mizuko Ito is a cultural anthropologist of technology use, focusing on children and youth´s changing relationships to media and communications. She is part of a research project supported by the MacArthur Foundation, "Kids´ Informal Learning with Digital Media," a three year ethnographic study of kid-initiated and peer-based forms of engagement with new media. She is also conducting ongoing research on Japanese techno-culture, looking at how children in Japan and the US engage with post-Pokemon media mixes. Her research on mobile phone use in Japan appears in a book she has co-edited, *Personal, Portable, Pedestrian: Mobile Phones in Japanese Life*. She is a research scientist at the School of Information and Computer Science at the University of California, Irvine, and a visiting associate professor at Keio University in Japan.

Tom Erik Julsrud, Ph.D. works as a research scientist at Telenor Research and Innovation and is also associated with the Norwegian University of Science and Technology (NTNU). His research areas of interests include social networks, distributed work, mobile work, workplace changes, trust in organizations, and social capital. He has co-authored books on telework and distributed work and has published several articles and papers on collaboration in distributed and virtual teams. His latest work focuses in particular on the development of trust in virtual environments and distributed groups.

James E. Katz, Ph.D. is professor and chair of the Department of Communication at Rutgers University, and founder and director of the Center for Mobile Communication Studies. Professor Katz is currently investigating how personal communication technologies, such as mobile phones and the Internet, affect social relationships and how cultural values influence usage patterns of these technologies. His award-winning books include *Machines That Become Us: The Social Context of Personal Communication Technology* (Transaction, 2003, editor), *Perpetual Contact: Mobile Communication, Private Talk and Public Performance* (co-edited with Mark Aakhus), *Connections: Social and Cultural Studies of the Telephone in American Life*, and *Social Consequences of Internet Use: Access, Involvement, Expression* (co-authored with Ronald E. Rice).

He is the author of more than forty peer-reviewed journal articles and his works have been translated into five languages and re-published in numerous edited collections.

Christian Licoppe, Ph.D. is professor of Sociology in the Department of Social Science of Telecom ParisTech, which is the main engineering school for telecommunications in France. Trained in history of science and technology, he moved ten years ago into the field of new media with emphasis on the interactional and relational aspects of communication practices and an interest in activity theories. His research in mobile technologies ranges from studies of "connected presence" to location awareness games. Recently he has investigated communication practices in activity settings such as service call centers and courtrooms.

Ann Light, Ph.D. is a reader in Interaction, Media, and Communication at Sheffield Hallam University and a senior research fellow in the Drama Department at Queen Mary, University of London. She is primarily interested in the social impact of technology and the politics of participation in design, explored in a range of projects including "Democratising Technology" (DemTech: www.demtech.qmul.ac.uk), "Fair Tracing" (www.fairtracing.org), and "Practical Design for Social Action" (www.technologyandsocialaction.org). She also helps run a charity using ICT for cultural exchange between Africa and Europe (www.fiankoma.org). Her recent research has taken a phenomenological perspective, developing methods for analyzing meaning-making, changes in attention, and experience of new media. She is published widely in the areas of human computer interaction, usability, interactive media, and design.

Rich Ling, Ph.D. is a sociologist at Telenor's research institute located near Oslo, Norway. He has also been the Pohs Visiting Professor of Communication Studies at the University of Michigan in Ann Arbor, and he now holds an adjunct position in that department. He is the author of the books *New Tech, New Ties: How mobile communication is reshaping social cohesion* (2008, MIT) and *The Mobile Connection: The cell phone's impact on society* (2004, Morgan Kaufmann) and co-editor of *Mobile Communications: Renegotiation of the Social Sphere* (2005, Springer).

Daisuke Okabe is a cognitive psychologist specializing in situated learning theory. His focus is interactional studies of learning and education in relation to new media technologies. He also studies Japanese technology geek culture. He is a co-editor of "Personal, Portable, Pedestrian: Mobile Phones in Japanese Life," which covers mundane mobile communication in Japan. He works as a research associate at Keio University in Japan.

Fernando Paragas, Ph.D. is assistant professor of Communication Research at the University of the Philippines Diliman (UPD), where he also earned his bachelor's and master's degrees. He completed his doctoral degree at Ohio University as a Fulbright fellow. Dr. Paragas was awarded the 1997 AdAsia-Newsweek Research Grant for his work on overseas Filipino workers, the 2002 Outstanding UPD Web site Award for the College of Mass Communication, and a 2006 New Ph.D. Incentive Grant from the UPD Office of the Vice Chancellor for Research and Development for his work on communication technology, mobility, and migration—his primary areas of research. His papers have been published or presented in Asia, Europe, and North America.

Sandra Pöschl is an academic staff member at the Department of Media Design and Media Psychology at the Institute for Media and Communication Studies at Ilmenau University of Technology. Her professional interest lies in personality dimensions of mobile communication and gender research, statistics, and research methods.

Marc Relieu is senior lecturer in Sociology at Telecom Paris Tech, Department of Economics and Social Sciences. Over the last fifteen years, he has sought to develop ethno-methodological studies of mobility and technology in France. Marc Relieu's recent studies have investigated the social organization of conversations on mobile phones (either vocal or textual) and the impact of the micro-mobility of tele-presence of collaborative systems' users on their remote interactions. The underlying issue he is interested in is how hybridization of digital and proximate activities is methodically achieved in ordinary settings. Prior to joining Telecom Paris Tech in 2005, Marc Relieu conducted research at Orange Labs and at the Ecole des Hautes Etudes en Sciences Sociales (Paris).

Zbigniew Smoreda is a senior researcher in Sociology and Economics of Networks and Services Department of Orange Labs R&D (Paris, France). His research interests include the study of everyday sociability and social network configurations, life cycle, and urban mobility and communication patterns.

Molly Wright Steenson researches the intersections of technology, urbanism, and architecture. She was a research intern at Microsoft Research India in the Technology for Emerging Markets group in 2006. Molly is an architecture doctoral student at Princeton University's School of Architecture and holds a Master's in Environmental Design from Yale School of Architecture. She was also an associate professor at the Interaction Design Institute Ivrea in Italy and has worked with design and technology since 1994.

Eva Thulin, Ph.D. is a research fellow in Human Geography at Göteborg University, Sweden. Her research interests primarily concern the role of virtual mobility (use of computers, the Internet, mobile phones) in people's lives, especially focusing on aspects of time and place, patterns of social communication, travel, and migration. Her research appears in *Environment and Planning*, *Netcom*, *Journal of Economic and Social Geography*, and *Young—Nordic Journal of Youth Research*.

Bertil Vilhelmson is professor in Human Geography at University of Gothenburg, Sweden. His research interests are in the fields of personal mobility (virtual communication and physical transportation) human activity patterns in time and space, and environmental geography. He is heading the Mobility Research Group (http://www.handels.gu.se/hgeo/mobility) in his department. His research appears in *Environment and Planning A*, *GeoJournal*, *Young*, *Tijdschrift vor Economische en Sociale Geographie*, *Netcom*, *Cybergeo*, *Geografisk Annaler B*, *Journal of Transport Geography*, and *Transport Policy*.

Cezary Ziemlicki is an R&D engineer in Sociology and Economics of Networks and Services Department of Orange Labs R&D (Paris, France). His main domain of activity is telecom traffic data collection, analysis, and data-mining algorithm development for the purpose of sociological and economic studies.

Index